Wrestling with
DARK ANGELS

TOWARD A DEEPER
UNDERSTANDING OF THE
SUPERNATURAL FORCES IN
SPIRITUAL WARFARE

C. PETER WAGNER & F. DOUGLAS PENNOYER, EDITORS

Regal Books
A Division of Gospel Light
Ventura, California, U.S.A.

Published by Regal Books
A Division of GL Publications
Ventura, California 93006
Printed in U.S.A.

Library of Congress Cataloging-in-Publication Data

Wrestling with dark angels / [edited by] C. Peter Wagner, F. Douglas Pennoyer.
    p.   cm.
    Papers represented at the Academic Symposium on Power Evangelism held
Dec. 13-15, 1988, at the Fuller Seminary School of World Mission.
    Includes bibliographical references.
    ISBN 0-8307-1385-9
    1. Missions—Theory—Congresses. 2. Evangelistic work—Philosophy—
Congresses. 3. Power (Christian theology)—Congresses. 4. Powers (Christian
theology)—Congresses. 5. Demonology—Congresses. 6. Holy Spirit—
Congresses. I. Wagner, C. Peter. II. Pennoyer, Fredrick Douglas. III. Academic
Symposium on Power Evangelism (1988 : Fuller Seminary School of World Mis-
sion)
BV2063.D26   1990
269—dc20   90-31281
                                                                    CIP

3 4 5 6 7 8 9 10 / 91

Rights for publishing this book in other languages are contracted by Gospel
Literature International (GLINT) foundation. GLINT also provides technical
help for the adaptation, translation, and publishing of Bible study resources
and books in scores of languages worldwide. For further information, contact
GLINT, Post Office Box 488, Rosemead, California, 91770, U.S.A., or the
publisher.

Contents

Introduction 5

1. Power Evangelism Definitions and Directions
John Wimber 13

    Response by Paul Watney 43

2. We Are At War Ed Murphy 49

3. Territorial Spirits C. Peter Wagner 73

    Response by Byron D. Klaus 92

4. Deception: Satan's Chief Tactic
Timothy M. Warner 101

    Response by James D. Simpson 115

5. Finding Freedom in Christ
Neil T. Anderson 125

    Response by John D. Ellenberger 160

**6. The Holy Spirit and Power:
A Wesleyan Understanding**
Donald Hohensee 169

    Response by Opal L. Reddin 184

**7. Pentecostal/Charismatic Understanding
of Exorcism** L. Grant McClung, Jr. 195

8. Sickness and Suffering in the New Testament
Peter H. Davids 215

    Response by Walter R. Bodine 238

84977

9. In Dark Dungeons of Collective Captivity
   F. Douglas Pennoyer   249

   Response by Charles H. Kraft   271

**10. Power Evangelism in Pioneer Mission
   Strategy**   John Louwerse   281

   Response by Edgar J. Elliston   297

11. Out of Africa: Evangelism and Spiritual Warfare
   Donald R. Jacobs   303

**12. The Relevance of Power Ministries for
   Folk Muslims**   J. Dudley Woodberry   313

   Response by Dean S. Gilliland   332

**13. Trends and Topics in Teaching Power
   Evangelism**   F. Douglas Pennoyer   339

Index   359

BY
C. PETER
WAGNER

Introduction

The transition from the 1980s to the 1990s is an awesome period of time for the Christian community. Skilled analysts and prophets alike are affirming that the decade of the '90s is shaping up as an arena for the greatest outpouring of spiritual power at least in living memory if not in all of Christian history. The fruition of the 90-year-old Pentecostal movement, now joined by the charismatic movement and the Third Wave, is one of the chief contributing factors. Combined with that are new and powerful emphases on church growth, compassion for the poor and oppressed, prayer, prophecy and other aspects of the supernatural.

A striking feature of this build-up of what may result in a historical revival near or just after the turn of the century is the new openness to the miraculous works of the Holy Spirit across the lines of historic Christian traditions. For years many evangelicals shunned the reported manifestations of signs and wonders, healings, demonic deliverances and miracles in the Pentecostal and charismatic movements. A few still rather staunchly adhere to their traditional anti-Pentecostal positions, but their ranks are becoming notably thin.

The great Lausanne II Congress on World Evangelization, held in Manila in July 1989, was in itself a highly visible and prophetically symbolic stepping stone into the decade of the '90s. In dramatic contrast to Lausanne I, held in
Switzerland in 1974, Lausanne II embraced leaders of the
Pentecostal/charismatic movements at all levels from the
Lausanne Committee itself through the plenary sessions
and workshops to the thousands of participants who regularly worshiped with raised hands. Remarkably, the three
most attended workshop tracks (of 48 offered) were on
the Holy Spirit, spiritual warfare and prayer. Speakers
such as Paul Yonggi Cho, Jack Hayford, Omar Cabrera,
Dick Eastman, William Kumuyi and many others like them
reflected the lowering of the barriers between evangelicals and charismatics over the 15 years between the two
congresses.

The Fuller Symposium

A much smaller, but also highly significant, meeting of
evangelicals, Pentecostals and charismatics was convened
by the Fuller Seminary School of World Mission seven
months previous to Lausanne II. Under the title "Academic Symposium on Power Evangelism" it brought
together 40 scholars representing Christian institutions of
higher learning in the United States and Canada on
December 13–15, 1988.

The consortium was brought together because of a
growing awareness on the part of many academicians that
curricula in certain Bible schools and seminaries were not
adequately dealing with the issues being raised by these
new movements. Several institutions, however, had
begun to introduce courses, sections of courses and lectures dealing with power ministries—not without varying

degrees of opposition from more traditionally inclined faculty colleagues who did not wish their institutions to be identified with what they regarded as Pentecostal excesses. Those who participated in the symposium were chiefly faculty members from the schools which had already begun to experiment with power-oriented teaching.

Because of the unusual degree of media coverage given to the Fuller School of World Mission's MC510 course, taught from 1982–1985 by John Wimber and me, it was fitting for Fuller to take the initiative in hosting the symposium. John Wimber's term "power evangelism" was selected as the theme, partly because his book, *Power Evangelism* (Harper & Row) had emerged as the most commonly used textbook in these new courses. The book is based on lectures given by Wimber in the MC510 course. Wimber also assumed the role of keynote speaker in the symposium, and his presentation, "Power Evangelism: Definitions and Directions," is the first chapter of this book.

Of the 40 participants, 7 represented classic Pentecostal/charismatic institutions, 4 represented Wimber's Vineyard movement, and 29 came from what would be regarded as traditional evangelical institutions. Most, but not all, who attended were desirous of seeing substantially expanded offerings related to power ministries in future curriculum designs in their schools. They regarded this symposium as a public legitimizing of academic pursuits in fields related to the supernatural power of God both for local church ministries and for world evangelization.

Participants in the symposium included: John L. Amstutz and John Louwerse, LIFE Bible College, a Foursquare institution in Los Angeles; Neil T. Anderson and Lloyd E. Kwast, Biola University/Talbot School of Theology in La Mirada, California; Walter R. Bodine and Jack Deere, two professors who had recently left the faculty of Dallas Theological Seminary; Betty Sue Brewster, Edgar J. Elliston, Eddie Gibbs, Dean S. Gilliland, Arthur F. Glasser, Paul G. Hiebert, Charles H. Kraft, Paul E. Pierson, R. Daniel Shaw, Charles Van Engen, C. Peter Wagner, and J. Dudley Woodberry, the Fuller Seminary School of World Mission in Pasadena, California; Peter H. Davids, Regent College, Vancouver, British Columbia; John D. Ellenberger, Alliance Theological Seminary in Nyack, New York; Wayne Grudem and Timothy M. Warner, Trinity Evangelical Divinity School in Deerfield, Illinois; Donald Hohensee, Western Evangelical Seminary in Portland, Oregon; Byron D. Klaus, Southern California College, an Assemblies of God school in Costa Mesa, California; L. Grant McClung, Jr., Church of God School of Theology in Cleveland, Tennessee; Jeffrey J. Niehaus, Gordon-Conwell Theological Seminary in South Hamilton, Massachusetts; F. Douglas Pennoyer, Seattle Pacific University; Peter E. Prosser, CBN University in Virginia Beach, Virginia; Opal L. Reddin, Central Bible College, an Assemblies of God school in Springfield, Missouri; Edward Murphy, San Jose (California) Bible College; James D. Simpson, Lee College, a Church of God school in Cleveland, Tennessee; Paul B. Watney, Oral Roberts University School of Theology and Mission in Tulsa, Oklahoma; Philip Thornton and Mark Nysewander, Asbury College in Wilmore, Kentucky. Those not representing academic institutions included Johan Engelbrecht, Donald R. Jacobs, Knud Jorgensen, George Mallone, Elizabeth R. Moberly and John Wimber.

Several of the key leaders were invited to speak to the group on topics of their choice related to power evangelism. Immediately following each presentation, a respondent discussed the issue further. This book brings together, in edited form, this treasury of information and inspiration. It ends with an up-to-date summary of what is being thought and taught in our academic institutions across the board, by co-editor F. Douglas Pennoyer.

The Real Battle

This material could not be more timely. Over the past 20 years enormous strides forward have been taken by missiologists, strategists and mission executives in advancing the technology for fulfilling the Great Commission. Church growth has become a science. Unreached people groups are being identified, analyzed and adopted as evangelistic targets. Demographic information is becoming readily accessible to all through computers. Communication networks are growing in sophistication. Methodologies for new church multiplication are being refined. Quality training is now available in modern language learning techniques, cultural anthropology, leadership selection and training, ethnomusicology, cross-cultural communication, the use of media, contextualization of theology and many other fields directly applicable to world evangelization.

Now that these pieces are in place as they never have been before, they appear to many as a rocket on the launching pad ready to take us to new dimensions of effectiveness in advancing the kingdom of God through the 1990s. But at the same time there has been a growing awareness that the rocket itself, with all of its state-of-the-art technology, will go nowhere without the fuel. The pieces for unprecedented effectiveness in world evangelization are in place, but only the power of the Holy Spirit will properly activate them for the massive spread of the gospel that God desires.

None of this should be interpreted to mean that the gospel has not been spreading rapidly in many parts of the world, especially since 1950. We are already well into the greatest ingathering of souls that history has ever seen. Much of what we have been doing has been working well. Pentecostal and non-Pentecostal missionary efforts alike are flourishing. I do not see in the recent past anything we need to be ashamed of.

However, I believe that the best years are yet ahead. I believe that God wants to increase our effectiveness in geometric proportions. I see our addition becoming multiplication and our multiplication becoming exponential.

The power evangelism symposium and this book which has emerged from it symbolize a new consciousness that the weapons of our warfare are not carnal but mighty in God for pulling down strongholds (see 2 Cor. 10:4). The real battle is not one of intellectual brilliance or technical superiority, but of spiritual power. We do not war according to the flesh, but according to the Spirit. "Not by might nor by power, but by My Spirit, says the Lord of hosts" (Zech. 4:6, *NKJV*).

Jesus and the apostles describe our ministry as warfare. "We do not wrestle against flesh and blood, but against principalities, against powers, against the rulers of the darkness of this age, against spiritual hosts of wickedness in the heavenly places" (Eph. 6:12, *NKJV*). If the real battle for the advancement of the kingdom of God is spiritual, we need to learn as much as we can about the rules of the war, the battle plans, the nature of our enemy, the resources at our disposal and the best tactics for employing them.

Pentecostals and charismatics have been exploring these areas of spiritual power for some time. But those of us who have chosen to be "non" or even "anti" in the past are discovering that we have much to learn about the real battle. Four of the most prominent areas of ministry that we are beginning to learn more about from our Pentecostal/charismatic colleagues are (1) praise and worship as power, (2) effective prayer, (3) power evangelism and (4) cosmic-level spiritual warfare. This book encompasses the power evangelism and the cosmic-level spiritual warfare categories.

Moving Ahead

The power evangelism symposium helped us to see that we ought to be training our students for the spiritual battle as we never have before. As we move into the '90s, we must do so as warriors on the offensive. "The kingdom of heaven has been forcefully advancing, and forceful men lay hold of it" (Matt. 11:12, *NIV*). Jesus is building His Church and the gates of hell themselves are not powerful enough to stop its forward movement (see Matt. 16:18).

As we move into battle, we do so with the assurance of final victory. Satan and all his armies were decisively defeated on the Cross. There, Jesus "having disarmed principalities and powers, He made a public spectacle of them" (Col. 2:15, *NKJV*). Through His death and resurrection, Jesus Christ "has gone into heaven and is at the right hand of God, angels and authorities and powers having been made subject to Him" (1 Pet. 3:22, *NKJV*).

While we are assured of final victory, we are also warned that it will not be easy. As Paul said, "We must through many tribulations enter the kingdom of God" (Acts 14:22, *NKJV*). No warrior expects to win a battle without pain, suffering, difficulty and discouragement.

But Jesus has given us the resources we need. He has delegated to us spiritual authority for healing the sick, casting out demons, tearing down strongholds, binding and loosing and, most of all, for sharing the good news of Jesus Christ so that men and women can be born again and have their names written in heaven. He has given us the full armor of God with the sword of the Spirit which is His Word. Martin Luther had it right when he wrote in "A Mighty Fortress," "We will not fear, for God has willed His truth to triumph through us."

The authors of this book have caught the vision of the real battle for world evangelization. They help us to be more fully prepared to move forward into it for the glory of God.

CHAPTER

1

Power Evangelism: Definitions and Directions

JOHN WIMBER

JOHN WIMBER is director of Vineyard Ministries International, and pastor of the Vineyard Christian Fellowship in Anaheim, California. He is widely known for his leadership in the deliverance ministry movement, especially through his influential book, *Power Evangelism*, and the national and international conferences he has conducted on the topic.

Personal Pilgrimage

I was converted to Christ in 1963 through the ministry of Gunner Payne, a man whose zeal for Jesus compelled him to share the gospel with anything that breathed. He went door-to-door in our town of Yorba Linda, California, telling virtually every resident about salvation in Jesus. Most nights of the week he taught evangelistic Bible studies, patiently answering seekers' questions into the late hours of the night. My wife Carol and I were the fruit of one of those studies.

For the first year of my Christian life I followed Gunner around, learning to do everything he did. Part of that involved telling people about Jesus. I couldn't go to the market or a hardware store without evangelizing someone. By the end of the year I too was teaching evangelistic Bible studies. Between 1963 and 1970 Carol and I led hundreds of people to Christ, and by 1970 I was leading several Bible studies a week, with over 500 people involved. I was appointed to the Yorba Linda Friends Church staff in 1970, because we had personally brought so many new Christians into the church. They were truly our sheep. I served as pastor until 1974.

The majority of people whom I led to Christ from 1963 through 1974 came under "normal" circumstances, at least as measured by typical evangelical criteria: I preached the gospel and answered some questions, and they repented and trusted Jesus. But occasionally I led someone to Christ in an unusual way. In some instances I received remarkable insights into their lives (for example, knowledge of a specific serious sin or deep hurt). At other times I experienced what seemed to be a supernatural force going out with my sharing and drawing people to

God.[1] When I described these experiences to colleagues, they encouraged me not to talk about them. My colleagues were uncomfortable (so was I!), and felt I would lose stature if other leaders heard about it. They had no explanation for what had happened.

In 1974 I left the pastorate to become founding director of the Department of Church Growth at what is now called the Charles E. Fuller Institute of Evangelism and Church Growth. During the next four years I introduced several thousand pastors to church growth principles, traveling across America and visiting dozens of denominations. During this time I got to know some Pentecostals, a part of the church that previously I knew little about. (Most of what I did know was inaccurate.) The most notable groups were the Church of God (Cleveland, TN), the Assemblies of God (Springfield, MO), and the Pentecostal Holiness Church (Franklin, GA). Each group was experiencing dramatic growth, and each attributed it to combining the proclamation of the gospel with works of power of the Holy Spirit.

Because of my dispensational background, I was skeptical about their claims of healing. But I couldn't write them off, because of their undeniable growth. So I visited their bookstores and picked up literature written by or about men such as John G. Lake, William Branham, the Bosworth brothers and Alexander Dowey. Their writings might not have convinced me that they had great theological insight, but they did convince me that they were not frauds. And they awakened in me the memory of my earlier, unexplainable evangelistic experiences. It began to dawn on me that perhaps some of my experiences were somehow related to the ministry of the Holy Spirit.

While this was going on, I was getting involved at Fuller's School of World Mission, where I served as an adjunct faculty member. At Fuller I had the honor of meeting professors such as Donald McGavran, Chuck Kraft, Paul Hiebert, C. Peter Wagner and the School of Theology's Russell Spittler. I also was introduced to the writings of George Eldon Ladd, specifically his work on the kingdom of God. Seminary courses and reports of signs and wonders from the Third World softened my heart considerably toward the Holy Spirit and the charismatic gifts, especially as they were related to evangelism.

Also at Fuller, I met many pastors from the Third World who reported dramatic instances of signs and wonders and church growth. At first they were quiet about it, but as I probed them they opened up with remarkable stories. I realized that the power of God was working in the Third World in ways I didn't think possible today. Their experiences made my earlier unexplained evangelistic encounters pale in comparison. At this point I felt compelled to reexamine Scripture, looking more carefully at the relationship between spiritual gifts and evangelism.

Scripture Study

I turned to the Bible and tried to answer three questions. First, how did Jesus evangelize? Second, how did Jesus commission the disciples? Third, in light of their commissioning, how did the disciples evangelize? My book *Power Evangelism* is the fruit of my study. In this paper I will highlight only a few points that led to my coining the term "power evangelism," by answering each of the above questions.

1. *How did Jesus evangelize?* At the beginning of His public ministry Jesus, quoting from Isa. 61:1, 2, proclaimed in the synagogue in His home town, Nazareth, that:

The Spirit of the Lord is on me,
because he has anointed me
to preach good news to the poor.
He has sent me to proclaim freedom for the
     prisoners
and recovery of sight for the blind,
to release the oppressed,
to proclaim the year of the Lord's favor . . . .
Today this scripture is fulfilled in your hearing
     (Luke 4:18-19,21, *NIV*).

Throughout the Gospels a clear pattern of ministry unfolds, and it is repeated wherever Jesus went. First, *proclamation:* He preached repentance and the good news of the kingdom of God. Second, *demonstration:* He cast out demons, healed the sick, raised the dead—which proved He was the Anointed One, and that in Him the Kingdom was present.

The Gospels occasionally summarize His ministry. It is particularly interesting to read what Matthew thought was most significant about Christ's ministry:

Jesus went throughout Galilee, teaching in their syn-agogues, preaching the good news of the kingdom, and healing every disease and sickness among the people. News about him spread all over Syria, and people brought to him all who were ill with various diseases, those suffering severe pain, the demon-possessed, those having seizures, and the paralyzed, and he healed them. Large crowds from Galilee, the Decapolis, Jerusalem, Judea and the region across the Jordan followed him (Matt. 4:23-25; see also 9:35-36, *NIV*).

Here again we see the pattern of proclamation combined with demonstration of the kingdom of God, resulting in large crowds and many followers. Passages such as these, summarizing Jesus' ministry as they do, are significant in that they tell us what Jesus *did*. This is not surprising, however. For in the rabbinic way of thinking, what one did was as important as what one believed. This concept was clearly demonstrated by the Lord Jesus Christ. He passed along to the disciples His life *and His way of life*. This is critical information for understanding the Great Commission in Matt. 28:18-20.

Another important aspect of Christ's ministry was His emphasis on the kingdom of God. My first book, *Power Evangelism,* could just as easily have been titled *Kingdom Evangelism,* for its foundational premise (and the topic of the first chapter) is that the kingdom of God has come in Christ, and that every Christian is called to preach and demonstrate the Kingdom today.[2]

Jesus and the disciples did not consign the kingdom of God to a future millennium. Jesus began His public ministry by announcing that "the kingdom of God is near" and then describing it in detail to His followers. In Mark 1:15 (*NIV*) He said, "the kingdom of God is near. Repent and believe the good news!" Thus the heart of Jesus' message was both the proclamation of God's action—"the kingdom is near"—and the demand for a response from all who hear—"repent and believe."

"Kingdom" is translated from the New Testament Greek word *basileia,* which implies an exercise of kingly rule or reign rather than simply establishing a geographic realm over which a king rules. The kingdom of God is the dynamic reign or rule of God. When Jesus said that the kingdom of God had come in Him, He claimed for Himself the position of a divine invader, coming to set everything straight: "The reason the Son of God appeared was to destroy the devil's work" (1 John 3:8, *NIV*).

Jesus went beyond merely claiming to be the presence of the Kingdom; He demonstrated it by healing the sick, casting out demons and raising the dead. Every one of His miracles had a purpose: to confront people with His message that the Kingdom had come and that they had to accept or reject it. This powerful combination of the proclamation and the demonstration of the Kingdom was a key to His ministry.

Most people can understand how Jesus was able to preach and demonstrate the kingdom of God. After all, He was God come in human form. God heals, casts out demons and overcomes all forms of evil. But what about the disciples? How were they able to demonstrate the kingdom of God? And what about us? How can we add demonstration to our proclamation? The Holy Spirit and His gifts provide the answer to these questions.

2. *How did Jesus commission the disciples?* For three years Jesus taught the disciples how to minister from hearts of compassion and mercy, to hear the Father, to grow in dependence on the Holy Spirit, to be obedient to God's leading and to believe that God performs miracles through men and women. Even though they frequently forgot or misunderstood what they were taught, Christ's post-resurrection commission, as recorded in Mark 16:14-20 (*NIV*), was consistent with their training:

> Jesus appeared to the Eleven as they were eating; he rebuked them for their lack of faith . . . [and] said to them, "Go into all the world and preach the good news to all creation . . . And these signs will accompany those who believe: In my name they will drive out demons; they will speak in new tongues; they

will pick up snakes with their hands; and when they drink deadly poison, it will not hurt them at all; they will place their hands on sick people, and they will get well. . . . Then the disciples went out and preached everywhere, and the Lord worked with them and confirmed his word by the signs that accompanied it.

I find it remarkable that many Western Christians are surprised by the emphasis on signs and wonders in this commissioning. Some have challenged the genuineness of Mark 16:9-20. While it is true that some of the most reliable early manuscripts do not contain this passage, most Christian traditions have included it in the canon of Scripture, including the *Authorized Version* (King James). This raises a question: Why was such a text added—if it were, as evidence suggests (but does *not* confirm)—in the second century? Although the ending was questioned in the early Church by Eusebius, Jerome, Clement of Alexandria, Origen, Cyprian and Cyril of Alexandria, why did the Church continue to include it in the manuscripts? Why did Iranaeus cite Mark 16:9? And why did Justin refer to Mark 16:20 as authoritative?

Modern theologians are far from unified on whether to include 16:9-20 in Mark's Gospel. For example, J.W. Burgon, R.C.H. Lenski and E.F. Hills all defend its inclusion in the text. Is it reasonable to think that the Church was sufficiently infiltrated by fanatics to allow the Word of God to be tampered with? A better explanation for its inclusion may be that the *experience* of the early Church conformed to the teaching of Mark 16:9-20.

But let's say, for the sake of argument, that the Mark 16:9-20 commissioning is merely the work of a simple, second-century scribe-fanatic, and that it must be discarded. Does this really change the nature of our commissioning? Matthew's version of the Great Commission reads:

> All authority in heaven and on earth has been given to me. Therefore go and make disciples of all nations, baptizing them in the name of the Father and of the Son and of the Holy Spirit, and teaching them to obey everything I have commanded you. And surely I am with you always, to the very end of the age (Matt. 28:18-20, *NIV*).

Notice the three objectives:
(1) Make disciples from all nations;
(2) Baptize them (bring them into the Church);
(3) Teach them obedience to God's Word (discipleship).

Jesus is calling for us to bring people fully under His reign, into the kingdom of God. This is "kingdom conversion," in which people come into a new reality, a reality in which the "supernatural" is quite natural. Thought of this way, conversion involves both a change *in the person* (being "born again"), and a change of *citizenship* (leaving the kingdom of Satan and entering the kingdom of God; cf. 2 Cor. 5:16-17). In conversion we become new men and women, and we enter a new world.

The question at hand, however, is: Are *works of power* included in the Great Commission? A letter published in the August 1988, issue of *On Being*, a leading evangelical publication in Australia, captures the thoughts of some Christians on this question. (The publication received many letters in response to articles on power evangelism and a conference I led; and they were published in a forum section.) Phil Hancox of Alderley, Queensland, writes of Matt. 28:19-20: "No mention was made there of a healing ministry. His whole emphasis was on teaching, followed by baptism. If preachers are wise, they will follow the same pattern."³ So, Hancox and others say, if works of power are not mentioned by name, we are guilty of reading into Scripture if we include them in the Great Commission. At the very least, the burden of proof is placed squarely on the shoulders of those who believe that proclamation and demonstration of the gospel are part of the Great Commission.

The goal of making obedient disciples who are integrated into the Body of Christ is a high if not impossible ideal, apart from God. This is why Christ promised help to fulfill the task: "You will receive power when the Holy Spirit comes on you; and you will be my witnesses in Jerusalem, and in all Judea and Samaria, and to the ends of the earth" (Acts 1:8, *NIV*).

The promise of the Holy Spirit was implicit in the Great Commission of Matthew 28:18-20, where, just before calling the Eleven to make disciples, Jesus said, "All *authority* in heaven and on earth has been given to me" (Matt. 28:18, *NIV*). Then, after the commissioning, He said, "And surely I am with you always, to the very end of the age" (v. 20). The Greek word used for authority in this passage, *exousia*, denotes power, which was divinely given to Jesus. Through the indwelling Holy Spirit we receive the authority of Christ, which is the authority of the Father. "I tell you the truth," Jesus told the Jews who were persecuting Him, "the Son can do nothing by himself; he can only do what he sees his Father doing, because whatever the Father does the Son also does" (John 5:19, *NIV*).

Jesus proclaimed and demonstrated the gospel wherever He went; it is reasonable to conclude that the apostles followed His lead and did likewise. The early disciples cast out demons, spoke in tongues and healed the sick. Why is their behavior so difficult for us to accept? Why are we always dismissing their behavior as the exception— not the norm—for how we are supposed to live the Christian life? When Jesus commissioned His followers to baptize, and to make disciples, they understood that they were to go out and do exactly what Jesus had shown them. How else are we to interpret their subsequent behavior? This leads me to my next point.

3. *How did the disciples respond to the Great Commission?* An old adage goes, "The proof of the pudding is in the eating." This is certainly true of the Great Commission, because a close inspection of the book of Acts reveals that the disciples went out and spread the good news in the same fashion as Christ: proclamation and demonstration of the kingdom of God. Practice is as important as belief, because it communicates our faith. Orthodoxy (right belief) and orthopraxy (right practice) are interrelated, reinforcing and validating each other. The apostles not only taught what they heard, they did what Jesus did. [4]

At the beginning of Acts, Luke wrote that the purpose of his Gospel had been to write all that Jesus did and taught (Acts 1:1). In Acts, Luke continued the story of Jesus' works and teaching, only now they were done by the disciples (Acts 1:8). Clearly he implies that the continuation of Jesus' ministry through the disciples was the continuation of Jesus' ministry on earth, the fulfillment of the Great Commission. Notice, too, that power evangelism went beyond the first generation of disciples; there were also the apostles. Then a second generation, Stephen, Philip, and Ananias—none of them apostles—proclaimed and demonstrated the Kingdom (Acts 7; 8:26-40; 9:10-18). Barnabas, Silas, and Timothy represented a *third genera-*

tion of those who performed works of power. Finally, in every century of church history we have reliable reports of works of power.[5]

The key to advancing the kingdom of God, of course, was the outpouring of the Holy Spirit in Acts 2. When the Spirit came on them the disciples received God's power. Now they were able to do works of power and preach with power. Michael Green responds to the question, "Why did God send His Holy Spirit?" in his book, *I Believe in the Holy Spirit*. He writes, "There can be no doubt from a candid examination of the New Testament accounts that the prime purpose of the coming of the Spirit of God upon the disciples was to equip them for mission. The Comforter comes not in order to allow men to be comfortable, but to make them missionaries."[6] Green goes on to point out that this runs contrary to our assumptions, "namely that the Holy Spirit, however vaguely we conceive of him, is an internal gift for the faithful, appropriate only to be mentioned in church." A key to power evangelism is the Holy Spirit.

At least 10 kinds of sign phenomena in the book of Acts produced evangelistic growth in the church. Specifically called "signs and wonders" nine times, they include healing, expelling demons, resuscitation of the dead, sounds "like the blowing of a violent wind" from heaven, fire over the heads of people, tongues, and being transported from one place to another. Acts 5:12-14 (*NIV*) says, "The apostles performed many miraculous signs and wonders among the people . . . [And] more and more men and women believed in the Lord and were added to their number." In the book of Acts there are 14 instances where both apostles and non-apostles, for example, preached, performed works of power, and saw significant church growth. The following summarizes these instances:

Works of Power	Preaching	Church Growth
Pentecost (2:4)	Peter (2:14)	3,000 added (2:41)
Cripple healed (3:1)	Peter (3:12)	5,000 believed (4:4)
Miraculous signs (8:6)	Philip (8:6)	Men and women believe (8:12)
Philip appears (8:26)	Philip teaches (8:35)	Eunuch baptized (8:38)
Angel appears, vision falls (10:3, 12, 44)	Peter (10:34)	Gentiles baptized (10:47)
Lord's hand with them (11:20-21)	Men from Cyprus (11:20)	Many believe (11:21)
Evidence of God's grace (11:23,24)	Barnabas (11:23)	Great number believe (11:24b)
Holy Spirit falls (13:1-3)	Barnabas, Saul (13:1)	Churches in Asia, (14:23) Europe (17:11)
Miraculous signs and wonders (14:1-7)	Paul and Barnabas (14:3)	People divided (14:4, 21, 22)
Cripple healed (14:8-18)	Paul and Barnabas (14:15)	Disciples gather (14:21)
Cast out demon (16:16)	Paul and Silas (16:14)	Believers gather (16:40)
Earthquake, prison doors open (16:25, 26)	Paul and Silas (16:31-32)	Jailer and household saved (16:34)

God's power (18:1; cf. 1 Cor. 2:1, 4, 5)	Paul (18:5)	Many believed (18:8)
Extraordinary miracles (19:11-12)	Paul (19:10)	Churches in Asia (19:26)

Even more revealing is the contrast in evangelistic results between Paul's work in Athens (Acts 17:16-34) and Corinth (18:1-17). In Athens Paul argued eloquently at the Areopagus, with the results that "a *few* men became followers of Paul and believed" (17:34, *NIV*). In Corinth, the next stop on his apostolic tour, the results were that "many people in this city" believed (18:10, *NIV*). While there are several factors that explain the different responses (particularly the different degrees of receptivity found in the people of each city), Paul himself wrote to those in Corinth, "When I came to you, brothers, I did not come with eloquence or superior wisdom . . . My message and my preaching were not with wise and persuasive words, but with a demonstration of the Spirit's power, so that your faith might not rest on men's wisdom, but on God's power" (1 Cor. 2:1, 4, 5, *NIV*). It appears that in Corinth Paul combined proclamation with demonstration, as Christ had done throughout His ministry. We are dealing here with both content (proclamation) as well as context (the situation impregnated with God's mighty presence). The Word and works of God were coupled in an expression of His divine will and mercy, culminating in the conversion of individuals as well as groups.

The combination of experiences at Fuller and in the field, plus a rethinking of Scripture, led me to begin praying for the sick. Around this time I returned to the pastorate, leading a small home group that my wife started. I have written extensively about my experience in the book *Power Healing,* but one aspect bears repeating. I discovered that as people were healed and as I encouraged members of my congregation to pray for the sick (and open themselves up to other works of power), evangelism took off. Put simply: the church exploded. Today we have 5,000 people attending the Anaheim Vineyard, and 240 Vineyards (with some 50,000 attendees) scattered across North America.

New Term

After I completed my study I concluded that while proclamation of the gospel is the heart and soul of evangelism, adding a demonstration of works of power can be a catalyst to the evangelistic task. Now, I was aware that I was proposing a new kind of evangelism, at least new to many Western Christians. In fact, since my book *Power Evangelism* was published, I have been accused of "adding to the gospel"—claiming that evangelism apart from signs and wonders is invalid. This claim is untrue. So, I will again say here: *the heart and soul of evangelism is proclamation of the gospel.* Many people come to Christ after hearing a simple presentation of the gospel; I imagine most of you reading these words did. And, why not? There is great power in the gospel. All effective evangelism is impregnated with the Holy Spirit (1 Cor. 1:21-24; 2:6-16). "I am not ashamed of the gospel," Paul writes in Rom. 1:16, "because it is the power of God for the salvation of everyone who believes" (*NIV*). The implication of Paul's words is clear: God's power for salvation is through the gospel alone. Its content, Paul writes, is "that Christ died for our sins according to the Scriptures, that he was buried, that he was raised on the third day according to the Scriptures"

(1 Cor. 15:3, 4, *NIV*). In power evangelism we don't add to the gospel, or even seek to add power to the gospel. But we do turn to the third Person of the Triune God in our evangelistic efforts, *consciously* cooperating with His anointing, gifting and leading. Preaching and demonstrating the gospel are not mutually exclusive activities; they work together, reinforcing each other.

The Bible, my experience and the experience of many fine Christians indicate that proclamation and demonstration produce dramatic results. After I became convinced of this, I knew I needed a term to capture the heart of what I had learned. I could have called it "signs and wonders evangelism," but that sounded audacious. Or, I could have called it "more-powerful evangelism," but that would have implied that the gospel itself was weak and in need of "signs and wonders Geritol." Then I asked myself, *What one word sums up what this is all about?* And I saw it: *power.* The key to what I saw was power. So I coined the term "power evangelism." This term is also open to much misunderstanding, but I have concluded that the nature of what I am doing will be attacked and misunderstood no matter what it's called. Let's face it, though—label it what you like, power evangelism is controversial.

For example, some draw the wrong conclusion that power evangelism excludes programmatic evangelism, the hallmark of twentieth-century evangelism. Many fine Christians have devoted their lives to programmatic evangelism—message-centered communication of the gospel primarily through rational arguments. Programmatic evangelism comes in many forms: organized crusades or revivals, door-to-door saturation campaigns in which tracts are presented, media campaigns, personal evangelism contacts and friendship evangelism are only a few examples. Of course, I am not against programmatic evangelism. Quite the contrary, I endorse and encourage it. As I have written in *Power Evangelism*, "My contention is not that programmatic evangelism has been wrong. After all, power evangelism employs the heart of programmatic evangelism, a simple presentation of the gospel."[7]

Properly understood, power evangelism can make all other approaches to evangelism more effective. I define power evangelism as a *presentation of the gospel that is rational but also transcends the rational*. The explanation of the kingdom of God comes with a demonstration of God's power through works of power. It is a spontaneous, Spirit-inspired, empowered presentation of the gospel. It is usually preceded and undergirded by demonstrations of God's presence, and frequently results in groups of people being saved. Signs and wonders do not save; *only Jesus saves.*

Because power evangelism cannot be reduced to a technique or method, I will describe it through illustrations and explanation of its key characteristics.

Kingdom Conflict

Eph. 6:12 says, "For our struggle is not against flesh and blood, but against the rulers, against the authorities, against the powers of this dark world and against the spiritual forces of evil in the heavenly realms" (*NIV*). This verse applies to every aspect of the Christian life, including evangelism. People engaged in power evangelism are self-conscious members of God's army, sent to do battle against the forces of the kingdom of darkness. They *expect* conflict, because they are always looking to overcome the works of Satan in order to set people free.

The difficulty in the Western Church is that most people don't know that there is a war going on. They do not see the relationship between God and Satan that the Bible sees. They are only minimally aware of conflict between the two kingdoms, and, due to their secularized, empirical perception of the Christian experience, they believe that they are living in a world unaffected by the two kingdoms and their existences. They are insensitive to God's kingdom because at best they are only minimally converted to it. They may have repented of their sin and trusted in Christ, but they are unaware that they are now members of a new kingdom that is opposed to everything the world says is important. In a word, Western Christians are highly individualistic and privatized; thus they see little significance in the kingdom of God.

This world view gap has led to the erroneous assumption that the spirit world is somehow less real than the tangible, materialistic one in which we live. Therefore, since the "real" world is more easily controlled (according to scientific assumption based on Western world view) we think we need have no fear of the less real (spiritual) world. The spirit world is thereby relegated to myth and superstition.[8]

Because Christians are not fully converted to the kingdom of God, they are influenced by the world's values of materialism and anti-supernaturalism. This inhibits Western Christians from experiencing evangelistic power as illustrated in the New Testament, thus they exclude from their thinking categories for understanding how to experience works of power.

In the kingdom of God "supernatural" and "natural" are not treated as separate realities that we slip in and out of, like entering and leaving the twilight zone. In the kingdom of God, angelic visitations, dreams, visions and prophecies are a natural way of life, some of the means God uses to communicate His desires and direction to His people. In contemporary society Christians frequently screen out the possibility of supernatural interaction with the natural. We refuse, for the most part, even to study or allow for the possibility of supernatural activity in our day.

Power Encounters

By accepting the supernatural as a natural part of kingdom living, we consciously encounter Satan's kingdom daily. It is here that we must take on Christ's authority, as given in the Great Commission, to heal diseases and cast out demons, to demonstrate God's reign.

These conflicts are called *power encounters,* the clashing of the kingdom of God with the kingdom of Satan. They may occur in many circumstances, the expulsion of demons being the most dramatic form, although power encounters are far from limited only to the demonic. When unbelievers either have a power encounter or witness one, they are moved to a new level of awareness in making a decision for Christ. God is present and they know it. Power encounters are doorways to the kingdom of God.

Jesus' public ministry began with a power encounter. In Mark 1:21-28 we read of His casting a demon out of a man in the synagogue in Capernaum. This created quite a stir among the people. Later that day the whole town "brought to Jesus all the sick and demon-possessed" (v. 32). He healed many, cast out many demons, and commanded the demons not to speak. The presence of the kingdom of God met Satan head to head, and Satan was soundly defeated.

Over the 11-year history of the Anaheim Vineyard Christian Fellowship we have seen numerous outpourings of the Holy Spirit, resulting in seasons of great evangelistic harvest and blessing. (On several occasions we have baptized hundreds of new Christians during these seasons.) These spiritual outpourings—revivals—have had such an impact on church members that many have spent days on end evangelizing under a supernatural compulsion. The Holy Spirit leads them from place to place and person to person in an overwhelming expression of God's love, and with remarkable responses.⁹

Supernatural Insights

Many power encounters begin with *supernatural insights,* called words of knowledge in Scripture. For example, in Acts 5:1-11 we read of Peter receiving a word of knowledge regarding Ananias. Ananias died because of unconfessed secret sin, sin that was premeditated. Scripture says, "Great fear seized the whole church and all who heard about these events"(v.11, *NIV*).

People who are constantly in communion with the Holy Spirit receive insights, inklings, sometimes even strange thoughts about complete strangers, and act on them with startling results. Is this really that different from the way the disciples operated in the book of Acts? I think not.

In my own experience, I once led someone to Christ by asking him an odd question: "Do you know what a breech baby is?"

After receiving the Lord he said, "How did you know?"

"Know what?" I asked.

"That I was a male nurse in the army," he replied. "I've helped to deliver many breech babies. Nothing you could have said to me could have made me understand any more than that."

How do you include that in an evangelistic training manual? "First you say . . . , then he says . . . . " No technique or method can teach this! This is the sovereign activity of a loving God giving spiritual insight to a yielded servant, willing to risk making a fool of himself.

The key to receiving God's inklings is a constant openness to His Spirit. I think this is the openness that Paul writes about in Eph. 6:18: "Pray in the Spirit on all occasions with all kinds of prayers and requests" (*NIV*). Paul is describing an attitude, a mind-set of communion with God that permeates every activity of the day. When we yield our hearts to Him in this way, He gives us "kingdom eyes," spiritual insight into the hearts and minds of men and women.

Simple and Direct

Power encounters are exciting experiences. But occasionally they lead to spiritual pride in those who receive them. This happens when they forget that the Holy Spirit provides wisdom and insight. Our job is to remain open and faithful.

I don't imply, though, that we don't have a significant role to play. In 2 Cor. 3:3 Paul says, "You show that you are a letter from Christ, the result of our ministry, written not with ink but with the Spirit of the living God, not on tablets of stone but on tablets of human hearts." Paul likens us to living Bibles—walking, talking testimonies of the kingdom of God!

We shouldn't be surprised when the Holy Spirit encourages us to say and do things we wouldn't ordinarily do. Under the anointing of the Holy Spirit, Jesus manifested all of the gifts of the Holy Spirit. Often He healed with a word or a gesture, and He converted some simply by knowing their names.

"Zacchaeus, come down from there immediately. I must stay at your house today," Jesus said. Zacchaeus responded by promising to give half of his possessions to the poor, and to pay back anyone four times the amount he had cheated them. Jesus said, "Today salvation has come to this house" (Luke 19:5, 9, *NIV*).

Jesus' prayers for the sick, His evangelistic messages, even His recruiting techniques ("Come, follow me . . . ") are notable for their simplicity. Obviously, He was operating in an unction greater than personal words. In drawing comparisons between us and Jesus we must always keep in mind that He was *the* Son of God—fully God, fully divine—while we are sons and daughters by adoption. We do not possess a divine nature as Jesus does.

Simplicity and directness mark Christ's approach to ministry. Jesus raised the young man from the dead in the town of Nain by simply saying, "Young man, I say to you, get up" (Luke 7:14, *NIV*). I have read through the Gospels and Acts, writing down all of the power-encounter prayers that Jesus and the apostles spoke. I found them straightforward and simple, excellent models for how we should minister.

Divine Appointments

A *divine appointment* is an appointed time in which God reveals Himself to an individual or group through spiritual gifts or other supernatural phenomena. God arranges these encounters—they are meetings He has ordained to demonstrate His kingdom power and His presence.

In Scripture we see many of these encounters: the Samaritan woman in John 4 (Jesus knew the secrets of her marital life); Zacchaeus and Jesus in Luke 19 (Jesus knew his name); Philip and the Ethiopian eunuch in Acts 8 (Philip was translated away from his encounter). In each instance God arranges a meeting in which His kingdom is demonstrated and explained, with startling results.

Usually divine appointments are effective because the Christian, by supernatural means, observes "felt needs" in the life of the person being evangelized. These needs vary: lack of self-control in areas like sex, food, drugs, alcohol; serious emotional problems; illness. But when a power encounter occurs, people are quickly converted.

As evangelicals we should always keep divine appointments. Frequently we miss them, which accounts for the poor evangelistic results many Christians experience. In power evangelism, what you do and say must be said at the right time and in the correct place.

Further Reflection

Many of the contributors in this volume have had a great influence on my thinking. I believe that their contributions in the area of theology will do much to shape the thinking of younger leaders in what is called the Third Wave. With this in mind, I have given thought to areas in which I believe serious theological reflection needs to be done by qualified scholars.

Please understand that in raising these questions I neither offer answers nor do I feel qualified to discover them. I am a pastor, not a theologian. My hope is that some of these concerns may stimulate the interest of people more qualified than I, and bring new insights that will bless the body of Christ.

1. *Can we sharpen the definition of the Kingdom paradigm?* I have become uncomfortable with speaking of the "supernatural," "miracles" and "signs and wonders," as though they are abnormal events or dimensions in the "real" world of material cause and effect. In part this has to do with my growing understanding of the radicalness of the kingdom of God. It seems that when we enter Christ

we come under a new rule and reign; we enter and live in the kingdom of God.

My question is: Should we not begin thinking about the kingdom of God in more radical ways, defining ultimate reality as God's Kingdom, and the world in which we live as, to borrow C.S. Lewis's term, a "shadow world"? This raises questions about what it means to enter and live under the kingdom of God. For example, what does it mean to have a Kingdom paradigm shift? I suspect further thinking on the kingdom of God is a key to future Third Wave theology and practice.

2. *How has the scientific method infiltrated evangelical theology and practice and what should we do about it?* In the foreword to the book *Power Encounters* I write:

> The historical-critical method itself is not responsible for this departure (the denial of the supernatural today by evangelicals), though I believe at times it inclines Christians away from a deeper spirituality. Commenting on the historical-critical method in *The Use of the Bible in Theology—Evangelical Options,* New Testament scholar Russell P. Spittler says, "The historical-critical method when applied to Scripture, is both legitimate and necessary—but inadequate . . . inadequate because . . . the end of biblical study cannot consist in historical dates or tentative judgments about complicated and conjectured literary origins. The end of biblical study consists rather in enhanced faith, hope and love both for the individual and the community" (p. 97). Reliance on this method of Scripture study, which dominates most Western conservative evangelical theological seminaries and graduate schools, can produce *intellectual* but not necessarily *spiritual* Christian leaders.[10]

Now, my point is not to downgrade serious biblical studies. But I ask: Does the historical-critical method, especially as practiced in most seminaries, produce the kind of fruit that we are looking for? Is it pointing students (especially future leaders) toward a relationship with Jesus Christ? And is it strengthening that relationship?

The historical-critical method is rooted in scientism, a way of thinking that has captured the Western mind in this century. Scientism is the principle that scientific methods can and should be applied in all fields of investigation—including religion. We have much to be thankful for from the scientific method; because of it many foolish and hurtful ideas have been discarded (for example, false ideas about the races), and it has paved the way to scientific and technological discovery. But have we allowed it to invade our approach to Scripture study to the degree that it now *controls* our thinking, in many instances excluding from the realm of thinking and faith those things that should be a part of the Christian life?

I also have questions about how the scientific method influences Christians' practices. For example, I have heard more than one Christian say that all healings must be validated by modern medicine before they will consider them true. I am not fearful of modern medicine scrutinizing healings, but I am afraid of the mentality that sets science up as the standard by which Christian practice is judged. It is as though doctors are the new priestly caste; only they are qualified to validate religious experience.

Think of this a little differently. What if someone walked into a pastor's office and said, "I have been a sinner all my life—drug user, hater of my parents, fornicator. This morning I repented and turned my heart to Christ. I feel like a new person!" Now, I ask, how many pastors would send this person to a psychologist to be tested to "prove" he was truly converted and is now emotionally well-adjusted? Or would they send him to an ethicist to verify in fact that he now believes Judeo-Christian ethics? Here is my point: Our skeptical responses to reports of signs and wonders show we are more affected by modern scientism than we want to admit.

Science has become the primary ideology in the Western world, replacing Christianity as the predominant religion. And, the religion of modern science is quite intolerant of any views that challenge its presuppositions. Certainly this is true of most colleges and universities today, as Allan Bloom argues in his book, *The Closing of the American Mind.* To question modern scientific presuppositions is to commit heresy, which is one explanation for Christianity's loss of stature in Western society over the past 50 years.

Finally, the scientific method of Bible study tends to control areas of theological exploration. It does this in two ways. First, it *eliminates some areas of investigation.* Among many liberal Christians, topics like demons and healing are not worthy of serious consideration. They are ruled out as incompatible with a modern world view. The issue here is plausibility; some subjects are acceptable within a scientific world view, others are not. The latter are discarded, and anyone interested in studying them is labeled a "fundamentalist" (horrors!) and a narrow-minded person.

Second, and this is far more difficult to combat, *the scientific method of Bible study alters how we study certain topics.* That is, it controls the nature of our investigation. Few theologians give serious consideration to topics like healing, demons or tongues. If they do, their approach frequently is framed in scientifically acceptable criteria. For example, studies of tongues may include "tongues from a psychological perspective," "the history of tongues, 1869 to present," or "the sociological effects of tongues." (In fact, I own books that treat tongues in these fashions.) Theologians who treat a topic like tongues with the assumption that it is a supernatural gift from God that is possible to experience today, lose professional stature in the eyes of their colleagues. They especially are in hot water if they suggest ways to put into practice subjects like divine healing or tongues. It is when one adds practice to theory that you find out what people truly believe.

Here is my question: What are our presuppositions as we approach theology? It may be acceptable to employ psychology, sociology, anthropology, medicine and other disciplines in the theological task, but what are our controls? If Scripture conflicts with modern medicine or modern psychology, which wins out?

3. *Should we be reviewing some basic assumptions regarding the education, training, and evaluation of future pastors?* Are our seminaries and Christian colleges really producing Kingdom empowered and equipped leaders? It is hard to answer a question like this. James Davison Hunter, after conducting extensive surveys, suggests we are failing. He makes many stinging remarks, such as the following:

We can see the multiple ironies of Christian higher education. On the one hand, Christian higher education historically evolved into precisely the opposite of what it was supposed to be, that is, into bastions of secularity if not anti-Christian sentiment. Contemporary Christian higher education, on the other hand, produces the uninteded consequences of being counterproductive to its own objectives, that is, it produces individual Christians who are either less certain of their attachments to the traditions of their faith or altogether disaffected from them. Education, to the degree that it is not indoctrination, weakens the tenacity with which Evangelicals hold on to their world view. In sum, Evangelical education creates its own contaminating effects. And the more Christian higher education professionalizes and bureaucratizes (that is, the more it models itself institutionally after secular higher education), the more likely this process will intensify.[11]

These are damning conclusions, but they are based on an impressive study of trends and effectiveness of the major Christian colleges and seminaries. If we choose not to write off Hunter's insights, what is our response? C. Peter Wagner has said the problem with Christian seminary training is we have "the wrong students, wrong teachers, wrong curriculum, and wrong places."[12] That's a bold statement, but one that bears a closer look. I will break it down into four parts and comment on each.

1. *Students:* Currently the primary criteria for admission to seminaries is academic achievement. Small wonder that a large percentage of students graduating from most evangelical seminaries do not go on into ministry. But as a pastor and leader of a fast-growing church movement, I must point out that most successful church growth pastors are not the best academic achievers. What do these men hold in common? They have a clear call, mature character and gifting. These are the kinds of people who should be in seminaries.

2. *Curriculum:* Curriculum that equips to both understand and minister effectively is needed. Seminaries place a strong emphasis on theology and academic achievement,

but is this alone really producing effective leaders?

3. *Teachers:* Many teachers in seminaries are ineffective trainers/equippers/disciplers. They may be good at theology, but should this be their primary purpose for being at the seminary? I think not. Instead, we need more emphasis on recruiting staff who can produce pastors who are able theologically, not theologians who later may find out if they are pastors. In other words, our emphasis should not be so much on theological education as on ministerial training.

4. *Places:* Is it possible to train effective pastors through the classroom method alone? Or, do our methods reflect once again a capitulation to the modern scientific approach to learning, especially the idea that once we intellectually know something, we truly know it?

"Power evangelism" raises concerns that reach far beyond personal evangelism. It touches the nature, the very core, of how we live the Christian life. I hope the remaining chapters will challenge you to reevaluate and renew your walk with God, resulting in a deeper and more intimate trust in Jesus.

Notes

1. For an example of one of these instances, see John Wimber with Kevin Springer *Power Healing* (San Francisco: Harper & Row, 1987), pp. 23-24.
2. I have written a booklet titled "Kingdom Evangelism" (Ann Arbor, MI: Vine, 1989). Also see Don Williams, *Signs, Wonders, and the Kingdom of God* (Ann Arbor, MI: Vine, 1989).
3. Phil Hancox, "Between the Lines" (Letters), *On Being* 15 (7): 52.
4. I am not claiming that the disciples were equal in nature with Jesus. He was God; they (and we) are one with Him in the sense that we are regenerated, and possess His human nature. The works that we do, we do in the power of the Holy Spirit. Also, I am not claiming that the disciples (or we) do works of power to the degree that Jesus did them. But that the disciples did them at all, that they healed the sick, raised the dead, cast out demons, and—in Peter's case—even walked on water, indicates that we are to do as Jesus did.

5. See Wimber and Springer, *Power Evangelism* (San Francisco: Harper and Row, 1986), Appendix A ("Signs and Wonders in Church") and Appendix B ("Signs and Wonders in the Twentieth Century").
6. Michael Green, *I Believe in the Holy Spirit*, Rev. ed. (Grand Rapids, MI: Wm. B. Eerdmans Pub. Co., 1985), p. 68.
7. Wimber and Springer, *Power Evangelism*, p. 47.
8. See Charles Kraft, *Christianity with Power*. (Ann Arbor, MI: Servant Publications, 1989).
9. For more examples of power encounters, read Kevin Springer's *Power Encounters Among Christians in the Western World* (San Francisco: Harper & Row, 1988).
10. Ibid., p. 26.
11. James Davison Hunter, *Evangelicalism: The Coming Generation* (Chicago: University Press, 1987), p. 178.
12. C. Peter Wagner (In personal conversation).

Power Evangelism: Definitions and Directions

John Wimber's paper starts with his own testimony, and keeps fairly close to this experiential dimension to the end. He follows the directives given to those who will contribute to this symposium by maintaining a popular style throughout. This enables him to be broad in his approach and to cover both the ministry of Jesus and of the early disciples in the New Testament. In his applications he is able to deal with cases from the Javanese to the modern Californian, and from animism to scientism. He is also able to suggest further theological and practical developments which he feels may be advantageous as this subject is developed.

The broad, popular approach has advantages and disadvantages. Wimber is able to introduce a number of issues and illustrate them at length. But it is obviously not his aim to deal in depth with any of them. This style will inevitably have a number of contentious, unsupported statements and a number of concepts unfinished or unexplained. It is even able to scrape by without a bibliography.

It is advantageous that near the beginning of the paper, the questions "How did Jesus evangelize?" "How did He commission the disciples?" and "How did the disciples respond to the Great Commission?" were dealt with. It is convincing to show Jesus' ministry as a combination of proclamation and demonstration, particularly in light of the reign of God having come in Him. The powerful ministry of the disciples does, of course, follow the model of Jesus, and uses the same power of the Holy Spirit. It sets the pattern for a powerful evangelistic thrust to continue in the Church. A highlight in this section is the brief challenge to concentrate on orthopraxy and not only on orthodoxy. Correct practice here is associated with the same demonstration of the power of the gospel as noted in the ministry of Jesus. This could have been developed into a telling argument. In between answering the two above questions, however, Wimber asks, "How did He commission the disciples?" In answering this question, in my opinion, he allows himself to get side-tracked into giving a great deal of attention to the problem of Mark 16:9-20. The section ended strongly, but still did not contribute a great deal to accomplishing any of his overall objectives.

Wimber follows this biblical treatment with a section primarily devoted to illustrative incidents. They begin with examples of power encounter in cultural groups which are either animistic or have an animistic core. This kind of incident seems to have done a great deal in the past decade to convince some missionaries and scholars of the need to seriously reexamine both the biblical basis and the missiological value of power encounters. In fact, the whole anti-supernaturalistic set of assumptions we have unsuccessfully endeavored to use in our Western hermeneutic has been exposed as inadequate. Wimber not only introduces this, but also uses some illustrations of power encounters of sorts having a possible effect on evangelization in American society today.

In Wimber's final section, "Further Reflection," he says, "I have given thought to areas in which I believe serious theological reflection needs to be done by qualified scholars. I neither offer answers, nor do I feel qualified to discover them. I am a pastor, not a theologian." Three suggestions are made, however. The first one, to *define the kingdom paradigm*, is a valid suggestion that we come to grips with the reality of the spiritual/supernatural nature of the kingdom of God. This would, however, probably be directed more at a debate with liberal theologians than with evangelicals, who would be loath to admit that they need this reminder. The question *How has the scientific method infiltrated evangelical theology and practice, and what should we do about it?* does, I believe, need investigation, although I do not feel that it is totally neglected by evangelical scholars. I believe that a similar problem has been dealt with to a certain extent by Paul Pommerville in *The Third Force in Missions* in his warning against the effects of a dead scholasticism on our approach to the Scriptures. Lastly, the question *Should we be reviewing some basic assumptions regarding the education, training and evaluation of future pastors?* is actually broader than the scope of this consultation. It is one which should cause such resonance among people like Dr. J. Robert Clinton, that the vibrations would be felt right back to the followers of Ivan Illich. Alas, perhaps the time is not yet ripe for such a radical change in pastoral formation, however necessary this seems to be. But let us keep on agitating until our church leaders, encrusted with, and deafened by, layers of ecclesiastical tradition, hear our challenge often enough, loudly enough, and from a sufficient number of different sources, to agree to really hear us out.

I feel that the greatest issue to arise out of this paper is Wimber's appeal for further investigation by competent theologians. A number of areas would provide fruitful research. One of these is a concept which has already inspired a great deal of scholarship. This is the contention that the Christian gospel is a wholistic message. It needs to be applied in particular to power evangelism. Neither the gospel nor the redemptive act of Christ can be limited to only one aspect of human existence. Jesus died for the whole man, and not just for his soul. If God's ancient covenant with Israel included the blessings of *shalom* or wholeness and well-being,[1] His ultimate covenant through His son would not include any less. His sacrifice included not only forgiveness, but also *shalom*.[2] Jesus died, rose again and sent us to preach a salvation which included the restoration of the whole man.[3] The scope of Christ's redemption is cosmic. It cannot be understood in a narrow, truncated way. As Wolter says, "The scope of redemption is as great as that of the fall."[4] Many have applied this, quite rightly to the way in which social structures and social ills are to be addressed by the gospel. It can be limited to this aspect just as little as it can be limited to the aspect of forgiveness. A wholistic message of salvation has to include the healing of the sick and the casting out of evil spirits.[5] This concept can be developed under the rubric of the kingdom of God with these aspects specifically in mind.

Another aspect of research that should be beneficial is related to the previous statements. It is the concept of the Church continuing with the same type of ministry as Jesus by using His authority or acting on His behalf. This is probably what is meant by Jesus teaching His disciples to pray to the Father in His name (John 14:13). For the ancient near Easterner, as well as the typical resident of the Roman Empire, a great deal of meaning was attached to the use of a name. An aspect of this meaning that is often seen to be prominent is, that to make a petition in someone's name is to do so as a right, or because it is being done as his or her representative. A name was used because of the power and authority that this name acquired.[6] To pray to the Father in the name of Jesus would be to do so as the representative of Jesus.[7]

This concept could be derived theologically from the close association of the believer with his or her Lord. We have Paul's teaching on the incorporation of the believer with Christ in His death and resurrection. We also have what was probably the most characteristic way in which Paul uses the expression *en christo:* We enjoy a sort of mystic corporate personality with him.[8] This attitude toward prayer, therefore, and a realization of the basis on which we act as Christ's representatives, would certainly enable Christians to deal with sickness and demon possession confidently and authoritatively.

The last aspect of research that I feel Wimber's paper calls for is an extensive theological treatment of the *charismata*. It is not his intention to provide even an introductory theology of the gifts, but he does deal with a great deal of charismatic activity. All of us who would like to have this emphasis would benefit from at least one definitive piece of scholarship on the subject. Most of the works which exist, however, are popular treatments, and make little attempt to provide an in-depth exegesis. Neither do they investigate honestly and thoroughly all the major perspectives concerning the *charismata* in the New Testament. My colleague, Siegfried Schatzmann, in *A Pauline Theology of Charismata,* has done some useful exegesis, as has also Gordon Fee in his *New International Commentary on 1 Corinthians.* However, both of these works simply serve as a foundation for a yet-to-be-written theology which investigates and analyzes major perspectives on the subject. Jack Gorman, in *The Gifts of the Spirit,* makes a

48   *Wrestling with Dark Angels*

useful contribution, but he neither attempts to be exhaustive, nor does he deal with and analyze all the perspectives. The same can be said about another good book also written during the '70s, *Spiritual Gifts and the Church,* by Donald Bridge and David Phypers. We have tremendously detailed theology on consubstantiation vs. transubstantiation, and *anomoios* vs. *homoousios.* What about more thinking concerning issues related to the gifts God wishes to use to help evangelize the world?

I would like to applaud John Wimber for his paper. He writes as a dear brother in Christ, a humble but anointed servant of God. He fascinates us, challenges us and encourages us. I believe he also stimulates us to do more sympathetic theological investigation into an extremely important subject.

Notes
1. William S. LaSor, *Epochal Events in the Bible.* Unpublished Syllabus for Fuller Theological Seminary, Pasadena, CA. 1977.
2. Claus Westermann, *Isaiah 40-66: A Commentary* (London: SCM Press, 1969), p. 263.
3. Colin Brown, "Redemption," *Dictionary of N.T. Theology* Vol. 3, ed. Colin Brown (Grand Rapids: Zondervan, 1979), p. 212-3.
4. Albert Wolter, *Creation Regained* (Grand Rapids: Eerdmans, 1985), p. 57.
5. Francis MacNutt, *The Power to Heal* (Notre Dame: Ave Maria Press, 1977), p. 4, 5, 6.
6. R. Youngblood, "The Significance of Names in Bible Times," *Evangelical Dictionary of Theology,* ed. Walter Elwell (Grand Rapids: Baker, 1984), p. 750.
7. Barbnabos Lindors, *The Gospel of John,* New Century Bible Commentary (Grand Rapids: Eerdmans, 1981), p. 476.
8. C. Leslie Mitton, *Ephesians,* New Century Bible Commentary (Grand Rapids: Eerdmans, 1981), p. 46.

We Are at War

ED MURPHY

ED MURPHY is vice president and director of the International Ministry Team of Overseas Crusades. He teaches Bible and missions part-time at San Jose Bible College and trains Christian leaders in spiritual warfare throughout the world. A former missionary to Latin America, Dr. Murphy is the author of three books.

A local newspaper announced the tragic fall of a world famous televangelist with the words of King David found in 2 Sam. 1:25: "How are the mighty fallen in the midst of the battle!" (*KJV*). The newspaper was correct. That man, and millions like him, was a war casualty.

We are at war. As to the origin of this war, all we know is what the Bible tells us. It began in the cosmic realm, evidently before the creation of man, in an angelic rebellion against the Lordship of God (Job 4:18; Matt. 25:41; 1 Cor. 6:3; 2 Pet. 2:4; Jude 6; Rev. 12).

How could such a rebellion occur in the presence of a God who is almighty, sovereign and all-knowing? God has not told us. All He has declared is that it was in this manner that evil was born within His universe.

For problems like this one the Scriptures have a helpful word for us. "The secret things belong to the Lord our God, but the things revealed belong to us and to our sons forever" (Deut. 29:29, *NASB*).

It is interesting, however, that demons will openly confess to their participation in such a rebellion. On more than one occasion while expelling demons from a person's life they have exclaimed,

> We rebelled against God. We were deceived by our master. We are doomed! For us no provision has been made for redemption as it has for mankind. We are doomed! Doomed! We are afraid. But we will fight God and you Christians until the end. We hate Him. We hate you Jesus. We hate you!

Of course, we do not build theology upon the confessions of lying spirits. It is interesting to note, however, that on every occasion when a demon spoke in the presence of Jesus he always told Jesus the truth. Look at the Gospel record.

The experienced deliverance minister can compel evil spirits to tell the truth. I do so all the time. This is not to say that it is wise to carry on long conversations with demons. We only obtain from them the information we need to proceed with the deliverance and then expel them to the place where Jesus wishes to send them.

What began as a cosmic rebellion soon became a cosmic-earthly rebellion. Mankind was deceived by the same master of the fallen angels, the devil (Matt. 25:41), to also rebel against the Lordship of God. The universe has never been the same since then (Gen. 3 with John 8:44; 2 Cor. 11:3 and Rev. 12:3-17).

The important point to emphasize here is that everything from Gen. 3 to Rev. 20 occurs within the context of this cosmic-earthly spiritual warfare dimension of reality. I call this the *spiritual warfare dimension of a biblical world view*. This is present reality from God's perspective.

We are at war. That war will not end until the final judgment of evil supernaturalism (Satan and his kingdom of fallen angels, Matt. 25:41) recorded in Rev. 20. We are all involved in this warfare whether we like it or not and, whether we are aware of it or not.

We need to condition ourselves, so to speak, to put on our spiritual warfare eyeglasses to correctly view present reality. Isn't this what the apostle Paul is trying to tell us in 2 Cor. 4:3-6 and Eph. 6:12?

A Threefold Description of the War

First and foremost, *it is a sin war.* Sin wars against us and we, in turn, must learn to war against sin.

Since I am writing to Christians I will not bother to

define sin. As to the cross-cultural dimensions of sin, each missionary must wrestle with that crucial question from within the context of both Scripture and local culture. That is what I have had to do.

I will affirm, however, that sin—moral evil in contrast to natural evil—is not a passive something that appears where righteousness is absent. Sin is at war with righteousness. It is like an active, dynamic, negative spiritual energy field that seeks to carry away everything with it. It will oppress, enslave and eventually destroy everything that stands in its way.

It releases *sin energy,* or negative spiritual force, for lack of a better word, that easily overpowers the best of men. It tempts, seduces, deceives, delights and captivates, only in time to torment, torture and finally destroy.

Perhaps the best description of the sin energy released by sin is in Heb. 12:1: "Let us also lay aside every encumbrance, and the sin which so easily entangles us" (*NASB*).

Sin both weighs us down and entangles itself around us. The writer says that to avoid such entrapment we must learn to lay sin aside, to refuse to allow it to entangle us. In other words, if we do not learn to war against sin it will easily oppress and eventually overcome us.

We are to declare a state of war between ourselves and sin, the writer implies in verse 4: "You have not yet resisted to the point of shedding blood in your striving against sin" (Heb. 12:4, *NASB*). These are warfare words—*resist, strive, shed your blood,* rather than being defeated by sin.

It is hard to live a holy life, the writer of Hebrews is admitting. The very atmosphere we breathe is saturated with sin. We must not give in just because everyone else is doing it. We are to resist, strive, die, if necessary, before allowing sin to entangle itself with our Christian life. We do so by fixing our eyes on Jesus, not on sin (see Heb. 12:2).

Second, it is a multidimensional sin war. Sin affects us on three levels: the *personal* level, the *social* level and the *supernatural* level.

1. *Sin is personal,* it comes from *within.* This is the problem of the flesh. The word *flesh* has a variety of uses in Scripture. For the purposes of this study we use the word only in its negative moral context, to refer to our inner humanity which is always inclined toward evil, toward actions of independence from the will of God. The classic description of the inner warfare of our flesh against the indwelling Holy Spirit of God is Gal. 5:16-21.

2. *Sin is social,* it comes from *without.* This is the problem of *the world.* We will define the world, as does William Vine, as present human society "in alienation from and opposition to God."[1]

Perhaps the classic description of the world as the enemy of God and the children of God is found in 1 John 2:15-17, (*NASB*):

> Do not love the world, nor the things in the world. If anyone loves the world, the love of the Father is not in him. For all that is in the world, the lust of the flesh and the lust of the eyes and the boastful pride of life, is not from the Father, but is from the world. And the world is passing away, and also its lusts; but the one who does the will of God abides forever.

3. *Sin is supernatural,* it comes from *above.* This is the problem of evil supernaturalism, Satan and his kingdom of demons, principalities and powers. This is the most difficult dimension of our multidimensional sin problem to understand and learn to handle. At the same time it leads

to the third and final description of the war in which we are engaged.

Third, it is a spiritual warfare sin war. That is, behind the wickedness of flesh and the corruption of the world is the true original source of all sin, Satan. This is exactly what the apostle Paul is affirming in Eph. 2:1-3, (*NASB*).

> And you were dead in your trespasses and sins, in which you formerly walked according to the course of this world, according to the prince of the power of the air, of the spirit that is now working in the sons of disobedience. Among them we too all formerly lived in the lusts of our flesh, indulging the desires of the flesh and of the mind, and were by nature children of wrath, even as the rest.

This spiritual warfare dimension of our sin war is the main theme of this study. To be biblically understood, however, the war in which we are engaged must be viewed, as we have been examining it, in its multidimensional nature. The flesh and the world are the channels through which evil supernaturalism oppresses and seeks to destroy the human race, both believers as well as unbelievers.

Three Levels of Spiritual Warfare

We are all to be involved in spiritual warfare on at least three levels. First, there is the objective level, reaching unbelievers with the gospel. Next is the subjective level, protecting ourselves and our families from succumbing to the demonic warfare directed against us. Finally, there is the Christian level, helping to free demonized Christians from demonization.

The Objective Offensive Level of Spiritual Warfare

The Church is not only the community of the redeemed, it is also the redeeming community. We are both commanded by our Lord and impelled by the indwelling Holy Spirit to declare the message of God's redeeming love in Jesus Christ to all peoples (Matt. 24:14; 28:18-20; Acts 1:8). That task is easier stated than it is accomplished. Not only do we face the overwhelming logistical complexities of such a mission and the incredible cross-cultural and cross-linguistical barriers involved; something even more tenacious challenges our best efforts.

Satan holds the nations in bondage to himself and will not easily let them go. Indeed, he will resist us each step of the way. World evangelism is spiritual warfare.

The Scriptures are emphatically clear at this point. All human beings who live without the true God are in bondage to evil supernaturalism.

Jesus repeatedly called Satan the ruler of this world (John 12:31; 14:30; 16:11). He did not challenge the devil's boast about the kingdoms of the world, "I will give You all this domain and its glory; for it has been handed over to me, and I give it to whomever I wish. Therefore if You worship before me, it shall all be Yours" (Luke 4:6-7, *NASB*). In His missionary commission to Paul, Jesus declared that the unredeemed must be delivered "from the dominion of Satan to God" (Acts 26:18, *NASB*).

The rest of the New Testament only expands this negative view of mankind's plight. The apostle Paul, after revealing the human cause of unbelief, hardened minds and veiled hearts (2 Cor. 3:14-15), describes in even greater detail the superhuman dimensions of unbelief:

> And even if our gospel is veiled, it is veiled to those
> who are perishing, in whose case the god of this
> world has blinded the minds of the unbelieving, that
> they might not see the light of the glory of Christ,
> who is the image of God (2 Cor. 4:3, 4, *NASB*).

As we seek to evangelize, Satan resists us (1 Thess.
2:18). He snatches away the Word sown into human
hearts (Matt. 13:19). He sows tares among the wheat
(Matt. 13:24). These tares are "the sons of the evil one,"
the Lord declares.

Sonship implies commonalty of nature. Thus, even
religious people, theists, who oppose the claims of our
Lord are described by Jesus as children of the devil (John
8:44).

Therefore, all of those we seek to bring to Christ are
potentially demonized to one degree or another, most only
mildly so, but some severely so. They are not demon possessed. They are not all demonized. All are potentially
demonized, however.

Fortunately, the words *demon possession* are gradually
being eliminated from our vocabulary in referring to the
demonic dimension of present reality.[2] It is doubtful that
any of the accounts of demonization revealed in Scripture
are true demonic possession.

Possession refers to the voluntary reception of a control spirit by a spirit medium. The spirit rides, mounts or
temporarily possesses the medium for a specific purpose
and time. During that time the person is in a trance-like
state. The spirit probably totally controls the medium—
his body, soul, mind, emotions, will and spirit at that point.
When the spirit leaves, however, the medium is once
again back in control of himself.

This is not the type of demonic activity described in

Scripture. Thus, the traditional practice of Bible translators, in translating the various Greek expressions describing the demonized by demon possession, has produced nothing but negative results for both the Church and the demonically afflicted.

Possession implies total ownership. Satan and his demons don't own anything in this universe except their own evil. They are usurpers. God owns all.

Possession also would imply unaccountability. If the demonized are totally possessed by evil spirits, then they are not responsible for their actions. They can truthfully declare "the devil made me do it." Yet, God holds all persons responsible for their actions.

Possession also conjures up the image of only the more severe types of demonization. The Gerasene demonic of Mark 5, or the severely demonized child of Mark 9, come to mind.

Such extreme cases of demonization do exist. They are the exception, however, not the norm. Most demonized persons are only mildly demonized and do not display such wild antisocial and/or self-destructive behavior. Their deliverance can usually be accomplished in a quiet, orderly manner and be carried out by any instructed godly Christian or group of praying believers.

By *demonization* I mean that *Satan, through his evil spirits, exercises direct partial control* over one or more areas of the life of a human being. The exact location of these attached demons is not always as important as some believe it to be. That is, partial control can be exercised from without as well as from within the victim.

It is true that most demons seem to want to enter the body of their victim. They are evidently more effective working from within. Yet some demons seem to prefer to remain attached to their victim from outside. They may be more difficult to detect in this manner. Others are able to slip in and out of the more severely demonized, almost at will.

It is important to stress five facts at this point. *One,* while all unbelievers live under demonic dominion, *not all unbelievers are demonized.*

Two, some unbelievers, however, *are demonized,* and should be set free from these demons when they are brought to faith in Christ.

Three, demonization can range from very severe to very mild. There are many complex factors leading to this difference in demonization which cannot be mentioned in this brief study.

Four, when dealing with the potentially demonized, the typical Western, analytical, reasoned approach toward evangelism will be ineffective. Only a gospel of power will set them free.

Finally, to evangelize the demonized we must learn how to bind demonic activity from the minds of demonized unbelievers. Demons cause confusion and resistance, hindering unbelievers from understanding the responding to the gospel. We can take control over these demons, allowing the unbeliever to exercise his or her will to accept or reject Christ without direct demonic interference.

The Subjective Personal Level of Spiritual Warfare

Before developing this point, I must strongly affirm two foundational truths declared everywhere in the New Testament. The Lord Jesus in His multifaceted redemptive act once and for all totally defeated Satan and his entire kingdom of evil supernaturalism;[3] and, the victorious Lord Jesus has delegated to all His disciples full authority over the kingdom of evil supernaturalism. We war with foes who are not only already totally defeated by our reigning Lord; they are already forced into subjection to our shared authority with the Lord.

One of the greatest joys in an otherwise often wearisome deliverance ministry is to take this position of authority in Christ. In the case of severe demonization, part of the joy is to see demons change from a posture of threats, boasts and attempts to injure us, to that of fear of us. This soon leads to their spontaneous confession of our authority over them. Soon they will be pleased that we released them from their sufferings, and send them quickly out of their victims—anywhere, that is, except to the abyss.[4]

It is for this reason that while we are told to fear God, we are never told to fear Satan or his demons. In Christ, we are more than a match for them. While we are *not* told they will submit easily to our authority in Christ, we *are* told not to fear them. They will eventually submit (Mark 9:14-29; Matt. 17:21).

Although this is the most important side of the coin, it is only one side. The other side is that, while Satan and his demonic hosts are totally defeated, they are not dead. They are very much alive and continually active in promoting evil wherever they can find responsive hearts and/or ignorance of their schemes of deception. Thus, the title of Hal Lindsay's popular 1974 best-seller is accurate, *Satan Is Alive and Well on Planet Earth.*

Contrary to popular opinion, true believers are the main objects of Satan's subtle deceptions. The apostle Paul warns us of this reality in 2 Cor. 11:3. While spoken specifically to the Christians at Corinth, his words have universal application to all believers: "But I am afraid, lest as the serpent deceived Eve by his craftiness, your minds should be led astray from the simplicity and purity of devotion to Christ" (*NASB*).

In the same epistle he writes, "in order that no advantage be taken of us by Satan; for we are not ignorant of his schemes" (2 Cor. 2:11, *NASB*). By implication we hear him saying, if we are ignorant of Satan's schemes, he will take advantage of us.

The popular notion that if we just focus all our attention on the Lord Jesus we can ignore the devil and his demons is thus revealed to be contrary to the teachings of Scripture. What adversary would not be delighted if those he seeks to deceive chose to totally ignore his tactics of deception?

Satan's goal is, through deception, to entice believers to sin or commit any act which quenches the Holy Spirit in their lives and/or to lessen their effectiveness in glorifying God through both personal conduct and Christian service.[5] His desire is to find any area of our lives to which he can attach himself (Eph. 4:27). Through his demons (Eph. 6:10-12) he seeks to find any *sin handles* which give him the right to influence us into actions of disobedience to God. Satan was unsuccessful in his attempts to do so with the man Christ Jesus.[6] He did, however, have success in the life of the apostle Peter (Luke 22:31-34). And, he continues to be successful in the lives of many believers.

Paul warned the Corinthians of the satanic dimension of sexual temptation (1 Cor. 7:5). He also expressed his fear that Satan would be successful in drawing the Thessalonian believers away from a life of obedience to God (1 Thess. 3:5).

We tend to focus almost exclusively on the sins which have their origin within us, the problem of the flesh, or from without, the problem of the world. We tend to ignore, or at least minimize, the incredible power of the sin energy released against us directly from Satan through the demons he has assigned against us as individuals, churches and Christian institutions.

Ray Stedman goes so far as to affirm:

> We often hear the idea "The *enemies* of the Christian are the world, the flesh and the devil," as though these were three equally powerful enemies. But there are not three. There is only one enemy, the devil, as Paul brings out in Ephesians 6 . . . But the channels of his . . . approach to men are through the world and the flesh. [7]

This failure to understand the demonic dimension to the Christian's sin problem is perhaps the weak point, the Achilles' heel, in our evangelical theology of evil and temptation. We would do well to heed the apostle Peter's warning:

> Be of sober spirit, be on the alert. Your adversary, the devil, prowls about like a roaring lion, seeking someone to devour (1 Pet. 5:8, *NASB*).

If this is true, then it must be possible for a true Christian to be devoured by the devil (1 Tim. 3:6, 7; 5:15; 2 Tim. 2:26). This statement prepares the way for the consideration of the third level of spiritual warfare.

The Christian Level of Spiritual Warfare

The Christian level of Satan's activity and demonization is the most troublesome for us to understand and/or accept. It is also the one that divides us most as Christians. Yet, it represents one of the most critical areas of ministry need facing the worldwide Church today.

I call this level of spiritual warfare the Christian level because it deals with the need to bring deliverance to demonized Christians. Such afflicted believers are probably found in every local church and Christian institution.

1. *The Enigma of Demonized Christians.* First, a word of *clarification.* True believers cannot be demon possessed. Satan cannot possess or totally control the children of God.

Next, a word of *affirmation.* True believers, through unusual conditions of sin—either their own or that of others against them—can become demonized. When this occurs they need to experience deliverance from these demons.

If the demonization is severe, the believer will usually need the help of others to become fully free. If it is mild demonization, any group of godly, sharing-praying believers who have received basic instruction in spiritual warfare can effect a healing (James 5:16 with 4:1-8). Often the afflicted believer can practice *self-deliverance* with just a little instruction in this area.

It would be helpful to state again my definition of demonization. Demonization means that Satan, through his demons, exercises direct, partial control over an area or areas of a person's life, a believer or unbeliever.

Traditionally, the Protestant Church has denied the possibility of demonized believers. While admitting that believers can be harassed, oppressed, afflicted and tempted by Satan through his demons, it has denied that demonization can occur with one who is truly a child of God. The usual basis of this negative position is the assumption that the Holy Spirit will not or cannot dwell in the same body with demons.

Again, the issue is not always that of demonic indwelling, but more of demonic attachment. Having said this, however, it must also be stated that demons can enter the body of some sinning Christians. The presence of the Holy Spirit does not, in itself, prevent demonization just as it does not, in itself, prevent the Christian from sinning.

It can also occur the other way around. The Holy Spirit will enter the body of an individual even if there are demons dwelling there. The Holy Spirit is not afraid of the demons. Nor do they contaminate Him by their sinfulness any more than He is contaminated by the sinfulness of the believer's flesh. The Holy Spirit's presence there is the only guarantee of the new believer's final deliverance from demonization.

The negative view denying the possible demonization of some Christians is being successfully challenged on at least three essential levels: *Scripture, church history* and *worldwide contemporary experience.*

The argument from *Scripture* is relatively simple. It follows at least two lines. There is not a single verse of Scripture which states that true believers cannot under any circumstance of sin become demonized; and, the Scripture presents both case studies of demonized believers and warnings of the possibility of such demonization. [8]

The argument from *church history* is even simpler. A study of the writings of the early church fathers reveals they understood that true Christians could be demonized. Because of this they created a lay order of exorcists who took new believers through deliverance after their conversion to Christ and before their public baptism. [9]

The argument from *worldwide contemporary experience* with demonized believers is unanimous. This point is so crucial, I feel I must look at it in more detail in the rest of this study.

I refer you to one of the most thorough, scholarly, biblical and exhaustive studies of this issue in print today, C. Fred Dickason's monumental work *Demon Possession and the Christian*. Dr. Dickason who is professor of New Testament Theology at Moody Bible College, has been involved for years in an active deliverance ministry. He is a fair-minded scholar, and he presents in detail the major arguments on both sides of the issue.

His personal position, however, corresponds exactly with what I am presenting here. From Scripture, logic, church history and contemporary worldwide experience with the demonized, he supports the position that some true Christians, under unusual conditions of sin, can become demonized.

One of the most valuable sections of Dickason's book deals with the great number of case studies of demonized believers that he presents. These come from the experiences of various theologians, pastors, counselors, missionaries and lay believers worldwide who work with the demonized.

I believe it would be accurate to affirm that anyone worldwide who is actually involved in a ministry of helping to deliver the demonized will agree that true believers can be demonized. It is only those who are not actively involved in such a ministry who affirm the opposite.

It is also important to recognize that it is not a matter of winning a theological argument that is in question. It is a matter of ministering to afflicted believers and delivering them from their sufferings caused by the demons attached to their lives. That is, after all, all that really matters.

2. *Two Explanations for the Enigma of Demonized Christians.* First, they were *demonized before their conversion* to the Lord Jesus. What I am affirming is that all demons do not automatically leave the body of demonized

unbelievers the instant they turn to Christ. This is especially true when the demonized are brought to Christ by the traditional Western world's logical-analytical approach toward evangelism already mentioned.

In the case of severe demonization, even when unbelievers are brought to Christ through a gospel of power, there is still no guarantee that *all* of the demons attached to the victim's life will immediately release their hold on the new believer. Thus, the importance of post-conversion deliverance counseling.

I follow what I call a *45-10-45 percent deliverance procedure*, with 45 percent of the time spent in pre-deliverance counseling, 45 percent of the time in post-deliverance counseling and only 10 percent of the time spent in the initial deliverance.

Post-deliverance biblical counseling will usually involve ongoing deliverance. This must continue until the new convert is firmly enough established in his faith and the Word of God, prayer, spiritual warfare, warfare praying and the use of his spiritual armor to be able to live in freedom without the continued help of the counselor.

Second, *the believer picked up demons after his conversion through his own sin and/or the serious sin of others committed against him.*

For the believer who finds it difficult to accept these possibilities biblically, I would again encourage the serious study of Dickason's book, *Demon Possession and the Christian.* As to how demons may be able to attach themselves to or penetrate the life of true believers, I present figure 1 as a possibility.

As figure 1 reveals, the believer would seem to have at least a threefold protection against the attacks of the enemy. They are the *hedge of God* (Job 1:10), *the angels of God* (Ps. 34:7; Zech. 3:1; Heb. 1:14) and the *shield of faith*

(Eph. 6:16). Although all are available to all believers, nothing is automatic.

God, in His grace, however, continually protects us from many of the flaming missiles of the enemy. If this were not so, none of us would survive his relentless attacks. Most carnal Christians are also protected. Otherwise, our churches would be filled with demonized believers. In some cases, however, because of sin a demon may be able to gain a foothold in the believer's life.[10]

Satan and his evil spirits are sin personified. They thrive on sin, love sin and live sin. They exist to spread sin among God's people. Where possible, they will attach themselves to sin areas of a believer's life and work continually to increase their control over these areas. If possible they will try to gain entrance into the believer's life.

That control is only partial, however, never total. Thus, demonized believers are able to, and, are responsible to turn against the demons attached to their lives. This is one of the purposes of pre-deliverance counseling—to lead believers to confess and reject the sin in their lives and turn against Satan and his demons (Jas. 4:1-7).

If the demon succeeds in entering the body of the believer, he will usually try to draw other demons into the believer's life—and they are usually successful in doing so. Most cases of demonization in our day seem to involve multiple demonic invasion. These demons will affect the believer's inner life, disturbing his emotions, his mind, his will and his spiritual well-being. The internal spiritual warfare all believers face will become intensified. With multiple invasion the believer's condition begins to deteriorate.

The rest of figure 1 is self-explanatory. Although it is based on a trichotomous view of the human personality, with minor changes it can be used by one who holds a dichotomous view.

The Three Levels of Protection Around Us

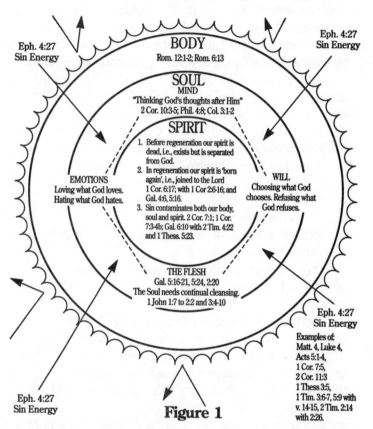

Eph. 4:27
Sin Energy

BODY
Rom. 12:1-2; Rom. 6:13

Eph. 4:27
Sin Energy

SOUL
MIND
"Thinking God's thoughts after Him"
2 Cor. 10:3-5; Phil. 4:8; Col. 3:1-2

SPIRIT
1. Before regeneration our spirit is dead, i.e., exists but is separated from God.
2. In regeneration our spirit is 'born again', i.e., joined to the Lord 1 Cor. 6:17; with 1 Cor 2:6-16; and Gal. 4:6, 5:16.
3. Sin contaminates both our body, soul and spirit. 2 Cor. 7:1; 1 Cor. 7:3-4b; Gal. 6:10 with 2 Tim. 4:22 and 1 Thess. 5:23.

EMOTIONS
Loving what God loves.
Hating what God hates.

WILL
Choosing what God chooses. Refusing what God refuses.

THE FLESH
Gal. 5:16-21, 5:24, 2:20
The Soul needs continual cleansing.
1 John 1:7 to 2:2 and 3:4-10

Eph. 4:27
Sin Energy

Examples of:
Matt. 4, Luke 4,
Acts 5:1-4,
1 Cor. 7:5,
2 Cor. 11:3
1 Thess 3:5,
1 Tim. 3:6-7, 5:9 with
v. 14-15, 2 Tim. 2:14
with 2:26.

Eph. 4:27
Sin Energy

Figure 1

3. *Primary Sin Areas of Demonized Christians.* While the percentage of demonized believers in our churches may be low in comparison with those who are not demonized, it is much higher than most of us realize. These believers need help. They need deliverance from these binding demons.

Fortunately, the demonic condition of most demonized believers is mild. Most are able to maintain a somewhat normal life. They usually realize, however, that something is wrong with them, though they seldom suspect they are suffering from demonization. Many are very sincere Christians. Many are Spirit-filled Christians. Yet they are *bound* by unexplainable fears, confusion, uncontrollable emotions and other disturbing phenomena. Usually certain sins dominate their lives, if not in actual, open sinful activity, at least in their thought life, their imagination or fantasies. They are often very disturbed, even obsessed, in four primary sin areas.

One, *illicit sexual practices or fantasies.*

Two, *deep-seated anger, bitterness, hatred, rage and rebellion,* often leading to destructive and/or self-destructive impulses.

Three, *a sense of rejection, guilt, poor self-esteem, unworthiness and shame.*

Four, *strange attraction* to the *occult and to the spirit world,* often, but not always, with a desire for illicit power over their circumstances and over other people.

Fortunately, most demonized believers do not need dramatic, spectacular, prolonged deliverance sessions. They often need only to be counseled by believers who know the spirit world and can help set them free, teaching them spiritual warfare and self-deliverance (Jas. 4:1-8; 5:13-20).

4. *Doors to Demonize Christians.* For both mild and more severe forms of demonization of believers, there seem to be at least three major doors through which demons enter a human life.

The first door is *at birth.* Some Christians were born demonized. This is often called by different names, such as generational sin, familial sin, demonic transference, demonic inheritance or the law of the inheritance of evil. Direct and clearly defined biblical teaching or examples of demonic transference are not found in Scripture. What is found are divine warnings that the sins of parents do have potentially devastating consequences upon their children, up to four generations (Exod. 20:5; 34:6-7; Deut. 5:5-10). The Jews interpreted this warning in this manner, at least by the time of the divided kingdom (Jer. 31:27-30; Lam. 5:7; Ezek. 18:1-20). The negative approach of the prophets toward this law of the inheritance of evil was not to deny its reality, but to correct its abuses. Plumtre states: "Men found in it an explanation of their sufferings which relieved their consciences. They were suffering, they said, for the sins of their fathers, not for their own."[11]

William H. Brownlee, in his commentary, *Ezekiel 1-19* in *The Word Biblical Commentary*, agrees, but adds another insight.

> In society, this would be a popular maxim for cautioning parents with regard to their behavior, lest they bring harm to the next generation. It is not this, however, to which Ezekiel objects, but to the perverse usage by which one infers that if past generations were as wicked as Ezekiel claims (2:3, chapter 16, 20, 23), then it will be of no use to repent in order to avert the doom he predicts. They say, in effect: "Of what use is repentance? Our fate is already sealed by the sins of the fathers." Against this Ezekiel directs a lengthy disputation.[12]

Plumtre declares that the Scriptures support both laws: "the law of heredity tendencies and punishments that fall not on the individual responsibility."[13]

This law of the inheritance of evil is not automatically binding. Neither is the opposite law that the children of godly parents will automatically love and obey the Lord

(Prov. 22:6). Both reflect general principles of order within God's kingdom which, under normal circumstances, will prove to be true.

In light of the biblical principle of the law of inheritance of evil, demonic transference or inheritance would not appear unlikely. The most obvious possibility would be within the occult realm, that is, parents who rebel against God and join themselves to the "no gods" of the spirit world. Studies in non-Christian religions and occultism reveal this transference to be a fact.[14] The experience of most, if not all, believers who are involved in deliverance ministry, including my own, would reveal this dimension of demonization to be a vivid reality.

The second door to demonize Christians is *through child abuse,* in at least four possible areas—sexual, physical, psychological and spiritual.

Spiritual child abuse demands a further word of explanation. It can occur when a child involuntarily receives demonic psychic/occult powers that are passed down through the family line. It can also occur when a child is voluntarily subjected to a spirit ceremony with the purpose of passing demonic psychic or occult spirits into its body. It can also occur when a curse is placed on a child by a malevolent spiritual practitioner, or by an angry person operating in the spirit realm. It can occur even in jest, or when one is not fully aware of the spirit forces activated by his or her anger or curse.

Ritual spiritual child abuse is the most horrible of all. This most horrible form of child abuse usually is a combination of the above: sexual, physical, psychological and spiritual abuse.

The third door to demonize Christians is through his or her own *willful sinful actions* in childhood, youth or adulthood. This usually occurs in the realms of sexuality, the occult and destructive interpersonal relationships. Sin has been the scourge of humanity since the Fall. With sin comes demons. They are drawn to sin like flies to filth. Indeed, their reason for being is to promote sin. Our age is excessively sinful. Both on a personal, national and international scale sin seems to be on a rampage. Increased demonic activity and increased sinfulness go together.

Demonic powers have come out into the open in most of the Western world, and especially in the United States. Our society seems to have been captured anew by the horrid, the brazen, sexual extremism, occultism, satanism and witchcraft. Christians are suffering demonic harassment and oppression at an alarming rate. Many are becoming demonized and are seeking for someone to help them.

Thus, it behooves us to learn the spirit world. We must not be ignorant of Satan's schemes. We must go on the offense and challenge and dethrone the evil powers afflicting so many believers, our homes, churches and Christian institutions. We are at war!

Notes
1. William Vine, *An Expository Dictionary of New Testament Words* (London: Oliphents, Ltd., 1966), Vol. III, p. 235.
2. C. Fred Dickason, *Demon Possession and the Christian* (Chicago: Moody Press, 1987), and Edward Murphy, *Spiritual Warfare Seminar* (Milpitas, CA: Overseas Crusades; 1988), and accompanying cassettes, are more detailed studies of the biblical words used to describe the activity of evil supernaturalism in human lives.
3. Out of the many Scriptures declaring this truth are Matt. 12:27-29 with Luke 4:18, 19; Mark 1:21-39; 5:7-13; 9:17-29; Acts 10:38; Eph. 1:18-23 with 1 Peter 3:22; 1 Cor. 15:24, 25; Phil. 3:21; Heb. 1:3,13; 2:14,15; 8:1; 10:12; 12:2; 1 John 3:8; and the book of Revelation.
4. Many verses declare our authority over the kingdom of evil. Some of the most important are Mark 3:13-15 with Luke 9:1 and 10:1,17-19 (Isa. 54:17); Acts 5; 8; 16:16-18; 19:11-20; 26:18; Rom. 16:20; Eph. 2:6; 3:10;

72   *Wrestling with Dark Angels*

6:10-20; Jas. 4:7,8; 1 Pet. 5:8-11 and 1 John 2:12-14; 4:4; 5:18,19; Rev. 12:7-11.

5. 2 Cor. 2:11; Eph. 6:10-13, 1 Tim. 4:1; 2 Tim. 3:13.

6. Matt. 4; Luke 4; John 14:30; Luke 22:53; Heb. 2:18; 4:15; 5:7-8.

7. Ray Stedman, *Spiritual Warfare* (Portland: Multnomah Press, 1975), p. 47.

8. Murphy, *Spiritual Warfare Seminar,* Tape 14.

9. J. Warwick Montgomery, *Exorcism, Is It for Real?* (Wheaton: Christianity Today, July 26, 1974).

10. Eph. 4:27; 1 Tim. 3:7,8; 5:15; 2 Tim. 2:26; Acts 5:3,4.

11. Bishop E. J. Plumtre, "Jeremiah," *Ellicott's Bible Commentary* (New York: Cassell and Company, n.d.).

12. William H. Brownlee, *Ezekiel 1-19, The Word Biblical Commentary* (Waco: Word Books, 1986) pp. 282-83.

13. Ibid, p. 108.

14. Merrill F. Unger, *Demons in the World Today* (Wheaton: Tyndale House, 1971), pp. 82-83; 177-78; 192, and *What Demons Can Do to Saints* (Chicago: Moody Press, 1977), pp. 135-158; 178-179.

CHAPTER

3

Territorial Spirits

C. PETER WAGNER

C. PETER WAGNER, who convened
the conference at which these
presentations were made, is the
Donald A. McGavran professor of
Church Growth at Fuller Theological Seminary in Pasadena,
California. Prior to coming to
Fuller in 1971, Dr. Wagner served
as a missionary to Bolivia for 16
years. He is the author of more
than 30 books on missions and
church growth.

THE annual Church Growth Lectures, sponsored by the School of World Mission of Fuller Seminary, were delivered in 1988 by Timothy M. Warner, professor of Mission at Trinity Evangelical Divinity School. At one point in his development of the theme, "The Power Encounter and World Evangelization," he stated, "I have come to believe that Satan does indeed assign a demon or corps of demons to every geopolitical unit in the world, and that they are among the principalities and powers against whom we wrestle."[1]

Until recently, such statements from evangelical missions leaders were all but non-existent. They would have been considered somewhat disreputable, expected perhaps from snake handlers or Holy Rollers, but not from professors in seminaries accredited by the Association of Theological Schools. No longer, however. The issue that I like to refer to as "territorial spirits" is indeed surfacing on the agendas of many church and mission leaders from across the theological spectrum.

Since it is a relatively new area of research, however, we are as yet far from enjoying consensus conclusions. The whole field of spiritual warfare, of which concerns relating to territorial spirits are a subset, is new—and somewhat scary—material for those of us who have come from a non-Pentecostal/charismatic background. Even among some of today's second- and third-generation Pentecostals, spiritual warfare is something that may have been done in the early days or back in the hills, but is no longer a prominent part of ministry in their congregations. Their theology teaches it, but their experience with it is considerably limited.

In the seven years of research on signs and wonders leading up to the publication of my book *How to Have a Healing Ministry Without Making Your Church Sick*, I came across very few individuals who had what could be considered a professional-level grasp of either the theory or practice of dealing with territorial spirits, and none who combined both. They may be out there, but I have yet to discover them. Many have been recommended to me through the years, but when I followed through by reading their books or listening to their tapes I found very little beyond the standard wisdom that has been accumulated on spiritual warfare in general. I will mention some exceptions to this as I go along.

My intention in this brief essay, therefore, is not to arrive at conclusions but rather to suggest hypotheses. I trust that the tentativeness of my research will be evident throughout.

A Working Hypothesis

My principal calling from God is to participate in fulfilling Jesus' Great Commission to make disciples of all nations. World evangelization is my focus, with the world including Jerusalem, Judea, Samaria and the uttermost parts of the earth, so to speak. Thus, I see issues relating to territorial spirits chiefly in terms of their alleged ability to prevent the spread of the gospel.

In this context, it is instructive to reread Paul's statement in 2 Cor. 4:4, *NKJV,* where he describes those who are perishing as having their minds blinded by the god of this age "lest the light of the gospel of the glory of Christ, who is the image of God, should shine on them." The chief end of humans is to glorify God and the chief end of Satan is to prevent God from being glorified. In the providence of God, Satan has the power to "veil the gospel" (see 2 Cor. 4:3), and thus prevent it from spreading.

Do we not have a responsibility as servants of Christ,

and stewards of the mysteries of God, to seek answers as to just how Satan goes about veiling the gospel? Paul himself said, "we are not ignorant of Satan's devices" (see 2 Cor. 2:11).

It is helpful to remind ourselves that Satan does not possess the attributes of God, and therefore he is not omnipresent. Although he may be able to move from one place to another very rapidly, he can still be in only one place at one time. Therefore, if he is intent on blinding the minds of the three billion who have yet to receive the light of the gospel of the glory of Christ, he must delegate this responsibility to others, namely evil spirits.

I do not know how many evil spirits there are around Planet Earth. One interesting set of figures comes from Friday Thomas Ajah, a Sunday School superintendent at the Assemblies of God church in Oribe, Port Harcourt, Nigeria. For years before his conversion he was a high ranking occult leader, given the name of Saint Thomas the Divine, purportedly by Satan himself. Ajah reports that Satan had assigned him control of 12 spirits and that each spirit controlled 600 demons for a total of 7,212. He says, "I was in touch with all the spirits controlling each town in Nigeria, and I had a shrine in all the major cities."[2] If this report is true, it would not be unreasonable to postulate that other such individuals, not yet saved, could be found in considerable numbers around the world.

It is commonly agreed that demons can and do attach themselves to objects, to houses or other buildings, to animals and to people. The Gospels record that Jesus found a legion of demons in one man and allowed them to enter into pigs when they left. Paul warns the Corinthians not to eat meat offered to idols in the idol temples, because by doing so they risk having fellowship with demons (1 Cor. 10:20). This is not to say that either an idol or a temple is

anything in itself (1 Cor. 10:19), but any demons attached
to them certainly are.

The hypothesis I am suggesting, then, is that which I
previously quoted from Timothy Warner; namely, that
Satan delegates high ranking members of the hierarchy of
evil spirits to control nations, regions, cities, tribes, people groups, neighborhoods and other significant social networks of human beings throughout the world. Their major
assignment is to prevent God from being glorified in their
territory, which they do through directing the activity of
lower ranking demons.

Warner tells that the village leaders in Sierra Leone,
where he worked, had rather maliciously offered the missionaries a place called "The Devil's Hill," on which to con-
struct their mission home. Being ignorant of "Satan's
devices" as the apostle Paul would say (2 Cor. 2:11), they
accepted the offer. The first family that lived there had to
leave the field after a series of illnesses. Subsequently vis-
itors who used the house would routinely become ill when
they arrived only to see the symptoms relieved when they
left the village. This all stopped abruptly two years ago
when the missionaries finally took seriously the demonic
occupation of that geographical spot, engaged the demons
in a power encounter and drove them out.[3]

One of the bedrock principles of the Church Growth
Movement is resistance-receptivity theory.[4] This postu-
lates that through analysis of certain indicators, the degree
of resistance or receptivity to the gospel on the part of a
given people group can be anticipated within certain
ranges of accuracy. It goes without saying that if this
hypothesis concerning territorial spirits is correct, and if
we could learn now to break their control through the
power of God, positions on the resistance-receptivity axis
could change virtually overnight.

Biblical Backgrounds

Our working hypothesis will be of little value for strategizing world evangelization unless there is some biblical warrant for suggesting it. I believe there is. A starting point is the apostle Paul's statement that "we do not wrestle against . . . the rulers of the darkness of this age, against spiritual hosts of wickedness in the heavenly places" (Eph. 6:12, *NKJV*). This helps us to recognize that high-level spiritual warfare is a reality.

Jesus, in His explanation of the coming of the kingdom of God, referred to the binding of the strong man (Matt. 12:29). It is clear that the strong man refers to evil spirits by Jesus' statement that leads into it: "If I cast out demons by the Spirit of God, surely the kingdom of God has come upon you" (Matt. 12:28, *NKJV*). Jesus illustrates this process by referring to the control the strong man has over the house. It would seem reasonable that the principle could be applied to a nation or a city or a people group as well as a house. The house is the territory controlled by Satan or his delegated authorities, and that territory cannot be taken unless the strong man is bound. But once the territorial spirits are bound, the kingdom of God can flow into the territory and "plunder the strong man's goods."

The idea of evil spirits dominating territories surfaces time and again throughout the Old Testament. For example, in the Song of Moses in Deut. 32, the Septuagint reading of 32:8 is as follows:

> When the Most High gave to the nations their inheritance,
> When he separated the children of men,
> He set the bounds of the peoples
> According to the number of the angels of God.

F. F. Bruce, who suggests that the Septuagint reading represents the original text, says, "This reading implies that the administration of the various nations has been parcelled out among a corresponding number of angelic powers. . . . In a number of places some at least of these angelic governors are portrayed as hostile principalities and powers—the 'world rulers of this darkness' of Eph. 6:12."[5]

Bruce goes on to point out that what is implicit in Deuteronomy becomes explicit in Dan. 10, where three princes are named. Two of them are evil princes, the prince of Persia and the prince of Greece; and one is a good prince, Michael, called one of the chief princes. As the story unfolds, a lesser unnamed angel who was sent by God to minister to Daniel battled the prince of Persia for 21 days and could not overcome him until Michael came to his rescue. If we take this account at face value, we begin to see the awesome degree of power that these world rulers of darkness can exercise (Dan. 10:10-21).

Territorial spirits and their dominance of geographical areas are taken for granted as the history of Israel unfolds. Joshua rebukes the Israelites for serving gods on the other side of the river and in Egypt (Josh. 24:14). Even in Canaan the Israelites did not cleanse the land as God commanded but "forgot the Lord their God, and served the Baals and Asherahs" (Judg. 3:7).

Names of some of the specific principalities are mentioned, such as Succoth Benoth of Babylon, Nergal of Cuth, Ashima of Hamath, Nibhaz and Tartak of the Avites, and Adrammelech and Anammelech of the Sepharvites (2 Kings 17:30-31). The occult power of these principalities is reflected in previous references in the same chapter to witchcraft and soothsaying (2 Kings 17:17). Jeremiah refers to the fall of Babylon by phrases such as "Bel is shamed" and "Merodach is broken in pieces" (Jer. 50:2).

Perhaps a specific instance of the breaking of the power of territorial spirit is seen in Paul's encounter with the sorcerer Elymas in Eastern Cyprus. Elymas's close relationship with the political authority, the proconsul Sergius Paulus, suggests a spiritual dominance of the region. Although the principality is not identified by name, when a power encounter breaks the power of Elymas (called a "son of the devil"), the proconsul believes. Satan's attempt to blind his mind failed (Acts 13:6-12).

Contemporary Examples

Research on territorial spirits is so new that the case studies that have surfaced tend to get told over and over again. I have no doubt that as time goes by credible stories of breaking powers over areas, both small and large, will multiply. Jamie Buckingham, for example, told me of sensing the presence of a specific power of evil over the city of Prague some time ago. He also reports that former Secretary of the Interior James Watt, through sensitivities acquired in his past association with the occult, perceives specific dark angels assigned to the White House. The implications such insights could have for social justice, peace and national righteousness, including evangelization, are obvious.

In two of my recent books, *The Third Wave of the Holy Spirit* and *How to Have a Healing Ministry*, I give eight contemporary examples dealing with territorial spirits. I do not wish to repeat them here, but I believe that it will be useful to catalog them:

1. *Thailand.* A wave of conversions followed when the

missionaries set aside one day a week for spiritual warfare.[6]

2. *Uruguay-Brazil border.* Individuals who were closed to the gospel on the Uruguay side of a town's main street became open when they crossed over to the Brazilian side.[7]

3. *Costa Rica.* Symptoms of mental illness left a patient when she traveled to the United States; they reappeared when she returned to Costa Rica. Christian psychologist Rita Cabezas was told by one of the demons that they were limited to their territory and could not go to the U.S.A.[8]

4. *Navajo reservation.* Herman Williams, a Navajo Alliance pastor, suffered serious physical symptoms which left as he crossed the reservation boundary for treatment in the city, and recurred when he entered the reservation. The spirits causing this were traced to a witch doctor whom they later killed.[9]

5. *Philippines.* Lester Sumrall cast a spirit out of an inmate in Bilibid Prison, followed by a dramatic change in the receptivity of Filipinos to the gospel.[10]

6. *Argentina.* Omar Cabrera, through prayer and fasting, exercises a regular ministry of identifying the spirits controlling certain cities, breaks their power, and finds little subsequent resistance to God's power for salvation and healing.[11]

7. *Korea.* Paul Yonggi Cho attributes the contrast in receptivity to the gospel between Germany and Korea to the victories in spiritual warfare gained through the ministry of prayer of Korean Christians.[12]

8. *Argentina.* Edgardo Silvoso reports the accelerated multiplication of churches within a radius of 100 miles of the city of Rosario after a team broke the power of the spirit of Merigildo in 1985.[13]

To reiterate the tentativeness of my research, I do not wish to go on record as attesting to the validity of these case studies. But they have been reported by persons of integrity who are looked upon as credible witnesses. Discernment is called for as they are further evaluated, but they need to be surfaced if they are ever going to be examined. Here are some other reports:

Greece. Loren Cunningham of Youth With a Mission relates an incident that took place in 1973. As 12 coworkers were praying and fasting for three days in Los Angeles, the Lord revealed to them that they should pray for the downfall of the prince of Greece. On the same day similar groups in New Zealand and Europe received the same word. All three groups obeyed and came against that principality. Within 24 hours a political coup changed the government of Greece, and for the first time YWAM workers could preach the gospel in the streets.

Evanston, Illinois. While teaching a doctoral class for me in 1985, John Wimber shared a report from Vineyard pastor Steve Nicholson. Steve had ministered in the Evanston area for six years with virtually no fruit. They prayed for the sick, but few got well. Then Steve went into a period of serious fasting and prayer. At one point a grotesque being appeared to him, saying, "Why are you bothering me?" It eventually identified itself as a demon of witchcraft who had supervision over the geographical area. In the heat of the battle, Steve named the city streets surrounding the area which he claimed for the kingdom of God. The spirit said, "I don't want to give you that much." Steve replied that through Jesus he was commanding him to give up the territory. The spirit argued with him, then left.

Immediately the sick began getting well. In a little over three months the church more than doubled from 70 to 150, mostly from new converts out of witchcraft. Almost every one of the new believers had to be delivered from demons as they were being saved.

Bermuda Triangle. Kenneth McAll spent many years as a missionary-surgeon in China, then returned to England as a consultant psychiatrist. While in China he began to be led into a deliverance ministry and has done considerable research and writing on the subject. As an Anglican he is very much in tune with the power of God channeled through the sacrament of the Eucharist.

In 1972 McAll and his wife were sailing through the Bermuda Triangle, knowing that many ships and airplanes had disappeared in that area without a trace, and thinking that such a thing could not happen to them. It did. They were overpowered by a fierce storm, the boat was crippled and set adrift, but fortunately they were rescued. McAll discovered through research that in the Bermuda Triangle area the slave traders of a bygone day, in order to collect insurance, had thrown overboard some two million slaves who were too sick or weak to be sold.

Sensing the leading of God to do something about this, McAll recruited several bishops, priests and others throughout England to celebrate a Jubilee Eucharist in July 1977. Another was held shortly afterward in Bermuda itself. The stated purpose was to seek the "specific release of all those who had met their untimely deaths in the Bermuda Triangle." As a result the curse was lifted. McAll reports that "From the time of the Jubilee Eucharist until now—five years—no known inexplicable accidents have occurred in the Bermuda Triangle."[14]

Identifying the Spirits

A common practice among those who exercise a ministry of deliverance is to discover the names of specific demons and deal with them on a personal basis. As He was ministering to the demonized Gadarene, Jesus asked the spirit's name and discovered it was Legion (see Mark 5:9). If this is frequently done with demons afflicting individuals, it might be reasonable to postulate that it could also be done with territorial spirits.

I first came into contact with this kind of spiritual warfare when I traveled around Argentina with Omar Cabrera, whom I have previously mentioned. Although he practiced identifying territorial spirits by name and breaking their power with regularity, his highly intuitive nature did not allow him to analyze for me the principles behind such ministry.

Another Latin American, Rita Cabezas, has done considerable research on the names of the highest levels of the hierarchy of Satan. At this point I will not describe her research methodology, except to mention that the beginning stages were associated with her extensive psychological/deliverance practice and that it later evolved into receiving revelatory words of knowledge. She has discovered that directly under Satan are six worldwide principalities, named (allowing that this was done in Spanish) Damian, Asmodeo, Menguelesh, Arios, Beelzebub and Nosferasteus. Under each, she reports, are six governors over each nation. For example, those over Costa Rica are Shiebo, Quiebo, Ameneo, Mephistopheles, Nostradamus and Azazel. Those over the U.S.A. are Ralphes, Anoritho, Manchester, Apolion, Deviltook and one who is unnamed.

Each of these governors has been delegated certain areas of evil. For example, the list under Anoritho includes abuse, adultery, drunkenness, fornication, gluttony, greed, homosexuality, lesbianism, lust, prostitution, seduction, sex and vice; while under Apolion we find aggressiveness, death, destruction, discord, dissent, grudge, hatred, homicide, violence and war.

None of the above is considered by any involved as final conclusions, but rather research in process. How valid are these findings? How can they be cross-checked? Apollyon is mentioned in Rev. 9:11 as "the angel of the bottomless pit." Beelzebub is mentioned seven times in the New Testament as a "ruler of the demons" (Matt. 12:24). Asmodeus is described in the Apocrypha as "that worst of demons" (see Tobit 3:8). Some of the others can be found in the *Dictionary of Gods and Goddesses, Devils and Demons.*[15] Azazel and Beelzebub are mentioned in Milton's *Paradise Lost,* and Apollyon in Bunyan's *Pilgrim's Progress.*

We have already seen that in the Old Testament the names of the principalities ruling over territories were known. We also recognize names of Greek and Roman principalities such as Jupiter, Aphrodites, Diana, Poseidon, Bacchus and Venus. Our most frequent categorization of these names is "mythology," by which we usually mean that they must have been figments of the imagination of prescientific people. If nothing else, the rise in popularity of the New Age Movement is now forcing many of us to reexamine these points of view.

In attempting to apply this to world evangelization, Jacob Loewen helps us by pointing out that "In many societies throughout Central and South America the spirit deities associated with various geographical or topographical phenomena are spoken of as their 'owners.'" Many nomads, for example, never make camp outside their own territory until they secure permission from the spirit owner. Loewen adds, "People never own the land; they only use it by the permission of its true spirit owners who, in a sense, 'adopt' them."[16] Although Loewen doesn't say so, I would imagine that among such animistic peoples the names of these spirit owners of territories are well known.

Recognizing the Dangers

I feel that it would be irresponsible to say this much about territorial spirits and the possibility of breaking their power without pointing out the risks of this type of ministry. Four clear dangers must be faced openly and honestly:

1. *Engaging in meaningless rhetoric.* Without mentioning names, many of those who write and speak on this subject tend to want to reduce the approach to speaking the right words. One of them suggests that to break the power of spirits over a city, you say, "I bind you, Satan, and I bind all of your emissaries and command them to cease their activity today. I place them in a state of confusion until they do not know what to do. I confess joy in the city today; I confess peace in the city today in Jesus' name."

There is nothing wrong with such a prayer per se, but my point is that a prayer like this can too easily be flippantly used, as if it were some sort of magic formula that would free an area from the power of the enemy for 24 hours or some other period of time. This can easily play into the devil's hands by giving a false sense of victory in spiritual warfare, and faith can be quenched when it becomes obvious that time after time the victory turned out to be illusory.

2. *Underestimating the enemy.* Unlike personal deliverance ministries, dealing with territorial spirits is major league spiritual warfare. It should not be undertaken casually. If you do not know what you are doing, and few who I am aware of have the necessary expertise, Satan will eat you for breakfast.

One of my students, Wilson Awasu, reports two tragic events involving Presbyterian ministers in Ghana. One of them, contrary to the warnings of the people in the area, ordered a tree which had been enshrined by Satanic priests to be cut down. On the day that the last branch of the tree was lopped off, the pastor collapsed and died. The second minister commanded that a fetish shrine be demolished. When it was, he suffered a stroke. Although he recovered from the stroke, he had lost several inches of height in the ordeal.

As the Fuller Seminary community heard Timothy Warner say recently, "Welcome to the war!" The purpose of power evangelism is to glorify God through demonstrations of divine power. But if the power of the enemy is underestimated, the opposite can occur.

3. *Expecting power without prayer.* I see the essence of prayer as a personal relationship with the Father. Prayer must accompany any attempt we make at invoking divine power, because only then will we know what the Father is doing in a given instance. Nothing could be more foolish than attempting to break the power of territorial spirits if the time, the place and the methodology turn out to be human ideas rather than God's. Only as we establish an intimacy with God will we gain the spiritual perception to know what is His will in a given situation. Without it we are sitting ducks for powers of darkness.

4. *Overemphasizing power.* Power evangelism is not some flawless formula for winning the world to Christ. Demonstrations of God's power by themselves never saved anyone. Jesus said as much to the 70 when they returned from their first practicum in exorcism: "Do not rejoice in this, that the spirits are subject to you, but rather rejoice because your names are written in heaven" (Luke 10:20, *NKJV*).

The apostle Paul puts it this way, "For I am not ashamed of the gospel of Christ, for it is the power of God to salvation for everyone who believes" (Rom. 1:16, *NKJV*). The gospel which Paul preached was "that Christ died for our sins according to the Scriptures, and that He was buried, and that He rose again the third day according to the Scriptures" (1 Cor. 15:3,4, *NKJV*). The communication of this gospel involves a delicate balance of weakness and power. Paul says to the Corinthians, "I was with you in weakness, in fear, and in much trembling." He then goes on to say that his preaching was not in words only but "in demonstration of the Spirit and of power" (1 Cor. 2:2-5, *NKJV*).

Even Jesus found that this power by itself did not always bring people to faith. Many of His mighty works were done in Chorazin and Bethsaida, but the cities did not repent (Matt. 11:20-24). Power certainly is important, but its importance must not be overestimated.

Moving Ahead

I could add a fifth danger to the four above, namely ignorance. It may be the most widespread danger of all among the evangelical community. Many are ignorant of the phenomenon of territorial spirits, some intentionally because of fear generated by the other dangers, and some unintentionally because they were never taught the kinds of things I have been mentioning. Among those who do recognize the phenomenon of territorial spirits, there is ignorance in the area of methodology. Few know how to go about breaking high-level powers of evil systematically, and fewer yet are doing it effectively. For this reason much more research is needed in this field. I consider it one of the top-drawer challenges in the years to come.

This challenge was heightened on a recent visit to Japan when I toured the ancient city of Kyoto for the first time. In that city, which is said to be the core from which Japanese culture radiates, I was enthralled by the beauty of the formal gardens. In them the entire landscape is a magnificent work of art. I was also impressed by the pervasive idolatry throughout the whole city, and began to suspect that Kyoto might be not only the seat of Japanese culture but also the seat of Satan, much as ancient Pergamos where Satan's throne was located (Rev. 2:13). It could be that powers of darkness, directed and coordinated from Kyoto, have succeeded in blinding the eyes of the Japanese people to the gospel of Christ.

For some reason, the investment in Christian missionary personnel, time, energy and money in Japan has produced perhaps the lowest return through the years of any nation of the world. Who knows how many conferences have been held to devise new strategies? Who knows how many theses and dissertations have been written to address the problem? Who knows how many prayer meetings have focused on Japan? And still far fewer than 1 percent of Japanese are practicing Christians, while just across the Sea of Japan churches are multiplying in South Korea and China with minimal missionary investment. I cannot help but feel that large-scale spiritual warfare could be a key to bringing Japanese people to Christ. I wouldn't be surprised if Satan knows this also, and has combatted it in part by erecting a formidable barrier between evangelicals on one hand and Pentecostals/charismatics on the other.

We have tried almost everything else. Why not try spiritual warfare? If God had called me to be a leader in the evangelization of Japan, I believe I would (1) seek God's power to tear down that barrier between the Christian factions; (2) train Japanese pastors and lay leaders in personal deliverance ministries; and (3) look to God for directions as to how to identify, engage and break the power of the territorial spirits that have had Japan in their clutches for centuries. I mention Japan simply as an example that I am personally acquainted with. I suspect that similar experiments could be attempted in other parts of the world.

Because of the dangers I have mentioned, the engagement of territorial spirits should not be undertaken lightly. Given the high degree of risk involved, it is not a ministry for the fainthearted. Nevertheless, the power of the Cross cannot be matched. On the Cross Jesus, "having disarmed principalities and powers, He made a public spectacle of them, triumphing over them in it" (Col. 2:15, *NKJV*). My prayer is that God will raise up a new army of faithful leaders who, filled with the Holy Spirit, will learn how to apply the power of the cross against the principalities and powers of darkness, thereby opening new pathways toward completing the Great Commission and bringing glory to God.

Notes
1. Timothy M. Warner, "The Power Encounter and World Evangelization, Part 4, The Missionary on the Attack." 1988 Church Growth Lectures audiotaped by Fuller Seminary Media Services, October 27, 1988.
2. Friday Thomas Ajah, "Saved at Last," *Testimonies*, Vol. 1. No. 4, August 15-30, 1985, p. 6. (P.M.B. 4990, Murtala Muhammed International Airport, Ikeja, Nigeria).
3. Warner, "The Power Encounter and World Evangelization, Part 3, The Missionary Under Attack."
4. See Donald A. McGavran, *Understanding Church Growth* (Grand Rapids, MI: Wm. B. Eerdmans Publishing Co., 1980), rev. ed., chapter 13, "The Receptivity of Men and Societies."
5. F. F. Bruce, *The Epistle to the Hebrews* (Grand Rapids, MI: Wm. B. Eerdmans Publishing Co., 1964), p. 33.
6. C. Peter Wagner, *The Third Wave of the Holy Spirit* (Ann Arbor, MI: Servant Publications, 1988), p. 60; and *How to Have a Healing Ministry Without Making Your Church Sick* (Ventura, CA: Regal Books, 1988), p. 201.

7. Wagner, *The Third Wave*, pp. 60-61; and *How to Have a healing Ministry*, pp. 201-202.
8. Wagner, *The Third Wave*, pp. 61-62.
9. Ibid., pp. 62-63.
10. Wagner, *How to Have a Healing Ministry*, pp. 197-198.
11. Ibid., pp. 198-200; and *The Third Wave*, p. 99.
12. Wagner, *How to Have a Healing Ministry*, pp. 200-201.
13. Ibid., pp. 204-205.
14. Kenneth McAll, *Healing the Family Tree* (London, England: Sheldon Press, 1982), pp. 60-61.
15. Manfred Lurker, *Dictionary of Gods and Goddesses, Devils and Demons*, (London, England: Routledge & Kegan Paul, 1987).
16. Jacob Loewen, "Which God Do Missionaries Preach?", *Missiology: An International Review*, Vol. XIV, No. 1, January 1986, p. 6.

RESPONSE
BY
BYRON D.
KLAUS

Territorial Spirits

The opportunity to respond to Dr. Wagner's paper has challenged me to read, learn and evaluate an area of ministry and topic for discussion that has received little formal attention. It is correctly observed that even Pentecostalism currently tends to avoid recognition and discussion of the practical elements of spiritual warfare. One of Dr. Wagner's recent books points to the glaring absence of the subject even in the articulation of leading Pentecostals.[1] As a third generation Pentecostal, however, the discussions in this paper certainly ring true to the assumptions for ministry with which I have been raised. Thus, I would feel more comfortable if Dr. Wagner's initial statements would differentiate between North American and Third World Pentecostals.

My response is divided into three sections: Observations on a Working Hypothesis, Implications for Ministry Strategy, and Areas for Further Study.

Observations on a Working Hypothesis

Dr. Wagner raises the issue of territorial spirits in an

appropriate context, that is, its impact on world evangelization. The twentieth century has had its fair share of examples emphasizing personal deliverance ministries that become self-serving and akin to circus sideshows. It is not a mere coincidence that this symposium happens under the auspices of Fuller's School of World Mission and with the capable representation of so many persons with considerable global missions experience. It might be even more forcefully argued that such discussion in this context, with wide-spread strategic implications for world evangelization, approximates most clearly the components necessary to give us the clearest insight into the issue.

A brief overview of selected biblical passages provides an introduction to foundational concepts of the topic. Particular emphasis is placed on the Old Testament passages where the concept of what may be termed "territorial spirits" can be seen as emerging. Dr. Wagner's conclusions are certainly corroborated by additional study in non-canonical literature of this period. Such study shows that the world view of this era affirms the "angel of the nations" idea represented in Deut. 32.[2] I think we would all agree that the biblical backgrounds of this topic need to be continually explored and hopefully matured. The subjects of the gods, angels, spirits, Satan, Lucifer, the devil, the world and the flesh are complex and require serious scholarly evaluation. Nonetheless, it is abundantly clear and particularly important for our purposes that the Bible always regards "the powers" as very real. This should be enough motivation for us to affirm that our efforts to "wrestle with principalities and powers" need not be mindless, sectarian activities. Rather, such efforts constitute a core component of the task of world evangelization.

Dr. Wagner's cataloging of contemporary examples is fascinating. I only wish I could have heard the full details of these accounts. Though serious research on territorial spirits is relatively new, the appeal to contemporary examples alone leaves the reader to wonder whether this is a new arena for spiritual warfare. Does not church history, modern missions history or the Pentecostal and charismatic histories of the twentieth century provide us any further insight with which to broaden our understanding?

It is briefly, though significantly, observed by Dr. Wagner that discernment becomes crucial to the church and its leadership who will move into the seemingly uncharted waters. The descriptive case studies provide more than research in process requiring validation. Implicitly, they call us to an equally necessary commitment: the reestablishment of discernment ministries and accompanying mature and valid verification processes. Lutheran charismatic leader Larry Christenson observes that "To take the reality of demons seriously is simply to ask the church—the whole church—to be as accurate as possible in the way it diagnoses and deals with evil."[3]

The section on *Identifying the Spirits* uses the Mark 5 account of the demonized Gaderene as a scriptural example. The biblical pattern Dr. Wagner observes is that the demons are named, that they may be identified, unmasked, subsequently engaged in battle and defeated. Whereas we can draw no final conclusions on the validity of these descriptive examples, (that is, particularly those of Rita Cabezas) using the pattern of Mark 5, a legitimate question can be asked: What ultimate spiritual conquests have resulted with the naming of the governors of six worldwide principalities? The areas of evil under Anoritho and Apolion read strikingly similar to those Paul suggested in Gal. 5:19-21. Paul seems to have observed that those are the products of the sinful nature that wars against life in the Spirit. I am not skeptical of the means by which our Lord may gift His people for purposes of identifying and defeating demonic forces. However, the excesses of recent personal deliverance type ministries do reveal a propensity to reduce most problems to the simple identification of a demon for the proverbial knock-out punch. *Identifying the spirits* certainly should be part of our strategic efforts toward global evangelization. How to validate and cross-check research in this area is crucial to its functionality in our efforts and is appropriately called for by Dr. Wagner.

The *Recognizing the Dangers* section concisely identifies clear and not so obvious dangers. The observation that we can reduce warfare against territorial spirits to a magic formula is a necessary corrective to over-zealous warriors. It rightly warns us of the tendency toward anthropocentric ministry efforts that can tempt most if not all of us.

The danger of misunderstanding the requirements of spiritual warfare in the *major leagues* and doing so without the proper spiritually disciplined life (particularly in prayer) is, thankfully, addressed. In order to wrestle with principalities and powers, one needs to wrestle with the flesh and blood of day-to-day Christian spirituality. Tenacity for intimacy with the Father results in a clearer focus that discerns Christ's continuing ministry among us by the power of His Spirit.

Dr. Wagner is to be thanked for his directive to avoid being owned by overemphasizing power. The history of both classical Pentecostals and the charismatic movement reveals the skeletons of tragedies attached to such overemphasis. The Azusa Street participant Frank Bartlemann understood such problems during the earlier part of the century. His wisdom is still worth observing. "Many are willing to seek power from every battery they can lay their hands on in order to perform miracles, draw attention to themselves, thus robbing Christ of His glory and making fair showing in the flesh . . . we must stick to our text, Christ!"[4]

Dr. Wagner rightly observes that the most pervasive danger to us all may be ignorance. Denying the facts surrounding spiritual warfare almost guarantees that these demonic powers can strike from their concealment and cripple us in our ministry efforts without our having the slightest comprehension as to what has happened.[5]

Implications for Ministry Strategy

1. The emphasis of this paper comes at a crucial time, not only in global evangelization, but because the mission field is coming to North America (Southern California is a prime example). Large numbers of immigrants come from parts of the world that are steeped in animism. Other immigrants bring syncretistic Christianity with indigenous religion components open to the demonic. Dr. Wagner's paper points us to the fact that this is not a problem of strategy for global evangelization alone. Territorial spirits will increasingly become an issue to contend with in North America, particularly in our urban centers.

2. The theme of this paper implores us to begin understanding the pervasiveness of the pagan resurgence implicit in the New Age Movement. The ploy of Satan has certainly taken a different route in the Western world, but the result has been a society increasingly drawn to the world of the demonic via channeling, psychic-healing or mind-altering meditation. We must realize that as we battle New Age influences, we dare not forget they are more than merely interaction with pluralism as ideas, individuals

or events. They are true power encounters.[6]

3. Discernment as giftedness and/or an integral part of a spirituality for ministry is paramount. The principalities and powers of darkness are clearly prime objectives for biblical discernment. We have for too long allowed this key component of spiritual warfare to be a domesticated task of prudence, character evaluation or sanctified common sense. We again need to see discernment as integral to a spirituality for spiritual warfare.

Areas for Further Study

At least three aspects of Dr. Wagner's presentation call for further study:

1. *Methods of validation and cross-checking of the case studies being presently examined.* Of particular importance is how revelatory words of knowledge are "tested" for their relationship to the discerning of territorial spirits. Is the ministry of *group discernment* a possible area of exploration in validation of case studies?

2. *Evaluation of appropriate historical documents that speak to the issue of territorial spirits from a historical perspective.* A deeper understanding of the Desert Fathers and church history throughout the Middle Ages up to the Enlightenment might be helpful.[7] The works of Ignatius Loyola are a literal goldmine on the issue of discernment. The theology and music of Martin Luther are also a rich source of insight into how another age dealt with similar issues.[8]

3. *Research into the issue of territorial spirits and related topics in spiritual warfare.* At the risk of seeming self-serving and certainly patronizing, I will make this final suggestion: The archives of classical Pentecostal groups offer an invaluable source for this research. Though the

documents in these archives represent a tradition more likely to produce oral history than conceptualized theologies, they nonetheless offer a solid source of a history of "power ministry" in the earlier part of this century. A rich heritage also exists in those first-generation Pentecostals still alive. The oral histories that may be obtained in interviews with these pioneers could prove invaluable to the development of this crucial area of study.

Concluding Remarks

Those who represent the Third Wave are very much at the forefront of this symposium. Your simple yet profound affirmation surrounding all facets of "power ministry" is a real source of inspiration to this Pentecostal. Might I be so bold as to suggest that the histories of Pentecostalism, the charismatic movement and the Third Wave are God's continuing reminder of a sovereign agenda He has been trying to develop in His Church throughout this century? Christo-centricity, giftedness for service and empowerment for Kingdom mission are concentric circles that God desires for His Church. Dr. Wagner rightly suggests that Satan's ploy, in counteracting the evangelism of Japan, may include erecting barriers between Christian groups in that country. My hope is that the three above mentioned groups may commit themselves to focus on their priorities in common, not their unique historical or theological nuances. Could it be that our Lord has brought us together "for such a time as this?"

Notes
1. C. Peter Wagner, *How to Have a Healing Ministry Without Making Your Church Sick* (Ventura: Regal Books, 1988), p. 20.
2. See Walter Wink's trilogy on the Power: *Naming the Powers, Unmasking the*

Powers, Engaging the Powers (Philadelphia: Fortress Press).
3. Larry Christenson, ed., *Welcome, Holy Spirit* (Minneapolis: Augsburg Publishing House, 1987), p. 344.
4. William Menzies, *Anointed to Serve* (Springfield: Gospel Publishing House, 1971), p. 58.
5. Wink, *Unmasking the Powers*, p.108. Though Wink's interpretation of the powers would tend to differ from many of those attending this symposium, his observation in this case is insightful.
6. Douglas Groothius, *Confronting the New Age* (Downers Grove: InterVarsity Press, 1988), p. 42.
7. See J. B. Russell, *Lucifer: The Devil in the Middle Ages* (Ithaca: Cornell University Press, 1984), pp. 313-30. This book provides a significant bibliography of sources for such a study.
8. See John Wimber, *Power Evangelism* (San Francisco: Harper and Row, 1986), for surveys of historical figures and events.

CHAPTER 4

Deception: Satan's Chief Tactic

TIMOTHY M.
WARNER

TIMOTHY M. WARNER is professor
of mission and director of professional doctoral programs at Trinity Evangelical Divinity School in
Deerfield, Illinois. He formerly
served as a missionary in Sierra
Leone, West Africa and was president of Fort Wayne Bible College
for 10 years. He has contributed
essays to several current books
in the area of "power encounter."

ONE of my strong memories from seminary study is a paper I wrote on the nature of evil in the Revelation of John. One of my chief conclusions was that the primary tactic of Satan is deception. In Rev. 12:9 he is called "the deceiver of the whole world" (*RSV*), and the book is a veritable chronicle of how he practices his deception.

Unfortunately, I did not pursue that study after the paper was turned in until recent years. I went to West Africa to minister in an animistic context with almost no functional knowledge of Satan and the demonic world, or of how Christian theology related to what I was encountering there. In reality, I was a victim of deception—the deception that as a Christian I had nothing to worry about from Satan and demons and that most of the African beliefs in such things were just superstition. It was only after I returned from Africa that I learned otherwise.

My main argument is that Satan's chief tactic is deception and that this deception operates both in the realm of truth and in the realm of power. Christian ministry must therefore have a proper balance of proclamation and demonstration—*proclamation* of Christian truth and *demonstration* of Christ's power. To limit the activity of demons to a few periods in history and to limit the exercise of Christian power against them to the Apostolic Era is to become the victim of one of Satan's deceptions, in my judgment. Two recent books from the Philippines speak clearly and forcefully to this issue as it has affected Christian ministry there.[1]

The Roots of the Problem

To understand the spiritual warfare going on today we need to understand where Satan came from and what motivates him. It is almost incomprehensible that a being who was one of the most powerful of the angels (perhaps with a special responsibility for the created world of which we are a part) could become dissatisfied with his position and develop an insatiable desire to become a God like Yahweh, the Creator. He at least wanted to share in the glory of the Creator and decided to challenge God over the issue of glory. There is not time to explore this in detail, but the result of his decision was that he did not become a glorious Being like God, but rather that he became a being who embodies all that is ungodly, even though he still presents himself as an angel of light (2 Cor. 11:14).

When that act of rebellion took place, God apparently did not deprive Lucifer of his power as an angel, nor did Lucifer turn from his lust for glory. The lust seemed rather to intensify to the point where the primary occupation of this fallen angel is now to deprive God of all the glory he can. He does this by working in the thinking and experience of God's children, children by creation and by redemption. He does this by telling them lies about God—something he is more than willing to do (John 8:44)—and by deceiving them through his shows of power.

Our introduction to Satan, as he has come to be called, is in the Garden of Eden where he comes on the scene to begin his war on God by attacking His children. Satan's very first approach is to impugn the character of God. He says to Eve (and I am obviously doing a little interpreting), "Did God really say that you would die if you ate of a certain tree? That's a lie. I am here to tell you the truth. The fact is, God is holding out on you. You can't trust Him. If you eat of that tree you will discover your true potential, namely that you are like God and really don't need Him to tell you what to do and not to do."

Notice how quickly and cleverly Satan deceived Eve to invert his role and the role of God. God became a liar and

Satan became a truth-teller. Such deception has been going on ever since that fateful day in Eden. Satan has, indeed, developed a considerable "bag of tricks" to impress people and to lead them astray. These tricks include clever lies, to which he has found us humans quite susceptible, and displays of power, which bring equally ready responses from us, especially when we have lost touch with the power of God.

The Nature of Deception

Deception is a most effective strategy. Without going into how it relates to the functioning of the human mind, we can say that, when we are deceived, we are convinced that what we believe is true. Because we have a tendency toward insecurity, we are constantly looking for things that are secure and dependable. This makes us especially susceptible to a voice that speaks with great confidence and sincerity. Satan has developed many approaches of this nature. And, the more thorough the deception the deeper the conviction with which the lie is held. We do not have to look far to find examples of those who are dying for their beliefs—beliefs that are patently false.

Another factor involved in deception that Satan uses effectively is that none of us respond warmly to being told that we have been gullible and are acting on what is false. Again, we do not have to look far to find examples, even within the Christian community, of groups being isolated from each other because they don't want to have to deal with the challenges to their belief system that would be required by meaningful contact with each other. Or, what may be even worse, the deep animosities and resentments held because of the suggestion that one may be deceived.

Beyond Deception

One of the deceptions we have to deal with is the idea that I am beyond temptation in some area—that I could not be deceived. I have had people very close to me tell me, after they had fallen into gross immorality, that they believed they were not subject to temptation in the moral area.

This is why we need a symposium like this. We need each other. We need lines of accountability. We need others to help us see where we have blinders on. I fear being a "lone ranger" in this area. Satan loves to tell us that we are so spiritual that we only need to listen to God. He doesn't tell us that God often chooses to speak to us through other members of the Body—and they are not always those members of the Body that we would like to listen to.

The Deceiver: Satan or the Flesh?

A question that is certain to be raised is, "But how do you know it is Satan who is deceiving you rather than just your own lower nature? Aren't you ascribing to Satan that which is really the flesh?" I think that most of the either-or kinds of questions are another strategy of Satan to deceive and to keep us from recognizing his role in such struggles. I would say that it is almost always both Satan and the flesh, rather than one or the other. Satan "prowls around like a roaring lion looking for someone to devour" (1 Pet. 5:8, *NIV*). If he finds a person, especially a Christian, having a struggle with the flesh, he would be a fool not to jump in and try to take advantage of the situation. His strategy is, in fact, to get us to think that we have the ability to run our own lives. He tells us that neither Satan nor God are really needed either to explain the problem we face or to find a solution for it.

This is the premise of our secular society, and it comes right from the pit of hell. Unfortunately it has been adopted to some extent by many counselors, even Christian counselors, and it is no wonder that such "therapies" do not produce better results.

We also need to face the fact that the either-or approach may work the other way—that is, that we blame everything on the devil and demons. Psychotherapists tell horror stories of people who come to them after some zealous Christians have tried to solve complicated problems by trying to cast demons out of them. Good deliverance counselors, on the other hand, can tell the stories of those who have spent a small fortune on therapy only to discover that they could be set free by the power of God. C. S. Lewis' famous statement in his *Introduction to Screwtape Letters* has been proved true again and again. Satan and the demons are pleased with either extreme and "hail a materialist or a magician with the same delight."

The point is, Satan does not care in which direction he perverts the truth. He only cares that we act on the basis of his deception rather than on the basis of God's truth. If he can get us to seek answers only in the realm of human responsibility or only in the realm of spiritual power, he can probably keep us from finding the answer we seek.

Deception in the Area of Truth

We have been talking primarily about deception in the area of truth so far, and we probably understand such deception better than deception in the area of power. Let me add or reinforce a few thoughts on this subject.

Satan's primary attack is always on the character of

God. We saw this, for example, in the case of Eve in the Garden. We see it today in persons such as those who have been seriously abused by others, especially in childhood. Two principle lines of thinking are usually involved in such cases. First, "Why didn't God prevent the abuse from happening?" or, second, "Is God really able to heal the pain and turn it into strength?" The questions may be asked in other ways, or they may not be verbalized at all; but they are almost certain to be there. Satan will see to that.

In the minds of some counselors, God and biblical truth may not be functional elements in the approach to healing, even when dealing with hurt and anger. In the final analysis, however, it is the character of God that is involved. When the person becomes convinced that the teaching of Scripture about God is true, healing can happen very quickly. The failure to go to this level in the counseling process often explains why the process becomes so long. The usual lack of a functional belief in the spirit world also helps to explain the inordinate success Satan has had in keeping us from the healing power of God in our lives.

Another observation is that deception is usually more effective when couched in a background of truth. Satan knows the Bible well and loves to twist it as he teaches the "doctrines of demons" (1 Tim. 4:1, *RSV*), but he is not averse to speaking the truth if it will contribute to his ultimate purpose to deceive. For example, when he tempted Jesus in the wilderness, he said, "If You are the Son of God, tell this stone to become bread" (Luke 4:3, *NASB*). John tells us that this is a confession that demons do not like to make and will not make on a continuing basis (1 John 4:1-3). If they can set us up for deception by giving us truth to which we can readily assent, however, they will speak the truth.

For example, some friends of mine with impeccable evangelical roots became involved in a group where the gifts were apparently operating, especially the gift of prophecy. At first the prophecies were thoroughly biblical—the truth—and a high trust level was developed. Gradually, however, the prophecies indicated that the group needed to cut off relations with those outside the group—those that might provide needed accountability. Then the wounds of prophecy began to include things like wives leaving their husbands. By this time, however, they were afraid to question the messages even though they were clearly contrary to Scripture; and, in the end, five Christian homes were broken by divorce, and the group ended in chaos.

I should add that I know of another case where the same process was underway, but the leader of the group recognized the drift away from biblical truth, identified the demonic roots of the deception, and took a scriptural path back.

There are numerous passages in the New Testament that speak of ways in which deception takes place, but we do not have time to mention them here.[2]

Deception in the Area of Power

Deception in the realm of power is somewhat more difficult for us to deal with because we are not in the habit of identifying spirits as the cause of phenomena here on earth. Because he is a powerful angel, however, Satan has the ability to manipulate things in the physical world. He uses this power to impress us and to get us to fear him. As our belief in the power of God has declined, Satan has been remarkably successful in getting Christians to treat him as if he had power with which they had no way of coping. The usual attitude seems to be that if we leave him alone, he will leave us alone. That, unfortunately, is another one of his lies.

While the purpose of his displays of power is to deceive, there is real power involved in them. They are not just someone's imagination. In 2 Thess. 2:9, 10 (*NIV*), we read that "the coming of the lawless one will be in accordance with the work of Satan displayed in all kinds of counterfeit miracles, signs and wonders, and in every sort of evil that deceives those who are perishing." This identifies the counterfeiting activity of our enemy in the realm of power. His work is characterized by "counterfeit miracles, signs and wonders, and in every sort of evil that deceives." This will especially be true in the time just prior to Christ's return, but I understand the passage to say that such deceptive shows of power are his standard mode of operation.

"But," you say, "apart from the activity of the Egyptian magicians, where are the biblical examples of such miracles?" It is true that there are not many direct references to such demonic activity, and I think there is a good reason for this. The Bible is not a book to glorify Satan by telling of his displays of power; it is a book to glorify God by telling of His displays of power—in creation, in redemption and in all areas of life. And from this we need to take a lesson: we need to be cautious in recounting the activity of the enemy. Some of the publications in this area may stimulate belief in Satan rather than belief in God. We need to establish the reality of the work of the enemy, but our emphasis needs to be on the truth and on the source of victory for the Christian.

The fact is that Satan's power is real power. In the final analysis, it is power delegated by God and being misused by one of His creatures. Just as God did not take back our freedom and the image of God in us when we sinned against Him, God did not take back Lucifer's power when he rebelled against Him. God's glory is seen supremely in His power to create—a power Satan does not have. Satan does, however, have the power to manipulate what God has created, and he has been very effective in getting us to look away from the revelation of God in creation and to focus on the manipulation of parts of that creation by the fallen angels.

Man has an inherent need for power, the power just to live as a significant human being, but especially power over the circumstances of life, power over people, and power over the future. God provides that power for us; but when we lose our functional relationship with Him and His power, we are open to offers from other sources. Satan's counterfeits take the form of such things as magic, sorcery, witchcraft and divination.

The manifestation of these areas of power is seen readily in societies where animistic beliefs are held. None of our Western explanations will convince people in such societies that there is not real spiritual power involved. I am not suggesting that such practices always work. Satan feels no obligation to deliver power on command from those he holds in his control. He delivers only so much as will keep them in his control. So, some magic doesn't work; some sorcery doesn't work; and some predictions don't come true. But these things work often enough that desperate people keep coming back to them.

Magical healing, for example, has a long history. Many societies have substantial catalogs of ways to heal through magical (demonic) power. "And why would Satan ever heal?" you ask. "Isn't that good? Does Satan ever do good?" Yes, Satan will do good if he can use it as a means to bring people into bondage to him. When Jesus said that if Satan cast out demons he would bring down his own kingdom, He was saying that if Satan cast out demons the way Jesus did, the destruction of Satan's kingdom would be the result. When Jesus cast out demons or when He healed, it was a pure, unmixed blessing. When Satan does such things, he always exacts a price. He offers something desperately wanted but requires bondage in another area as the price. So, when practitioners of voodoo cast out demons, they simply exchange control by one demon for control by another. And when healing is by demonic power, it either will not be a permanent healing or it will result in bondage in some other area of one's life.

For example, a Christian man was experiencing a deep spiritual depression from which he could not find relief. A counselor with whom he was consulting asked him if anything else significant happened in his life about the time of the onset of the depression. The man replied that, in fact, it was about the time someone prayed for him, and his congenitally shortened leg was made whole for the first time in his life. The counselor then suggested that it was possible that the healing was by demonic power and that the price of the healing was the depression. The man immediately said that if the healing was not from God he renounced it. Whereupon his leg shriveled up again, but he lost his spiritual depression.[3]

Another example of this is seen in the case of a couple who brought their nine-year-old son to a friend of mine because they had been unable to find any solution to the son's hyperactivity. In the course of talking with them, my friend discovered that five years ago they had taken the son to a doctor for the physical problem he was having—a legitimate physician but one who practiced holistic medicine. He used any powers, psychic or physical, that were available to him. The boy was healed, but he also became

hyperactive. Extensive treatment by a child psychiatrist
had produced no improvement. When the parents recognized what they had done in opening their son to demonic
activity, they renounced it and sought the Lord's forgiveness. The counselor commanded the demons to leave the
boy, and in a few minutes he said, "I feel so much better."
The next week the teacher wrote the parents a note saying, "What happened to your son? He's fine."

When it comes to sorcery, most Westerners have a
very difficult time accepting the idea that there is real
power involved. They are reluctant to accept the validity
of such things as curses. That there is real power operating in this area is demonstrated by something I heard
recently from a former student. A man from an animistic
background had become a Christian, and shortly after this
he came under conviction for curses he had placed on
three men, all of whom went insane and began to wander
about aimlessly. So he went to the place in the forest
where he had worked the sorcery against them, dug up
and destroyed the objects involved, and revoked the
curses in Jesus name. He then went into town to find the
men. When he found the first man, he was already clothed
and in his right mind. The power of suggestion had not had
a chance to work—only the power of God to defeat the
power of the devil.[4]

When it comes to divination, I don't think demons have
the ability to foretell the future in any sense other than
that they can tell a person what they plan to do in the
future. The problem is that they cannot always do what
they want to do. Therefore not all the predictions of fortune tellers and psychics come to pass, but enough do that
some people are impressed and come back for more. One
failure in such prophecies, however, indicates that the
source is not from God. The same principle applies in the

Christian realm in the exercise of the gift of prophecy. Any prophecy that does not agree with the Scriptures or does not come true must be rejected as not from God. This is why Paul says that when one prophesies, the others are to "judge." Satan loves to counterfeit spiritual gifts, and unless the judging is going on and the gift of the discerning of spirits is operating, it is doubtful whether the other gifts are from God.

Conclusion

Much more could be said about deception. I especially recommend Jessie Penn-Lewis' treatment of the subject in her classic *War on the Saints*. But to go back to where we started, we need to remember that Satan's fundamental attack is on the character of God. Good theology is therefore an absolute essential in talking about power evangelism or power encounter or any other concern with power. I do not use the term "theology" in the sense of systematic theology, but rather in the sense of knowledge of God. If we depend on demonstrations of power for our theology, we are especially prone to deception. This again is why we need to stay in the Word and why we need each other—why the Body of Christ must keep in touch with all its members.

Jesus had some strong words to say about deception in the Sermon on the Mount (Matt. 7:22, 23) and in His Olivet discourse (Matt. 24:4; 23-25). We need to take seriously His warnings and all the other biblical warnings concerning deception. They should spur us to commitment to mastery of the Scriptures and to familiarity with the Master's voice gained through long periods of meaningful time spent with Him.

Notes

1. See Rodney Henry, *The Filipino Spirit World*, 1986, and Melba Maggay, *The Gospel in Filipino Context*, 1987, both published in Manila by OMF Literature, Inc.
2. See 1 Cor. 6:9; 15:33; 2 Cor. 11:13-15; Gal. 6:7; 1 Tim. 4:1; 2 Tim. 3:13; Jas. 3:15; 1 John 4:1; 2 John 7; Rev. 20:10.
3. Source verifiable but confidential.
4. Documentation in personal files.

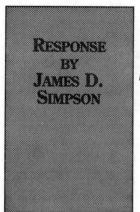

RESPONSE
BY
JAMES D.
SIMPSON

Deception: Satan's Chief Tactic

It is very easy in our modern, materialistic and mind-over-matter society to become insensitive and even oblivious to Satan's tactics, especially deception. If Satan can keep us so busy in the natural realm as we scurry off to work, scamper up the success ladder and settle back in the recliner with one hand grasping the remote and the other clinching the *Daily Reporter,* we will soon forget altogether the reality of the supernatural. And so goes our work-a-day world, the supernatural engulfed by the natural. No wonder humanism becomes so cozy and comfortable in the midst of such sophistication. It is much easier to "leave the driving to Greyhound" and become intoxicated with getting ahead while letting the rest of the world pass by. Consequently, Satan becomes delighted with people, especially Christians, who live out their lives in a spirit of apathy rather than in a spirit of authority (Matt. 28:18-21). As Warner so avidly states:

> His strategy [Satan's] is in fact to get us to think that
> we have the ability to run our own lives. He tells us
> that neither Satan nor God are really needed either

to explain the problem we face or to find a solution for it. This is the premise of our secular society and it comes right from the pit of hell. Unfortunately it has been adopted to some extent by many counselors, even Christian counselors, and it is no wonder that such "therapies" do not produce better results.

If Satan can convince us that there is no alarm, that all is well and that the supernatural is a product of the simple-minded and not for the up-and-coming intellectual, he will ultimately cause us to relax with overwhelming reluc-tance. This is the unfortunate reality of much of Western Christianity: "Having a form of godliness, but denying the power" (2 Tim. 3:5, *KJV*). Western Christianity has con-tacted a powerless disease that I call "non-rockaboatus." If you leave the devil alone, he'll leave you alone. Warner states that "As our belief in the power of God has declined, he has been remarkably successful in getting Christians to treat him as if he had power with which they have no way of coping."

As a result, we simply avoid reality for illusion. The truth of the matter is that by philosophically limiting Satan's power we make his deception all the more power-ful. The trade-off is a mere message of Mickey Mouse mentality that further rejects the truth for a lie. Satan can only pretend to be what he isn't. Consequently, all of his glitter and glaze serves only to lure his victims until after being so close they become blinded by his lustrous light which is only a deceptive reflection of what he really is. What he is is "a roaring lion" that "walketh about, seeking whom he may devour" (1 Pet. 5:8, *KJV*). "Therefore hell hath enlarged herself, and opened her mouth without mea-sure: and their glory, and their multitude, and their pomp, and he that rejoiceth, shall descend into it" (Isa. 5:14,

KJV). "But if our gospel be hid, it is hid to them that are lost: for whom the god of this world [Satan] hath blinded the minds of them which believeth not" (2 Cor 4:3,4).

Satan is a supernatural being, although limited in power yet still greatly effective in fulfilling his malicious purpose, at least for a time. Because he is limited in power he has to rely upon clever delusion and allusion. Warner states that Satan: "did not become a glorious being like God but rather he became a being who embodies all that is ungodly, even though he still presents himself as an angel of light" (2 Cor. 11:14).

Deceptiveness implies that one is not altogether all-powerful. Consequently, what is often said, "The best line of defense is a good offence," Satan has construed within a complex network of deception. Being limited in his power and unable to confront God one-on-one, he has chosen to impact what is nearest to God's heart, His creation (us). We are "the apple of His eye," but the "worm" is not dead yet. "Where their worm dieth not, and the fire is not quenched" (Mark 9:44, *KJV*). In fact, he never dies; he is simply at the time appointed going to be transplanted to a place prepared especially for him and all who follow. It is to this extent that Satan's limited power will be fully realized once and for all.

As always, Satan's lust for power and glory has been the motivating factor behind his attack on the character of God. Warner advocates, "Satan's primary attack is always on the character of God. The lust seemed rather to intensify to the point where the primary occupation of this fallen angel is now to deprive God of all the glory he can." The best way to accomplish that is to kill, steal and destroy what was originally intended to return glory and honor to God only, that is, mankind (John 10:10). Satan is a liar and the father of lies (John 8:44). And all liars, those who follow his example, will, as Scripture warns, be cast into the lake of fire along with Satan and his fallen co-hosts (Rev. 21:8).

It is easy to fall prey to the lies of Satan, especially, as Warner writes, "when we have lost touch with the power of God." Spiritual renewal is necessary for bold, visionary spirituality. Daily warfare demands a daily walk with God! I believe to a great extent the Western Church is out of touch with the power of God. The fact is, unless we begin to rely upon the supernatural power of God as "normal," as Dr. Kraft points out, we will never impact the society in which we live. It is time to take authority in the name of Jesus Christ. Dr. Lasmar Vest says:

> The power of God operated in the early Church in much the same way it operated in the life of Jesus Christ. Those early believers discovered that they were linked with all the power of omnipotence, whether it was waiting before God, reaching out with compassion to suffering men and women, or challenging the power of darkness. What has become of the Church's power? In many cases the Church—now prudent, self-admiring, self-protecting—talks bravely within her own borders while the powers of darkness go unchallenged. The Church too often reaches out with gimmicks of straw, and the sleeping world does not even wiggle an ear. A sick, struggling, and powerless Church will never change this world. The Church is more than moral men and planned programs. It is divine power in action. Do we take that power for granted?[1]

The Church must *confront* Satan if it wishes to obey the Great Commission. Reaching the lost in these last days demands a power encounter. "I will build my church;" says Jesus, "and the gates of hell shall not prevail" (Matt. 16:18, *KJV*). We must fight to win. Paul claimed, "I have fought a good fight, I have finished my course, I have kept the faith" (2 Tim. 4:7, *KJV*). Indeed it is a *good* fight because the ultimate outcome is *good*. Further, Jesus asked, "Why callest thou me good? none is good, save one, that is, God" (Luke 18:19, *KJV*).

Warner's comments on the section titled "Beyond Deception" are in much need of understanding today. We must fight the idea that we as Christians are above deception. Paul was not above admitting that he kept himself under subjection lest he become a castaway (1 Cor. 9:27). The Bible warns emphatically, "Be not deceived; . . . whatsoever a man soweth, that shall he also reap" (Gal. 6:7, *KJV*). Pride always precedes a fall (Prov. 16:18). And I quote Warner, "This is why we need a symposium like this. We need each other. We need lines of accountability. We need others to help us see where we have blinders on." The Bible is very clear, "We are our brother's keeper" (see Gen. 4:9; Matt. 25:35-46 and Jas. 2:14-26).

I have had the distinct privilege of working with several prominent ministers who are internationally known, yet both fell into gross immorality. One of these ministers, to my surprise, I met at the airport just before flying out to California to engage in this symposium on power evangelism. I asked him if what I had heard about him only a week prior was true. He admitted that he had repented and reestablished his relationship with God.

After looking back over the years I spent with both of these great men of God, I have concluded that there was a common denominator that plagued both of these world-renown evangelists—each felt that they were above correction. I can recall both of them admitting to having literally no friends outside of their immediate family members and time would not allow for much interaction even then. Sad but true, too many prominent Christians feel that all they need to listen to is God, not realizing that "iron sharpens iron" (Prov. 27:17, *NIV*). I can honestly say that in my earlier ministry I held myself above the need for accountability in friendship. I was even known to often say, "Shape up or ship out." They usually shipped out! In light of having worked with those mentioned above, all I can say is, "but for the grace of God there go I."

Warner's section on "Deception in the Area of Truth" is very important to our understanding. The Scripture soundly states, "Ye shall know the truth, and the truth shall make you free" (John 8:32, *KJV*), and "As he thinketh in his heart, so is he" (Prov. 23:7, *KJV*). Our actions are in direct proportion to the way we think. Therefore, Paul gives helpful advice in Phil. 4:8, to think on things that are true, honest, just, pure, lovely and of good report.

It has been said that "an idle mind is the devil's workshop." The real battlefield in Christianity today is in the mind. Spiritual warfare is mental warfare. We desperately need to know how to maintain the mind of Christ.

Warner states, "The usual lack of a functional belief in the spirit world [especially in the area of counseling] also helps to explain the inordinate success Satan has had in keeping us from the healing power of God in our lives." I contend that power evangelism does not need proof; it needs practice. Let us return to simplicity of faith and obey rather than sacrifice what we know and believe in on the altars of humanism. As Warner states, "Satan knows the Bible well and loves to use it to teach 'the doctrines of demons'" (see 1 Tim. 4:1), but when resisted with obedient application of truth, he cannot stand but flees away.

Truth can only be a defense when practiced. Truth is like a good tool of the trade, useless unless used. Theory must be converted into application. Paul said, "And my speech and my preaching was not with enticing words of man's wisdom, but in demonstration of the Spirit and of power" (1 Cor. 2:4, *KJV*). James says that demons believe that there is a God (Jas. 2:19). Believing that there is a God is one thing; putting into practice the precepts about that God is another.

We certainly need a functional theology again, a new Pentecost or perhaps just putting into practice what we have known for a long time. Sad but true, time often erodes the high peaks of our faith. Jesus said that if we have as much faith as a grain of mustard seed, we can effectively move mountains (Matt. 17:20). He was not talking about the amount of one's faith as compared to another's, but the individual and corporate application of using what we already have no matter how small the amount. The implication being that what would increase would not be the amount of faith but indeed the amount of miracles in our lives. The key was simply using what you've got—that's enough! Here again, the Word of God does not need proof, it needs practice.

On another topic, I do not believe that Christians per se can be demon *possessed.* I do believe that they can backslide in a progressive sense. They can be oppressed. Also, demon spirits can gain habitual hold of a Christian who in such case will be in need of repentance, deliverance and spiritual instruction. Let me explain: In classical Pentecostal circles, the phrase "the devil cannot cross the bloodline" is used quite often. This means that there is no fear of any type of demonic possession as long as you maintain a faithful relationship with God and/or are born again. Christians can, however, through habitually yielding to temptation through the lust of the flesh, lust of the eyes and the pride of life, be led to demonic possession, in which case casting out demons may or may not be necessary. Of course, this state of the will, emotion and mind is the exception and not the rule among classical Pentecostal experiences.

A depressed and oppressed mind can be influenced over a period of time until a deviant pattern of behavior can be identified. This happens progressively until the believer grows weary with the fight and relaxes his/her stand against evil. This is why the Bible encourages or warns the believer to "not become weary in well doing" (see 2 Thess. 3:13). Realizing that the thoughts can influence the will, eventually a Christian can become susceptible to demon spirits, even to the point of "possession." Again, I firmly believe backsliding is the exception and not the rule. Let me also say again that backsliding is a progressive state of being and not instantaneous. Until this point is reached, oppression and obsession are forerunners to this dilemma.

In conclusion I offer the following definition of terms:

1. *Oppression*—Depressing influence / temptation / wain in spiritual disciplines, growing weary in well doing, etc.
2. *Obsession*—Deeper level of yielding to the lust of the flesh, lust of the eye and the pride of life in regard to whatever the problem/temptation may be. Still, this stage is difficult to detect outwardly depending upon the ego of the person. Sinful habitual behavior is beginning to take place.
3. *Demonic attachments*—This is a worsening of the habitual state of the person into evil practice until a particular life-style is taking shape. This life-

style may reflect itself in attitude and/or action. A person at this level is in danger of "falling out of grace," and taking authority over the problem is necessary. Repentance also is necessary! The Bible says, "Neither give place to the devil" (Eph. 4:27, *KJV*).

4. *Possession*—This state of being describes a non-Christian; complete break from true commitment to Christ into a willful, deliberate pattern of behavior or life-style that is in dire need of repentance. Deliverance and casting out demons may or may not be necessary for complete healing.

Note
1. James D. Simpson, *The Pentecostal Evangelist* (Cleveland, TN: Pathway Press, 1988), pp. 34-35.

CHAPTER

5

Finding Freedom in Christ

NEIL T. ANDERSON

NEIL T. ANDERSON is associate
professor of practical theology
and chairman of the department
at Talbot Theological Seminary,
Biola University, in La Mirada,
California. He is in wide demand
for conferences and seminars on
discipling and spiritual growth,
and is the author of *Victory Over
the Darkness.*

Last summer I was speaking in a large Southern California church on the subject of the New Age Movement. My text was 1 Tim. 4:1, "The Spirit explicitly says that in later times some will fall away from the faith, paying attention to deceitful spirits and doctrines of demons" (*NASB*). I was inundated afterward by people seeking help for themselves or their friends and relatives. Halfway back in the church was a young girl emotionally overcome, but not willing to let anyone approach her. Finally one of the staff cut through the crowd, saying, "I'm sorry folks, but we need Dr. Anderson back here." As I approached I could hear her say, "He understands, he understands!" We were able to get her out of the sanctuary and into a private office where we scheduled an appointment. The next week we heard her story.

When Louise arrived for her appointment her face was marked with open wounds! Sheepishly, she admitted, "I have been scratching myself uncontrollably, until my boss suggested that I take the day off." Louise identified her grandmother as a black witch, and described a horrible childhood that saw two of her sisters die at the hands of her father.

She continued, "When I was three years old, I received my guardians." Never once in those early years did she question that those spirit guides were anything other than normal. They were her companions, who told her how to live and what to say. It wasn't until her mother took her to Sunday School that she began to suspect that her companions may not be good. When she asked her parents about it, her father beat her. She never asked again! In order to cope with the increasing mental torment, she resorted to mental discipline. In her high school years she trusted in Christ, but the only substantive change was that the demons took on her face!

After high school she turned to the Marines, and determined to become the toughest of leathernecks. She won awards for her discipline, but the mind can take only so much pressure before it snaps. She was unable or unwilling to tell anyone of her mental torment for fear of being labeled insane. Quietly, she accepted a medical discharge and struggled living alone while eking out an existence. Twenty-two years old, sitting in a church, she heard someone talk about deceiving spirits; finally someone understood!

After she shared her story I asked, "Would you like to get rid of them?"

There was a long pause, "Would I be three again?"

"No, you have been developing all these years."

"Would they really go, or would I go home and be thrashed again?"

"No, you will be free."

An hour later she was free, and hugging us with an openness that she had never known before. "Now I can be hospitable, now I can have people over to my house," she exclaimed.

My own journey into the spiritual world has not come by choice. I was an aerospace engineer before God called me into ministry. I was never curious about the occult, I don't even know my astrological sign. The occultic lure of knowledge and power doesn't appeal to me, and I never felt that I needed a sign from God. It has been God's idea from the beginning. On the other hand, I have never been predisposed to disbelieve what the Bible has to say, especially about the spiritual world. About 15 years ago the Lord began to direct people my way who were spiritually oppressed. I fumbled my way through a lot of failure, but had enough success to know that the spiritual world exists, and that we are woefully unprepared to minister in it. From the beginning my interest has been pastoral, sparked by the desire to see God's people free and living productive lives. What follows are several misconceptions that I labored under, a pastoral procedure that has proven effective, concluding with steps to freedom in Christ.

Misconceptions

1. *There was a particular manifestation of demonic working when Christ was on earth, but it subsided.* This misconception is postured by a simplistic form of dispensational thinking. I happen to belong to the dispensational school of thought, but it would take a particular form of blindness to hold to this extreme view in light of all that is transpiring today. The fact that the Church is going to wrestle with principalities and powers is unavoidable. The only option we have is to determine how, and to what extent. If our Christian world view does not include the kingdom of darkness, then either God or man is going to take a bum rap for all the corruption in this world.

2. *The early Church knew nothing of mental illness and simply diagnosed it as demonic.* One would have to hold to a low view of inspired Scripture to believe this. This position comes from a Western world view that has accepted the definitions of secular psychology. One counselor argued, "There is no way that it can be demonic; that person is paranoid schizophrenic." Labeling doesn't explain anything, it is only a means of classifying symptoms. What is a hallucination? Multiple personalities? What is a person hearing when they hear voices? All these classifications come from a secular source that has no concept of God, much less the demonic. We should not be surprised that secular psychologists with a Western world view offer an inadequate explanation of mental problems.

3. *We need to have some definitive way to know when a problem is psychological and when it is spiritual.* This may be one of the biggest errors. There is no problem that is not psychological. There is never a time when the person's mind, will and emotions are not involved. Experiences of early childhood are always a factor. Likewise, there is no time when God is not present, nor is there a time when it is safe to take off the armor of God. It is never "not spiritual." If our Christian world view does not include the "god of this world," "the prince of the power of the air," it is simply wrong. The fact that theologians can't agree whether man is two or three parts illustrates how difficult it is to separate the spiritual from the psychological. The tendency is to polarize into a deliverance ministry that ignores the other realities of life, or to a psychotherapeutic ministry that ignores the reality of the spiritual world.

4. *Deliverance ministry is a power encounter, and only mature leadership of the Church should be involved.* Actually it is a truth encounter. It is truth that sets people free. Satan is a deceiver, and will work undercover at all costs. His demons are like cockroaches that run to the shadows fleeing from the light of God's Word. One psychotherapist that attended my conference on "Spiritual Conflicts and Counseling" said, "I have never seen any evidence of demonism in all my years of counseling until I came to your conference. When I returned to my practice I discovered that two-thirds of my clients were being deceived and so was I." Satan is a defeated foe, and yet he renders the Church powerless. How does he do this?

When I was a boy on the farm, my dad, my brother and I would drive over to our neighbors to share produce and labor. They had this yappy little dog that would scare the socks off me. When he came around the corner barking, I ran. Guess which one the dog chased! I escaped to the top of our pickup. That dog had no power over me except that which I gave it. Furthermore, it had no inherent power to throw me up on top of that pickup. It used my muscles, my mind, my emotions and my will. Finally I screwed up my courage, stood my ground, kicked a rock at it, and low and behold it ran away! Satan deceives the whole world (Rev. 12:9), and through deception the whole world lies in the power of the evil one (1 John 5:19).

5. *Christians can't have this type of problem.* The prevailing belief among evangelicals is that Christians can't be demon possessed. Nothing has done more damage in arriving at a diagnosis. Even suggesting that demonic influence may be part of their problem brings the disclaimer, "Can't be. I'm a Christian." No attempt has been made to define terms or explain how we wrestle with principalities and powers. If Satan can't touch the Church, why is the Church told to put on the armor of God? Why are we to "resist the Devil"? "Stand firm"? "Be alert"? What if we don't? If there is no kingdom of darkness that seeks to destroy the Church and blind the minds of the unbelieving, then our problems are only physical or psychological. That conclusion will leave a lot of people weeping.

6. *Demonic influence is evident only in extreme or violent behavior and gross sin.* Although there are extreme cases, most live comparatively normal lives, but experience serious personal and interpersonal problems for which no cause or solution has been found. "Satan disguises himself as an angel of light. Therefore it is not surprising if his servants disguise themselves as servants of righteousness" (2 Cor. 11:14, 15, *NASB*). Satan's strategy is first and foremost deception. The tendency is to point out an extreme case that all believers would call demonic, and then not see the subtleness of Satan's

deceptions. It is the latter that is causing the Church to be ineffective.

Pastoral Procedure

One objection to the ministry of deliverance is the lack of instruction in the Epistles. No direction seems to be given to do the kind of ministry that Jesus and the apostles did. A different perspective may clarify the issue and suggest how we would be ministering to those afflicted. Something radical happened at the Cross and in the Resurrection that changed the nature of spiritual conflicts forever. First, Jesus disarmed the rulers and authorities and made a public display of them, having triumphed over them (Col. 2:15). Second, every believer was made alive, raised up with Him, and is now seated with Him in the heavenly places (Eph. 2:5,6). Satan is a defeated foe, and Christians must understand and appropriate their position and authority in Christ. This is what Paul is praying for in Eph. 1:18-21 (*NASB*):

> I pray that the eyes of your heart may be enlightened, so that you may know what is the hope of His calling, what are the riches of the glory of His inheritance in the saints, and what is the surpassing greatness of His power toward those who believe. These are in accordance with the working of the strength of His might which He brought about in Christ, when He raised Him from the dead, and seated Him at His right hand in the heavenly places, far above all rule and authority and power and dominion, and every name that is named, not only in this age, but also in the one to come.

Satan can do nothing about our position in Christ, but if he can deceive us into believing a lie we will spend a lot of time on top of the pickup! Essentially we will be walking according to the flesh (his plane). The pastor/counselor needs to understand that the battle is for the mind, and that the path to freedom is to believe the truth and walk accordingly by faith. Notice the progressive logic of Scripture (*NASB*):

> You shall know the truth, and the truth shall make you free. John 8:32
> Jesus said to him, "I am the way, and the truth, and the life." John 14:6
> But when He, the spirit of truth, comes, He will guide you into all the truth. John 16:13
> I do not ask Thee to take them out of the world, but to keep them from the evil one . . . Sanctify them in the truth; Thy word is truth. John 17:15,17

When we put on the armor of God the first thing we do is:

> Stand firm therefore, having girded your loins with truth. Eph. 6:14
> Finally, brethren, whatever is true . . . let your mind dwell on these things. Phil. 4:8

When God first disciplined the early Church, He did it in such a dramatic way that if done today we should all be dead. What was the issue? Drugs? Sex? No, it was truth! God knows that the Deceiver can wreak havoc with the Church if he can get us to believe and live a lie. "Why has Satan filled your heart to lie to the Holy Spirit?" (Acts 5:3, *NASB*). Thus, the necessity for "taking every thought

captive to the obedience of Christ" (2 Cor. 10:5, *NASB*).
The implication is that this is not a power encounter,
but a truth encounter. When I first realized this, it had a
dramatic effect on my counseling. Previously, I would talk
to a counselee as with any other person, but when I
exposed the demonic influence it would turn into a power
encounter. Satan's strategy is always deception, but when
that strategy is exposed he resorts to a pretense of
power. I have seen people go catatonic, run out of the
room, and become generally disoriented. A power
encounter would ensue, and I would attempt to take
authority over the demonic influence.

My first approach was to get a demon to expose itself
and then command it to come out. Usually this resulted in
a great deal of trauma for the person, and one would have
to wonder who was more powerful. Although progress
was made, the episode would often have to be repeated
again. This is where the Epistles come in. It is the believer's responsibility to resist, renounce, forgive and confess.
It is not what the counselor does that results in freedom, it
is what the counselee believes, confesses and renounces.
The counselor acts as a facilitator. I have not attempted to
"cast out a demon" in several years, but, I have seen hundreds find freedom in Christ.

The procedure is to help the counselee understand the
battle for the mind. Virtually nobody exposes what they
are thinking, assuming that all the thoughts are their own.
Numerous times I have been invited to sit in with Christian
counselors, and after a short period of questioning I have
said, "You are not going crazy, there is a battle going on for
your mind." The typical response is, "Praise God someone finally believes me!" People don't share that they are
hearing voices, fearing that people will think they are
indeed going crazy. Others would not understand the ter-

minology of "hearing voices." When explained in terms of mental confusion, or conflicting thoughts, they identify. A wife of a student at Talbot School of Theology sat in on my class and sent the following letter:

Dear Neil,

I just want to thank you again for how the Lord has used your class to change my life. The last few years of my life had been a constant struggle for the control of my mind, but I was ignorant of my position and authority in Christ, and of Satan's ability to deceive me, and therefore I was open to all kinds of attack. Open areas such as bitterness and fantasy, though I had dealt with them, left me accustomed to accepting all kinds of thoughts as my own. Not knowing that these fears and thoughts could come from another source, I accepted them as my own. I was constantly afraid, my mind bombarded by hostile and angry thoughts that flooded my mind. Much of my life was paralyzed by fear of even little things. I constantly felt guilty and wondered what was wrong with me, but since I couldn't get into anyone else's mind to compare, I did not really understand how much in bondage I was until I came into your class. When you began to describe a person influenced by demons, I just about passed out in shock. You were describing me! I was also taught that demons didn't really affect Christians. Well anyway, for the first time in my life I can really resist Satan, because I can finally identify his attack and I know I am united with Christ and I don't have to sin. I'm not paralyzed by fear any more and my mind is much less cluttered. I could go on and on about the changes in my life. I don't have to be a slave to my sub-

*jective thoughts anymore. As you can tell I am pretty
excited about this. When I read the Scriptures I think,
"Why couldn't I see this before? It's obvious!" But as
you know I have been deceived.*

This problem is not evident just in the context of counseling, the battle is going on continuously. I will tell people who make appointments that they will have thoughts like: "Don't go, he can't help you," or first person singular thoughts such as : "I don't want to go," and "I have tried this before." Many never ask for help because of the mental battle. One person wrote this:

*Every time I try to talk to you or even think about
talking to you, I completely shut down. Voices inside
literally yell at me "No." The same thing happens
when I try to talk to my pastor, or when my father tries
to discuss God with me. I think I'm going insane so I
don't say anything to anyone. My old feelings of "life
isn't worth the trouble" come back and I've even considered killing myself to end this terrible battle going on
inside.*

I need help!

*Right now, even as I'm writing, there is this awful
struggle going on inside me. I want to run away from
it. It is physically and mentally exhausting. I'm scared,
I'm lonely, I'm confused, I'm insecure and very desperate. I know deep down that God can overcome this but
I can't get past this block. I can't even pray. When I try,
things get in my way. When I'm feeling good and begin
putting into action what I know God wants me to do,
I'm stopped dead in my tracks by those voices and a
force that is so strong I can't continue.*

> *I'm so close to giving in to those voices that I feel myself having less and less of a fight. I just want some peace.*

Those thoughts (voices) have no power over the person, but the mental torment is maddening. Somehow they have a right to be there, and the counselor has to find out what it is. You start by helping the person realize that those thoughts are not theirs. Then you ask for their cooperation to reveal what those thoughts are. This helps the person to understand what the nature of the battle is. Watch their eyes very closely. If they become clouded or start darting around, get the counselee's attention and ask, "What are you hearing right now?" The variety of thoughts range from, "They say you don't care," or "This isn't going to work," or "God doesn't love you," or "They're laughing at you." The last can be very intimidating until you expose it as a deception.

The power is gone as soon as the deception is exposed as a lie. The thoughts have no more power over the person than if they were coming from a loudspeaker hanging on the wall. The counselee will typically calm down so that you can proceed. They will try again, and again, each time the person shares what he or she is hearing, and each time the lie is refuted by the truth of God's Word. The one definitive passage in Scripture that describes the role of the pastor is 2 Tim. 2:24-26, (*NASB*).

> And the Lord's bondservant must not be quarrelsome, but be kind to all, able to teach, patient when wronged, with gentleness correcting those who are in opposition, if perhaps God may grant them repentance leading to the knowledge of the truth, and they may come to their senses and escape from the snare

of the devil, having been held captive by him to do his will.

Those demonically inflicted perceive themselves caught between two equal and opposite powers. In their experience Satan is more real and appears to be more powerful. One young lady wrote in her diary:

> *Dear God,*
> *Where are you? How can you watch and not help? I hurt so bad and you don't even care. If you cared, you'd make it stop or you'd let me die. I love you, but you seem so far away. I can't hear you, or feel you, or see you, but I'm supposed to believe you're here. Lord, I feel them, see them, and hear them. They're here. People tell me you're here, but I can't tell. I'm sorry if I'm that bad God, but I'm trying. Please love me and help me! I want to be a part of you. Why won't you help me to do that? I know you're real God, but they are more real to me right now. You know how real they are Lord, but no one will believe me. Please make someone believe me Lord. I'm alone in this and it hurts so bad. Why Lord? Why? I have no answers but I have so many questions. Why won't you give me some answers? Why won't you make it stop? Please Lord! Please! If you love me you'll let me die.*

Steps to Freedom in Christ

If the person that you are dealing with is not a Christian, then the whole procedure is to lead them to Christ. Again, if Satan has blinded the minds of the unbelieving, then the battle is for the mind. One young girl that was brought to me recounted a horrible background of ritual and sexual abuse. After sharing the gospel with her, I asked if she would like to make a decision for Christ. She said she would but couldn't right then. Realizing her background, I asked her if she was hearing a voice or having thoughts like "If you do I will kill you" or "It won't do any good." She nodded that she was. After I exposed it as a lie and showed her the truth from Scripture, she made her decision.

The first step is to pray that Satan and all his demons be bound to silence and commanded not to interfere with the process. The counselee is asked to reveal what, if any, interference they are receiving throughout the session. At this time it is inappropriate to ask the demons to leave. The one you want to deal with is the counselee. The demonic influence is rendered ineffective by exposing the lie or taking authority over them. When counselees make the right decisions of faith, they will command the demons to leave. Seldom will there be any manifestations that usually accompany deliverance sessions.

What follows is a "confidential inventory" that the counselee will fill out. This will help in the diagnosis, and uncover many of the reasons why they are having spiritual problems. The "steps to freedom in Christ" are self-explanatory. They deal with the seven major grounds that Satan uses to invade the Christian. They are cult and occultic involvement, deception, unforgiveness, rebellion, pride, sin and the sins of ancestors, including any curses.

Confidential Personal Inventory

I. Personal Information

Name _____ Telephone _____
Address _____

Church affiliation:
Present _____
Past _____
School:
Highest Grade Completed _____ Degrees earned _____
Marital Status: _____
Previous History of Marriage/Divorce _____
Vocation:
Present _____
Past _____

II. Family History

A. Religious

1. Have any of your parents, grandparents, or great grandparents, to your knowledge, ever been involved in any occultic, cultic, or non-Christian religious practices? Please refer to the enclosed "Non-Christian Spiritual Experience Inventory" and indicate what the involvement was.
2. Briefly explain your parents' Christian experience (that is, were they Christians and did they profess and live their Christianity?).

B. Marital Status

1. Are your parents presently married or divorced? Explain.

2. Was there a sense of security and harmony in your home during the first 12 years of your life?

3. Was the father clearly the head of the home or was there a role reversal where the mother ruled the home? Explain.

4. How did your father treat your mother?

5. Was there ever an adulterous affair to your knowledge with your parents or grandparents? Any incestuous relationship?

C. Health

1. Are there any addictive problems in your family history (alcohol, drugs, etc.)?

2. Is there any history of mental illness?

3. Is there any history of the following physical ailments in your family? (please circle)
   TB
   Heart disease
   Diabetes
   Cancer
   Ulcers
   Glandular problems
   Other

4. How would you describe your family's concern for:
   a. Diet

b. Exercise

c. Rest

D. Moral Climate

During the first 18 years of your life, how would you rate the moral atmosphere in which you were raised:

	Overly Permissive	Permissive	Average	Strict	Overly Strict
Clothing	5	4	3	2	1
Sex	5	4	3	2	1
Dating	5	4	3	2	1
Movies	5	4	3	2	1
Music	5	4	3	2	1
Literature	5	4	3	2	1
Free will	5	4	3	2	1
Drinking	5	4	3	2	1
Smoking	5	4	3	2	1
Church attendance	5	4	3	2	1

III. History of Personal Health

A. Physical

1. Describe your eating habits (that is, are you a junk food or health food addict, do you eat regularly or sporadic, is your diet balanced, etc.?).

2. Do you have any addictions or cravings that you find it difficult to control (sweets, drugs, alcohol, food in general, etc.)?

3. Are you presently under any kind of medication for either physical or psychological reasons?

4. Do you have any problems sleeping? Are you having any recurring nightmares or disturbances?

5. Does your present schedule allow for regular periods of rest and relaxation?

6. Are you adopted?

7. Have you ever physically been beaten or sexually molested? Explain.

B. Mental

1. Which of the following have you or are you presently struggling with? (please circle)

Daydreaming
Lustful thoughts
Inferiority
Inadequacy
Worry
Doubts
Fantasy
Obsessive thoughts
Insecurity
Blasphemous thoughts   (cont.)

Compulsive thoughts
Dizziness
Headaches

2. Do you spend much time wishing you were somebody else or fantasizing that you were somebody else or possibly imagining yourself living at a different time, place, or under different circumstances? Explain.

3. How many hours of TV do you watch per week? List your five favorite programs:

4. How many hours do you spend a week reading?

   What do you read primarily (newspaper, magazines, books, etc.)?

5. Would you consider yourself to be an optimist or pessimist (i.e., do you have a tendency to see the good in people and life or the bad)?

6. Have you ever thought that maybe you were "cracking up" and do you presently fear that possibility? Explain.

7. Do you have regular devotions in the Bible? When and to what extent?

8. Do you find prayer difficult mentally? Explain.

9. When attending church or other Christian ministries, are you plagued with foul thoughts, jealousies, other mental harassments? Explain.

10. Do you listen to music a lot, and what type do you enjoy the most?

C. Emotional

1. Which of the following emotions have you or are you presently having difficulty controlling? (please circle)

Frustration   Fear of death
Anger   Fear of losing your mind
Anxiety   Fear of committing suicide
Loneliness   Fear of hurting loved ones
Feeling worthless   Fear of terminal illness
Depression   Fear of going to hell
Hatred   Fear of _____
Bitterness

2. Which of the above listed emotions do you feel are sinful? Why?

3. Concerning your emotions, whether positive or negative, which of the following best describes you? (please check)

___ Readily express them
___ Express some of my emotions but not all
___ Readily acknowledge their presence but
reserved in expressing them
___ Tendency to suppress my emotions
___ Find it safest not to express how I feel
___ Tendency to disregard how I feel since I
cannot trust my feelings
___ Consciously or subconsciously deny them
since it is too painful to deal with them

4. Is there someone in your life whom you know that
you could be emotionally honest with right now
(i.e., you could tell this person exactly how you feel
about yourself, your life, and other people)?

5. How important is it that we are emotionally honest
before God, and do you feel that you are? Explain.

IV. Spiritual History

A. If you were to die tonight, do you know where you
would spend eternity?

B. Suppose you did die tonight and appeared before
God in heaven, and He were to ask you, "By what
right should I allow you into My presence?" how
would you answer Him?

C. First John 5:11,12, (*NASB*) says, "God has given
us eternal life, and this life is in His Son. He who
has the Son has the life; he who does not have the
Son of God does not have the life."

1. Do you have the Son of God in you (2 Cor. 13:5)?

2. When did you receive Him (John 1:12)?

3. How do you know that you have received Him?

D. Are you plagued with doubts concerning your salvation?

E. Are you presently enjoying fellowship with other believers and, if so, where and when?

F. Are you under authority of a local church where the Bible is preached, and do you regularly support it with your time, talent, and treasure? If no, why not?

G. Please fill out the Non-Christian Spiritual Experience Inventory below circling those items that apply.

OCCULT	CULT	OTHER RELIGIONS
Astral-projection	Christian Science	Zen Buddhism
Ouija board	Unity	Hare Krishna
Table lifting	Scientology	Buhaism
Speaking in trance	The Local Church	Rosicrucian
Automatic writing	The Way	Science of the
Visionary dreams	International	Mind
Intell. Telepathy	Unification	Science of
Ghosts	Church	Creative Intell.
Materialization	Church of Living	Hinduism
Clairvoyance	Word	Transcendental
Clairsentience	Mormonism	Meditation

Fortune-Telling
(Tarot cards,
  palm reading
  etc.)
Astrology
Rod and
  Pendulum
  (dowsing)
Amateur
  Hypnosis
Healing magnetism
Magic charming
Mental suggestions
Black and White magic
Blood pacts
Fetishism
Incubi and succubae
  (sexual spirits)

Jehovah Witness
Children of God
Swedenborgianism
Herbert W.
  W. Armstrong
  (Radio Church of
  God)
Unitarianism
Masons
New Age
Other _____

Yoga
Echkankar
Roy Masters
Silva Mind
  Control
EST
Father Divine
Theosophical
  Society
Islam
Black Muslim
Other _____

1. Have you ever been hypnotized, attended a "New Age" seminar, or seance?

2. Have you ever taken a class or read books on parapsychology? Explain.

3. Have you ever heard voices in your mind or had repeating and nagging thoughts that were foreign to what you believe or felt, as though a dialogue was going on in your head? Explain.

4. What other experiences have you had that would be considered out of the ordinary?

Finding Freedom in Christ

The above procedure is to be done with a trusted pastor
and/or Christian friends. The persons desiring freedom
must themselves pray the prayers and the affirmations of
faith. It is very important that the pastor or friends take
authority over all demonic forces, binding them to silence
and preventing them from inflicting any physical harm.
One person should be in charge of the counseling session,
and all others should support in prayer and, when appropriate, offer any insight that would contribute. Should any
spirit try to manifest itself, the person in charge should
take authority over the enemy and demand that the counselee be released.

The first step is to have the counselee renounce all
involvement with the occult, cults and other religions mentioned in the Non-Christian Spiritual Experience Inventory. After they have renounced those previous experiences and asked God to forgive them, then have them say,
"I renounce you, Satan, and all your works and all your
ways."

The following procedure is to remove all ground that
Satan can use as a foothold against them.

I. Deception vs. truth (John 1:4-2:2)

Prayer (to be read by the counselee):
Dear Heavenly Father, I know that You desire truth
in the inner man (Ps. 51:6) and that facing this truth
is the way of liberation (John 8:32). I acknowledge
that I have been deceived by the father of lies (John
8:44) and that I have deceived myself (1 John 1:8). I
pray in the name of the Lord Jesus Christ that You,
Heavenly Father, would rebuke all deceiving spirits

by virtue of the shed blood of the Lord Jesus Christ and His resurrection, and that I by faith, having received You into my life and now seated with Christ in the heavenlies (Eph. 2:6), I command all deceiving spirits to depart from me during this time of prayer to be sent wherever the Lord Jesus Christ sends them. I now ask the Holy Spirit to guide me into all truth (John 16:13), and ask that You would "Search me, O God, and know my heart; try me and know my anxious thoughts; and see if there be any hurtful way in me, and lead me in the everlasting way" (Ps. 139:23,24, *NASB*). In Jesus' name I pray. Amen.

A. Personal Affirmation

Affirmation (to be read by the counselee):
Because of the unconditional love and acceptance of the Lord Jesus Christ, I am free to accept truth and face reality. Since God is light and in Him there is no darkness at all (1 John 1:5), I choose to walk in the light in order to have fellowship with Him and other people. I understand that "walking in the light" is not emotional, mental or volitional perfection on my part but a willingness to be completely honest and in agreement with God concerning my present condition.

Personal Perspectives (to be guided by the counselor):

1. Beliefs and feelings toward God the Father, God the Son and God the Holy Spirit.
2. Beliefs and feelings toward self.

3. Memories or experiences so painful that it is difficult to talk about them. Is there an attempt to live as though they never happened?
4. Is there a lot of fantasizing, wishing they were somebody else, imagining doing things they probably will never do or be capable of doing?
5. Is there any guile, hypocrisy?
6. Is there a lot of projection, blaming others for their problems; or at the other extreme, a tendency to take the blame for everything?

B. Doctrinal Affirmations

(To be read by the counselee)
I choose to present my body as an instrument of righteousness, a living and holy sacrifice, and to renew my mind by the living Word of God in order that I may prove that the will of God is good, acceptable and perfect (Rom. 6:13; 12:1,2). I therefore make the following affirmations:

1. I recognize by faith that the triune God is worthy of all honor, praise and worship as the Creator, Sustainer and the Beginning and End of all things. I confess that God, as my Creator, made me for Himself. In this day I therefore choose to live for Him (Rev. 5:9-10; Isa. 43:1,7,21; Rev. 4:11).
2. I recognize by faith that God has proven His love to me in sending His Son to die in my place, in whom every provision has already been made for my past, present and future needs through His representative work, and that I am alive in Christ and seated with Him in the heavenlies, and

anointed with the Holy Spirit (Rom. 5:6-11; 8:28,29; Phil. 1:6; 4:6,7,13,19; Eph. 1:3; 2:5,6; Acts 2:1-4,33).

3. I recognize by faith that God has accepted me, since I have received Jesus Christ as my Lord and Savior (John 1:12; Eph. 1:6); that He has forgiven me (Eph. 1:7); and adopted me into His family. God has given me eternal life (John 3:36; 1 John 5:9-13); applied the perfect righteousness of Christ to me so that I am now justified (Rom. 5:1; 8:3,4; 10:4); made me complete in Christ (Col. 2:10); and offers Himself to me as my daily sufficiency through prayer and the decisions of faith (1 Cor. 1:30; Col. 1:27; Gal. 2:20; John 14:13,14; Matt. 21:22; Rom. 6:1-19; Heb. 4:1-3,11).

4. I recognize by faith that the Holy Spirit has baptized me into the Body of Christ (1 Cor. 12:13); sealed me (Eph. 1:13,14) and anointed me for life and service (Acts 1:8; John 7:37-39). He seeks to lead me into a deeper walk with Jesus Christ (John 14:16-18; 15:26,27; 16:13-15; Rom. 8:11-16), and to fill my life with Himself (Eph. 5:18).

5. I recognize by faith that only God can deal with sin and only God can produce holiness of life. I believe that in salvation my part was only to receive Him and that He dealt with my sin and saved me. In order to live a holy life, I surrender to His will and receive Him as my sanctification; trusting Him to do whatever may be necessary in my life so that I may be enabled to live in purity, freedom, rest and power for His glory (John 1:12; 1 Cor. 1:30; 2 Cor. 9:8; Gal 2:20; Heb. 4:9; 1 John 5:4; Jude 24).

Having confessed that God is worthy of all praise,

that the Bible is the only authoritative standard, that only God can deal with sin and produce holiness of life, I recognize my total dependence upon Him and I submit to Him. I accept the truth that praying in faith is necessary for the realization of the will and grace of God in my daily life (1 John 5:14,15; Jas. 2:6; 4:2,3; 5:16-18; Phil.4:6,7; Heb. 4:1-13; 11:6,24-28).

C. Decisions

Recognizing that faith is a total response to God by which the daily provisions the Lord has furnished in Himself are appropriated, I therefore make the following decisions by faith:

1. For this day I make the decision of faith to surrender to the authority of God as He has revealed Himself in the Bible and to obey Him. I reject the self-life, and choose to walk in the light (Heb. 3:6,13,15; 4:7).

2. For this day I make the decision of faith to surrender to the authority of God as revealed in the Scripture and to believe in Him. I accept only His Word as final authority. I believe that as I have confessed my sin He has forgiven and cleansed me (1 John 1:9). I accept at full value His Word of promise to be my sufficiency and rest, and will conduct myself accordingly (Exod. 33:1; 1 Cor. 1:30; 2 Cor. 9:8; Phil. 4:19).

3. For this day I make the decision of faith to recognize that God has made every provision so that I may fulfill His will and calling. Therefore, I will not make any excuse for my sin and failure.

4. I make the decision of faith to receive from God

that provision which He has made for me. I renounce all self-effort to live the Christian life and to perform God's service in my own strength. I renounce all sinful praying which asks God to change circumstances and people so that I may be more spiritual. I renounce all drawing back from the work of the Holy Spirit. I renounce all non-biblical motives, goals, and activities which serve my sinful pride.

a. I now ask Jesus Christ to be my sanctification, particularly as my cleansing from the old nature, and ask the Holy Spirit to apply to me the work of Christ accomplished for me in the Crucifixion. In cooperation with and dependence upon Him, I obey the command to "put off the old man" (Rom. 6:1-14; 1 Cor. 1:30; Gal. 4:16; Eph. 4:22).

b. I ask Jesus Christ to be my sanctification, particularly as my enablement moment-by-moment to live above sin, and ask the Holy Spirit to apply to me the work of the Resurrection so that I may walk in newness of life. I confess that only God can deal with my sin and only God can produce holiness and the fruit of the Spirit in my life. In cooperation and dependence upon Him, I obey the command to "put on the new man" (Rom. 6:1-4; Eph. 4:24).

c. I ask Jesus Christ to be my deliverance from Satan and I take my position with Him in the heavenlies, asking the Holy Spirit to apply to me the work of the Ascension. In His name I submit myself to God and stand against all of Satan's influence and deception. In cooperation with and dependence upon God, I obey the

154 Wrestling with Dark Angels

command to "resist the devil" (Eph. 1:20-23;
2:5; 4:27; 6:10-18; Col. 1:13; Heb. 2:14,15;
Jas. 4:7; 1 Pet. 3:22; 5:8,9).

d. I ask the Holy Spirit to empower me for every
aspect of life and service for today. I open my
life to Him to "be filled with the Holy Spirit"
(Eph. 5:18; John 7:37-39; 14:16,17; 15:26,
27; 16:7-15; Acts 1:8).

Having made this confession and these decisions of faith, I now receive God's promised
rest for this day (Heb. 4:1-13). Therefore, I
rest in Christ, knowing that in the moment of
temptation, trial or need, the Lord Himself will
be there as my strength and sufficiency (1 Cor.
10:13).

II. Bitterness vs. Forgiveness (Eph. 4:31,32)

Prayer (to be read by the counselee):
Dear Heavenly Father, I thank You for the riches of
Your kindness, forbearance and patience, knowing
that Your kindness has led me to repentance (Rom.
2:4). I confess that I have not extended that same
patience and kindness toward others who have
offended me, but instead I have harbored bitterness
and resentment. I pray that during this time of self-
examination that You would bring to mind only those
people that I have not forgiven from my heart in
order that I may do so (Matt. 18:35). I also pray that
if I have offended others that You would bring to my
mind only those people who I have need to seek forgiveness and to what extent I need to seek it (Matt.
5:23,24). I ask for Your guidance that I should not fall

short of Your will, and that in no way would I go
beyond it. I ask this in the precious name of Jesus.
Amen.

1. List in the following space every person that you
   in any way have feelings of resentment toward
   (may include God and yourself).

Having listed all individuals that you sense any bitterness or resentment toward, now as an act of
your will go through the list and one by one pray,
"I forgive (name) for (whatever he or she has
done or not done to offend you)." In so declaring
them forgiven, you are agreeing to live with the
consequence of their sins, and not to use it
against them. You are setting yourself free from
that person and the past.

2. List in the following space every person that God
   has brought to your mind from whom you need to
   seek forgiveness.

Make a plan to go to each individual and ask forgiveness. Be as specific as you can concerning
the nature of the offense. Do not mention their
offense or responsibility in the matter.

III. Rebellion vs. Submission (Rom. 13:1-5)

Prayer (to be read by the counselee):
Dear Heavenly Father, You have said that rebellion is as the sin of witchcraft and insubordination is as iniquity and idolatry (1 Sam. 15:23), and I know that in action and in attitude I have sinned against You with a rebellious heart. I ask for Your forgiveness for my rebellion and pray that by the shed blood of the Lord Jesus Christ that all ground gained by evil spirits because of my rebelliousness would be cancelled. I pray that You would shed light on all my ways that I may know the full extent of my rebelliousness so that I will choose to adopt a submissive spirit and a servant's heart. I pray that You would guide my examination in this area, that it would not be of self but of You. In Jesus' name I pray. Amen.

Examination:
Determine any ungratefulness, resentment or critical spirit either in active or passive rebellion on your part in the following lines of authority:

1. Civil government   1 Tim. 2:1-3; 1 Pet.
                       2:13-16
2. Parents   Eph. 6:1-3
3. Husband   1 Pet. 3:1-3
4. Employer   1 Pet. 2:18-21
5. Church leaders   Heb. 13:17

Now specifically ask God to forgive you where you have not been submissive, and declare your trust in God to work through His established lines of authority.

IV. Pride vs. Humility (Jas. 4:6-10)

Prayer (to be read by the counselee):
Dear Heavenly Father, You have said that pride goes before destruction and an arrogant spirit before stumbling (Prov. 16:18). I confess that I have not denied myself, picked up my cross, and followed You (Matt. 16:24). In so doing I have given the enemy ground in my life. I have believed that I could be successful and live victoriously by my own strength and resources. I now confess that I have sinned against You by placing my will before You and by centering my life around self instead of You. I now renounce the self-life and by so doing cancel all the ground that the enemies of the Lord Jesus Christ have gained in my members. I ask You to fill me with Your Holy Spirit and teach me to walk in faith by the Holy Spirit in order that I may glorify You in my body (1 Cor. 6:19,20). I crucify the flesh with its passions and desires (Gal. 5:24) and no longer place any confidence in the flesh (Phil. 3:3). I pray that You will guide me so I will do nothing from selfishness and empty conceit, but with humility of mind regard others as more important than myself (Phil. 2:3). I ask this in the name of Christ Jesus my Lord. Amen.

V. Bondage vs. Freedom

Prayer (to be read by the counselee):
Dear Heavenly Father, You have told us to put on the Lord Jesus Christ, and to make no provision for the flesh in regard to lusts (Rom. 13:14). I acknowledge that I have given in to fleshly lusts which wage war

against my soul (1 Pet. 2:11). I thank You that in Christ my sins are forgiven, but I have transgressed Your holy law and given the enemy an opportunity to wage war in my members (Eph. 4:27; Jas. 4:1; 1 Pet. 5:8). I come before Your presence to acknowledge these sins and to seek Your cleansing (1 John 1:9) that I may be freed from the bondage of sin (Gal. 5:1). I now ask You to reveal to my mind the ways that I have sinned and grieved the Holy Spirit.

List all the sins of the flesh:

I now confess these sins, and ask for Your forgiveness and cleansing. I cancel all ground that evil spirits have gained through deception or by my willful involvement in sin. I now put on the whole armor of God and ask that You, Heavenly Father, will fill me with Your Holy Spirit that I may be able to stand against the schemes of the devil (Eph. 6:10-18). I ask this all in the name of my Lord and Savior, Jesus Christ. Amen.

VI. Acquiescence vs. Renunciation

Prayer (to be read by the counselee):
As a child of God purchased by the blood of the Lord Jesus Christ, I here and now reject and disown all the sins of my ancestors. As one who has been delivered from the power of darkness and translated into the kingdom of God's dear Son, I cancel all demonic

working that has been passed on to me from my ancestors. As one who has been crucified with Jesus Christ and raised to walk in newness of life, I cancel every curse or spell that has been put on me or on any objects of my possession or dwelling. I announce to Satan and all his forces that Christ became a curse for me when He hung on the Cross. As one who has been crucified and raised with Christ and now sits with Him in the heavenly places, I reject any and every way in which Satan may claim ownership of me. I declare myself to be internally and completely signed over and committed to the Lord Jesus Christ. I now command every familiar spirit and every enemy of the Lord Jesus Christ that is in or around me to go to the pit and to remain there until the Day of Judgment. I now ask You, Heavenly Father, to fill me with Your Holy Spirit and I submit my body as an instrument of righteousness, a living sacrifice that I may glorify You in my body. All this I do in the name and authority of the Lord Jesus Christ. Amen.

Note
1. Some of the material in Section C has been adapted from Mark I. Bubeck, *The Adversary* (Chicago: Moody Press, 1975).

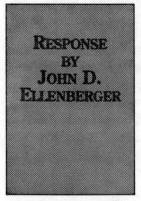

RESPONSE
BY
JOHN D.
ELLENBERGER

Finding Freedom in Christ

This is the classic case of the minnow evaluating the whale. I have had some exposure to deliverance ministry in Irian Jaya, Indonesia, and some more recently in North America among people just as needy. But as I read Neil Anderson's paper, I began to realize that God has given him a much-anointed and wide-ranging ministry in this area, and I have benefited from his insights.

All of us are concerned with the need to keep our understanding of power evangelism and deliverance under the authority and measure of God's Word. And, although we would express it in different ways and with different emphases, we are all concerned with achieving a balance. What one calls balanced will be excessive and unacceptable to another, and vice versa. But even our efforts to keep balanced need to be tested by Scripture, and our hermeneutical presuppositions need to be made explicit. I see this paper as a good exercise in examining some of those limits.

I will group my comments under three headings: Overall Emphases, Areas of Concern and Some Concluding Questions.

Overall Emphases

First, we owe a debt of gratitude to Neil for preparing for us a thought-provoking model that comes out of his wealth of experience in the areas of freedom and pastoral care. This is not just a paper about his ministry; this is a handbook of that ministry, complete with rational, step-by-step approach, check lists and a final section of prayers and affirmations for the counselee, covering each of the seven major grounds that Satan uses to invade the Christian.

I respond to certain broad-stroke emphases in this model with great approval, things that need to be a part of any such ministry:

1. *The importance of teaching the truth of the Word of God as an integral part of the ministry.* This is one place where the counseling session begins to sound like a seminary classroom, but the use of the Word throughout is an excellent feature.

2. *The need to tie in any deliverance ministry to an adequate, Christ-centered counseling program.* Often a deliverance session will turn up some demonizing influence from which the counselee is gloriously freed by the power of Christ. All are now rejoicing and saying "Praise the Lord" because the house has been swept clean. But too often the unresolved hurts, the emotional trauma and, in the case of sin, the compromised will, have not been adequately dealt with. Unless sensitive counseling brings inner healing and closure to memories and attitudes, many of them on a subconscious level, the swept house will be reinvaded by its former evil tenant, and perhaps by many more (Luke 11:24-26).

The only way to ultimate freedom is for the counselee to be led into inner healing, confession of sin, a rejection of what has bound him or her before and a stated affirmation of all that will be embraced in its place. What Neil has done here is to give us an insider's look at this counseling process.

3. *The importance of the counselee in the whole deliverance process.* It is easy to focus on the clash of powers, or our own role, or even the concern for the glory of God in the situation, and forget what a key party in this scene the counselee is. This is a child of God, whom He wants to see set free. Now, we probably will not all agree on all aspects of the role of the counselee in the healing process. Nonetheless, we can all applaud the reminder that the counselee is a key party in deliverance. Without his or her actively seeking to be free, without active participation in asking forgiveness, rejecting powers and affirming new allegiances, the whole process will not result in lasting freedom.

4. *The misconceptions that Neil labored under before he got into his present ministry.* These are biblical, theological and methodological hang-ups that other persons or groups may still have today, and they deserve our attention as well. Number 4 in this list introduces the paradigm for his paper, so we will be looking at it in more detail in the next section.

Areas of Concern

The image of God's people on the top of the pickup, cowering from the bluffing of a defeated foe, is for many an apt one. Even the youngest convert, standing his or her ground in the authority of Christ, can resist the devil and watch him flee (Jas. 4:7). I believe this is true because the authority of any convert—mature or newborn in Christ—is Christ's power and not his or her own.

It is here that Neil affirms that the reason the believer spends time on top of the pickup is because of the counselor's treating resisting the devil as a power encounter instead of a truth encounter. It may be difficult in the last hour of a symposium on power evangelism to hear that we are barking after the right cat but up the wrong tree, but it is valuable to follow the idea through his section on Pastoral Procedure. What I understand the *truth* encounter model to be is a battle for the *mind* of the counselee. In this the troubled believer is made aware of several theological verities:

1. Christ has conquered powers and authorities by His death and resurrection, and Satan is defeated,
2. Christ has raised every believer to share His position of power over all spiritual powers,
3. Therefore, the believer has Christ's power against Satan and demons as defeated foes.

Freedom comes from believing that truth and walking daily in an awareness of and faith in that truth.

In this model the counselor does not usually take authority over any Satanic power to effect deliverance, but acts as a facilitator in self-deliverance as the believer learns to apply the authority of Christ gained from knowing his or her position with Him in heaven. The person grows in understanding by affirmation, repentance, confession and renunciation. The problem of power is a delusion that collapses when the truth of our place in Christ unmasks the lie of Satan's bluffing power. The implication made is that deliverance done in the truth encounter model does not often have to be repeated (and implicitly, that the power encounter model deliverances are more often repeated). I trust I have been fair in describing the model rather than caricaturizing it.

I would like to make several points as we consider the model:

1. *The difference between the two models is a methodological one rather than a theological or truth one.* The theological framework outlined above is the basis of any deliverance, whatever the methodology used. The confrontations of Satan's defeated power by the victorious power of Christ is still in the equation, no matter by what name it is called or how the deliverance is actualized. I am not convinced by the presentation, and admittedly it was only mentioned in passing, that this methodology can effect a higher retention rate, or maybe we should say, expulsion rate! Whether counselees remain free seems to be more related to the inner healing ministry that accompanies it than by the deliverance procedure. However, it would be important to hear if Neil has a comparison of results.

2. *The counselor as catalyst instead of deliverer model seems to be considerably different from what appears to be a confrontational, power-encounter-oriented, counselor-dominated model used by Jesus* (for example in Mark 1:26,34; 5:8; 9:25; 16:9); *by the disciples* (for example in Mark 6:13; 9:18; Luke 10:17); *and by Paul* (Acts 16:18).

This counselor as catalyst model seems to fit quite well with the lower levels of intensity of demonized people. On Chuck Kraft's "Strength of Attachment Scale" of 1 to 10, he indicates that these weak to medium attached spirits (1-4) cause only mild manifestations, rarely talk through the person, and usually communicate to the person within his or her own head.[1] This level makes it more possible for the counselor to work through the counselee, who can be encouraged to take authority over the demonizing power in Jesus' name.

The paper has mixed signals as to what happens in a

truth encounter session with spirits manifesting a stronger attachment. Counselors often see attachments of 5-8 on the scale, which are often characterized by vocal manifestations, a great deal more writhing and possible violence. This setting is more difficult for the counselor serving as catalyst. The paper indicates that if a spirit with these characteristics manifests in the counseling session, the counselor is to "take authority over the enemy and demand that the counselee be released." Neil indicates that he has not had to do this for the last several years. This could mean that the counselor is breaking down the strength of the attachment by counseling and inner healing before attempting deliverance. This is also highly recommended in Chuck Kraft's work.

3. *The truth encounter methodology uses a highly cognitive approach.* It talks about the *battle for the mind,* about the progressive logic of truth in the Scripture and of working through the reasoning that proves to the counselee that he or she possesses the power of Christ that is now appropriated in the prayers and affirmations into the life of the believer. At the same time the power aspects are correspondingly minimized in an area most of us would agree is the *power zone* lying between our cosmic supernatural and our earthly natural, now lovingly known as our *excluded middle.* I am trying to figure out why it is so important to set this power-level encounter into such a highly rational package. Could it be the pressure of our own world view?

I think we need to ask if the locus of the battle is really in the mind. Is not knowing Jesus as the truth (John 14:6) experiencing Him in mind, emotions and will? Is not knowing the truth and being set free by it (John 8:32) talking about the impact of the whole of who Christ is upon the whole of our being, which results in a new allegiance to

Christ? That larger, holistic understanding is expressed in many of the prayers and affirmations of Neil Anderson's paper. Perhaps using Chuck Kraft's term *allegiance encounter* here would help us understand that the locus of the battle is in the total being of the person—will, mind, emotions and world view.

While the truth encounter model seems to have worked well enough for Neil in cognitively-oriented North America, can we assume this approach would have equivalent impact in the power-conscious areas of the rest of the world?

Deliverance and freedom can be seen on more than an individual level. A whole people group can be delivered from the bondage of Satan, and quite often this has a power encounter aspect (Matt. 12:29). In Irian Jaya, Indonesia, where my wife and I worked, the gospel had been preached for many months to the Dani tribespeople of the Ilaga Valley, with interest but no response. Then their neighbors, the Damal tribespeople, began to turn to Christ. The unbelieving Danis saw the son-in-law of their powerful headman burn his sacred charms and fetishes. Then the son-in-law strode into the sacred devil grove and chopped it down without so much as a single bolt of lightning to zap him! It was not long before the Dani headman along with his whole kin group turned to Christ. That was truth mediated through an encounter which the Danis perceived as a test of power.

That leads us to the final point. Often it is a demonstration of God's power that leads us to a new understanding of the truth, and a new step of allegiance to Christ. Witness the growing levels of commitment to Christ in the life of the blind man in John 9:1-38. Healed by a person whom, somehow, he did not know, he grew from seeing Jesus as some kind of prophet to confessing Him as Lord. Another example is John the Baptizer. When he asked a question of truth about the Messiah, he was given an answer about power ministry. This led to a new level of allegiance on John's part: trust even when you don't understand (Matt. 11:1-6).

Some Concluding Questions

Timothy Warner has reminded us that in power encounter we need to differentiate two levels: the one in which Satan is on the initiative attacking the believer, and the other in which God's servants take the initiative against Satan and his forces.[2] Neil Anderson's paper is about the defensive level and how we take victory in that situation. But at this symposium, and in our communities and our worldwide outreach, we need to be asking the right questions about that other level. The church must not be content with reacting defensively. While we deal with those whose lives have been invaded by Satan's power, we need to talk about the appropriateness of going on the offensive, about what would be involved in an aggressive strategy. How does one bind the strong man to liberate people held captive by him (Matt. 12:29)? Is it legitimate to strategize in relation to territorially based powers, like taking a "power walk" around your block or around your city? Are there "principalities" in charge of certain countries? How should we pray about principalities? Are there other measures in addition to prayer that can be used in going on the offensive? What are the dangers? I am not proposing answers. I am only saying that these are a logical extension of our inquiry into the deliverance ministry.

I close with a reminder to us given by Art Glasser 11 years ago: "No form of Christian teaching has any future before it except such as can keep steadily in view the reality of evil in the world, and go to meet the evil with a battle song of triumph."[3]

Notes
1. Charles Kraft, "Deep Level Healing." Notes prepared for Dealing Decisively with Spiritual Powers Seminar, Pasadena, 1988, p. 14.
2. Timothy Warner, "Power Encounter with the Demonic," ed. Robert Coleman, *Evangelism on the Cutting Edge* (Old Tappan: Fleming H. Revell, 1986), 91.
3. Arthur Glasser, "Culture, the Powers and the Spirit," *Missiology*, 5, (2): p. 137.

The Holy Spirit and Power: A Wesleyan Understanding

DONALD
HOHENSEE

DONALD HOHENSEE, professor of missions and church growth at Western Evangelical Seminary in Portland, Oregon, served as a missionary in Burundi, Africa, for 14 years. He is the author of *Church Growth in Burundi* as well as several journal articles on missiology.

JESUS was ready to return to His Father in heaven. He wanted a few last words with His followers before His departure, one last command. "Do not leave Jerusalem, but wait for the gift my Father promised, which you have heard me speak about. For John baptized with water, but in a few days you will be baptized with the Holy Spirit" (Acts 1:4, 5, *NIV*).

The disciples did not understand. They were still thinking about the earthly kingdom of Israel and its restoration with Jesus being the new King. Thus, they asked, "Lord, are you at this time going to restore the kingdom to Israel?" (v. 6). Jesus tried to bring them back with an assertion and a promise. "It is not for you to know the times or dates the Father has set by his own authority. But you will receive power when the Holy Spirit comes on you; and you will be my witnesses in Jerusalem, and in all Judea and Samaria, and to the ends of the earth" (vv. 7,8, *NIV*).

What kind of power, or what is the nature of this power, that Jesus gave to His disciples? The New Testament has two Greek words that are frequently translated power. *Dunamis*—power, or *dunamai*—to be able or possible, is one set. The other set is *exousia*—authority, power, right, strength, jurisdiction, or *exousiazo*—to exercise authority upon, to bring under the power of. *Dunamis* carries with it the idea of enabling, the power to do something. *Exousia* has the idea of the right of a sovereign to reign, to exercise authority.

In the New Testament these two terms are interchangeable when referring to Jesus or God. The Lord's prayer in Matt. 6:13 concludes with "for thine is the kingdom, and the power [dunamis] and the glory, forever. Amen" (*KJV*). When Jesus talked with the paralytic in Matt. 9:1-8 some of the religious leaders thought He was blaspheming when He forgave the man's sins. Jesus then healed the man so they would know that the Son of man has power or authority (exousia) to forgive sins.

Near the end of His life when Jesus stood before the Sanhedrin He said, "In the future you will see the Son of Man sitting at the right hand [of power—dunamis] of the Mighty One" (Matt. 26:64, *NIV*). In His final instructions to His disciples Jesus said, "All authority (*exousia*) [power] in heaven and on earth has been given to me" (Matt. 28:18, *NIV*).

Mark and Luke use both of these terms in writing about Jesus. John uses only exousia when speaking of Jesus' power and authority.

When applied to people there appears to be a distinction between dunamis and exousia. In all cases when Jesus sent His disciples out on a mission of casting out evil spirits (Matt. 10:1; Mark 6:7, Luke 9:1), He gave them authority (exousia) over evil spirits. Luke says Jesus gave them both power (dunamis) and authority (exousia) to drive out demons and to cure diseases. A ministry of exorcism is definitely based on the authority (exousia) of Jesus. A healing ministry could be based on either the authority (exousia) or power (dunamis) of Jesus.

Paul uses the term authority (exousia) when referring to the Christian life. The Christian has authority (exousia) over his will (1 Cor. 7:37), in this case whether to marry or to refrain from marriage. The Christian has authority (exousia) to eat and drink, to have a wife accompany him in ministry, to be supported by those he ministers to (1 Cor. 9:4-6). Paul also refers to his authority (exousia) which the Lord gave him for building up the Body of Christ. It can be said that the Christian has authority over evil spirits and has authority in some of the temporal affairs of this life.

Power (dunamis) is given to enable the believer to

serve God. Jesus promised this to the disciples both in Luke 24:49 and Acts 1:8. This was immediately manifested in Peter and others being able to preach on the day of Pentecost, and in the first healing he and John performed. The Sanhedrin in Acts 4:7 wanted to know by what power (dunamis) Peter and John were able to heal the cripple from birth. Peter had already testified that it was not by his own power (dunamis) that the man was healed (Acts 3:12). For Peter and John the power was in the name of Jesus. The name stood for the person of Jesus present among them through the indwelling Holy Spirit. The apostles continued to witness with great power (dunamai) (Acts 4:33). Stephen was a man full of the Holy Spirit and power (dunamis) (Acts 6:8).

Paul reminds the Ephesians of the power (dunamis) that is at work in them (Eph. 3:20). He tells the Thessalonians that the Word came to them with power (dunamis), with the Holy Spirit and with deep conviction (1 Thess. 1:5). Peter reminds his readers that they are kept by the power (dunamis) of God through faith (1 Pet. 1:5), and that God's divine power has provided for us everything we need (2 Pet. 1:3). Thus the disciples had power (divine enabling) to serve God. Christians have power enabling them to do the work God has assigned to them.

It is valid to ask what the relationship is between power and the Holy Spirit. The disciples obviously did not have this power before Pentecost, but they did have it after Pentecost. Wesleyans have consistently taught that the coming of the Holy Spirit in His fullness, or the baptism of the Holy Spirit, is both a cleansing and an empowering event.

Wesleyans, along with other Christians, have recognized the two-fold nature of sin. There are the acts of sin and there is the sin nature. We have maintained that the

person must be freed of both elements of sin before one
can enter a holy heaven. Other evangelical Protestants
maintain that the penalty for the acts of sin is removed at
conversion, but that the principle of sin or the sin nature
remains in the newly converted person.[1]

While many Protestants maintain that the sin nature is
removed at death or shortly before, Wesleyans hold that
the individual can be freed from the sin nature by faith.
They see the infilling or baptism of the Holy Spirit as an
event subsequent to the conversion experience, which
both cleanses the heart and empowers the life. Peter's
testimony at the Jerusalem Council (Acts 15:8,9) teaches
that Pentecost was both a purifying or cleansing event and
an empowering event.[2]

E. Stanley Jones affirms this when he writes,

> Something would persist from Jerusalem to the
> uttermost parts of the earth, namely, the power to
> witness effectively for Jesus. Not *power*—full stop;
> but power of a certain kind, the power to witness to
> Jesus Christ . . . .
>
> Two things, then, are permanent in the gift of the
> Holy Spirit: purity and power. Purity for myself and
> my own inner needs, and power to witness effec-
> tively to others . . . .
>
> So I'm grateful that I received the Holy Spirit
> without complications or *riders*. The Holy Spirit
> brought me purity, and he brought me power, for he
> brought me himself. I need and want no more.[3]

This frees the heart from the pollution of sin and
empowers the person to live the Christ life. Wesleyans
question the claim of those who profess this infilling with
power (psychic blessedness) that does not result in holy

living.⁴ It is also reasonable to question those who profess to be purified when there is no empowering. In recent years I believe the Wesleyan movement has put more emphasis on the purifying aspect and not sufficient on the empowering.

Type of Power the Holy Spirit Gives

What kind of power does the Holy Spirit-filled person have?

On the negative side:

1. *It is not an impersonal force or power.* It is not like the power of "May the Force be with you." It is not like the power present in animistic religion that is commonly called *Mana,* that adheres itself to the person who comes in contact with it, either on purpose or by accident, and who can then discharge it whenever it is most advantageous to the possessor. It is not like the impersonal power of eastern religions. It is not some spiritual static electric charge that can be released at the time that is most advantageous to the person possessing it.

2. *It is not some sort of spiritual energy that might be released in the person.* It is not like a charge in a battery that is disconnected from its source of power but continues to release energy until used up.

3. *It is not the type of power that is set off in an explosion.* Some have seen "dynamite" in dunamis, and therefore advocate the explosiveness of power. No doubt at times it may seem like dynamite, but the usual characteristics of the power of the Holy Spirit are different. Dynamite is exploded once and its power is used up. Spiritually, that kind of power would soon dissipate and leave the person with a spent feeling.

4. *It is not power that an individual can use for personal accomplishments* (Acts 8:18-23).

On the positive side:

1. *It is rather the power of a personal being, the power of a personal presence.* It is the presence of the person of the Holy Spirit. This power is inseparably linked to the Holy Spirit. The person who has the Holy Spirit in his fullness has this power. The person who does not have the Holy Spirit does not have this power.

2. *The power is found in the Holy Spirit and not some "package" of power the individual might receive.* The Spirit does not give us a battery that is severed from Himself.

3. *It is the power of an inner dynamic.* It is more like the dynamos in dams that constantly produce power because of the supply of water behind the dam. The person continually indwelt by the Holy Spirit has this power. Dayton says, "It is simply the grace of God at work through the Holy Spirit."[5]

4. *It is the power of the Spirit who gets mastery over the individual for His use as He desires.* God gives the Holy Spirit to those who obey Him (John 14:15,16). The more one submits to God and waits upon Him, the more of this power the individual possesses.

Samuel Logan Brengle, of Salvation Army fame, reports of the saintly John Fletcher, the early apologist of Methodism, that he expected a study of the doctrine of the Holy Spirit to be more like lightning in his soul. He found rather that it was more like a steady fire that was maintained by constant attention to the work of God.[6]

Manifestation of the Power

This power is given primarily for witnessing, for use in evangelism (Acts 1:8). In his *Explanatory Notes on the*

New Testament Wesley writes, "Ye shall be empowered to witness my Gospel, both by your preaching and suffering."[7] This is exemplified when Peter preached his powerful sermon on the day of Pentecost, and 3,000 people became believers. At least some of the 120 were enabled to preach in languages they had not learned so the people could more adequately understand the Word of God (Acts 2:5-11).

Secondarily, the power of the Holy Spirit is power for performing signs and wonders. The first sign, a healing, came as they were going about their regular ministry. They were entering the Temple to pray (Acts 3:1).

As one ponders the manner in which the power is manifested, it must be stated that it will not be manifested in a uniform manner. It will have as much variety as there are human temperaments.

For Paul Rees it is power in preaching that will be used by God to draw many to Himself. But not all Holy Spirit empowered people will be great evangelists.

Daniel Steele, the Greek exegete of the Holiness movement of the nineteenth century writes,

> It is generally supposed that the copious effusion of the Spirit upon the believer to his utmost capacity will render him like an electric battery emitting such shocks of power that sinners will instantly tremble, and fall down and cry for mercy, as did the thousands under the pentecostal preaching of Peter. Such phenomena do sometimes occur in modern times, but they are exceedingly rare.[8]

Dr. Steele believes it might be more common if the whole church were full of faith, "But even then all would not be endowed with equal measures of spiritual power, all not having suitable capacity." One needs to guard against confusing power with purity. Both of these are attainable by faith, but power seems to be dispensed in a sovereign manner by the "selfsame Spirit, dividing to every man severally as he will" (1 Cor. 12:11, *KJV*). Daniel Steele confesses that he had no marked degree of power to convert sinners although he had sought this "with intense desire, with strong cries and tears." He did find God empowering him to edify believers, perfect the saints, to constantly work for Christ in proclaiming "distasteful truths."[9] In this he found a wonderful increase of God's power.

This power will be manifested along the lines of spiritual giftedness. If it is teaching, there will be power in teaching. If serving, there will be a sense of being done in the power of the Spirit. If leading, there will be a sense of the Lord's direction in the leadership given.

This power will also be manifested in living the Christian life in an extraordinary way. When the world would expect the Christian to be cross, upset or angry, there is peace, joy and tranquility. As Richard S. Taylor observes, it is "power to be holy in the midst of defilement, to endure hardship not only courageously but triumphantly, and to rejoice because of being counted worthy of suffering disgrace for the Name."[10] Dayton notes that "the indwelling Comforter makes the Spirit-filled believer adequate and able for that which is not possible to ordinary human ability."[11] This is certainly not a part of the ordinary; therefore it can be called extraordinary.

Nancy Ashcraft reports how a Karen headman in Thailand was saved from a life given to drinking rice whiskey. This salvation was tested at a local wedding where the acceptable thing was to drink. He refused to drink because of his faith in Christ. This stunned his followers and they wanted to pull him back to his old ways. They used arguments, passed a bowl of rice whiskey under his nose in an attempt to lure him back. Finally a drunken young man poured a bottle of rice whiskey over his bowed head.

"He shook the whiskey from his hair and chin and spoke to his tormentors: 'You are right. If anything would cause me to drink, it would be this taste on my lips. But, no, I still refuse.'" The Karen people saw a man delivered from sin. They saw a change in a man of temper and pride to a man of patience and forgiveness. Throughout his lifetime the Christian headman would say, "I never knew what it was to truly love till that moment."[12] This is power to live the Christian life in an extraordinary way.

This power is power in temptation. No state of grace in this life exempts the person from temptation. There is a place in grace that enables, empowers the Christian to always triumph. This comes through the "expulsive power of a new affection." It is the "love of God being shed abroad in our hearts by the Holy Spirit" (see Rom. 5:5) which works in us a revolution in what brings us delight. Spiritual joys become more appetizing than sensual gratifications. This is not to suggest that one loses the appeal of the basic appetites for food, drink, sex, etc. These desires can be purified so that one does not seek fulfillment in unholy ways.

Some people attempt to handle temptation like Ulysses after taking Troy. The wind drove his ship near the island of the Sirens. It was reported that these famed singers had the power of enchanting all who heard so that the listeners died in the ecstasy of delight. Ulysses filled the ears of his companions with wax and tied himself to the mast until his ship had sailed out of hearing of these deadly charmers. When passing the Sirens with the Argonauts, Jason did not bind himself to the mast or stuff the ears of his crew with wax, but rather commanded Orpheus, who was on board, to play his lyre. His song so surpassed in sweetness the charmers that their music seemed like harsh discord, and Jason escaped. The purifying and empowering of the Holy Spirit changes what causes delight so that the old delights lose their appeal because of a new love.

It is power in the supernatural impact of one's testimony on the hearers. This comes not from the brilliance or cleverness of the speaker. A.M. Hills reported:

A Christian man full of the Holy Spirit sought an infidel's conversion. He filled his mind with arguments against infidelity and went to see him, hoping to argue him out of unbelief. When he reached the man's house, God kindly took all the vain arguments out of his mind, and he could not recall one of them. He laid his hand on the infidel's shoulder and wept, and could only say, "My dear brother, I am concerned for your soul." He went away filled with confusion over his failure; but God used it to the infidel's conversion.

A young man converted outside of Chicago, and wholly uneducated, was commended to Brother Torrey as one who might be invited to address one of his meetings in the city. Torrey asked the young man to address a certain meeting in a tent where a bigoted mob had assaulted them the week before. He began to speak, and Torrey says he could see nothing remarkable about the address but the grammatical blunders. Yet at the close of that blundering and crude speech men rose for prayers all over the tent. It was Holy Spirit power; not the power of human wisdom or eloquence, but the power of God.[13]

This power imparts to the person a holy courage, not naturally its own. Amanda Smith, the black evangelist said, "I used to be so afraid of white folks I couldn't speak before them, but when the Spirit came he took all that out of me."[14]

It is power in prayer. It is power to touch God's throne and to secure answers because the heart is pure and the motives have been purified. It produces confidence, even boldness to approach God with one's requests. Brengle expresses this so well:

> It may mean one prayer that gets hold of God and comes away with the blessing, or it may mean a dozen prayers that knock and persist and will not be put off until God arises and makes bare his arm on behalf of the pleading soul.
>
> There is a drawing nigh to God, a knocking at Heaven's doors, a pleading of the promises, a reasoning with Jesus, a forgetting of self, a turning from all earthly concerns, a holding on with determination to never let go, that puts all the wealth of Heaven's wisdom and power and love at the disposal of a little man, so that he shouts and triumphs when all others tremble and fail and fly, and becomes more than conqueror in the very face of death and hell.[15]

It is also power to face death with the glory of God on one's face, a prayer of forgiveness on one's lips, with poise before one's tormentors (Acts 6:15; 7:59,60).

This power may often be exercised when the individual is unconscious of it. The person may not feel it, though at times there is the awareness of a power descending on him or her. This gives the person divine insight or spiritual might. Peter Cartwright, the Kentucky Methodist evangelist, tells of meetings when "suddenly the power of God fell on the congregation like a flash of lightning and the people fell right and left; some screamed aloud for mercy, others fell on their knees and prayed out loud."[16] Nathan Bangs, a New England Methodist, was shocked when William McKendree from Kentucky was asked to address the Methodist General Conference in 1808. McKendree was sunburned and dressed "with a red flannel shirt which showed a very large space between his vest and his small clothes."

Bangs' opinion did not change when McKendree stammered through his prayer and seemed almost at a loss for words as he began to preach. Suddenly a magnetism seemed to emanate from him to all parts of the house. Bangs noted:

> He was absorbed in the interest of his subject; his voice rose gradually until it sounded like a trumpet. The effect was overwhelming . . . The house rang with irrepressible responses; many hearers fell prostrate to the floor. An athletic man sitting by my side fell as if shot by a cannon ball . . . Such an astonishing effect, so sudden and overpowering, I seldom or never saw before . . . There was a halo of glory around the preacher's head.[17]

Seth Rees, father of Paul Rees, and Bud Robinson, the Nazarene evangelist, likewise reported outpourings like this.[18]

Steele writes, "but ordinarily the Spirit's power, like gravitation, magnetism and electricity, is silent and unseen, giving a penetrating energy to the speaker's words, even when they seem powerless to himself."[19]

There are times when the speaker is so unaware of the

Spirit's work that she/he will be discouraged. The speaker may slip out the back door of the church so as to not meet the people. Later she/he finds that several were saved or filled with the Holy Spirit because the Spirit indeed was at work.

The manifestation of this power, as I've tried to illustrate, will differ from person to person. It is power that is related to the indwelling Holy Spirit. With Him one has the power, without Him one does not have it. It is power to witness for God and to Jesus that causes people to turn to Him in faith. This, Wesleyans hold, is the primary purpose for and of power. Secondarily, this power enables the person to do signs and wonders. Again the power is not in their person, but in the Holy Spirit working through a heart made clean and pure in the blood of Jesus (1 John 1:7). The signs and wonders come more in the ordinary course of ministry and almost seem incidental rather than of primary focus.

Notes
1. Henry E. Jessop, *Foundation of Doctrine* (University Park, IA: Vennard College, 1938), pp. 14,15.
2. Charles Carter, ed., *A Contemporary Wesleyan Theology* 2 Vols. (Grand Rapids: Francis Asbury Press, 1983), Vol. 1, 55,66,80.
3. E. Stanley Jones, *A Song of Ascents* (Nashville: Abingdon Press, 1968), pp. 56,57,59.
4. Timothy L. Smith, "A Historical and Contemporary Appraisal of Wesleyan Theology," ed. Charles Carter, *A Contemporary Wesleyan Theology*. Vol. 1. (Grand Rapids: Zondervan Publishing House, Francis Asbury Press, 1983), p. 96.
5. Wilber T. Dayton, "Entire Sanctification: The Divine Purification and Perfection of Man," Vol. 1 (Grand Rapids: Zondervan Publishing House, Francis Asbury Press, 1983), p. 536.
6. Samuel Logan Brengle, *Heart Talks on Holiness* (London: Salvationist Publishing, 1897), p. 78.
7. John Wesley, *Explanatory Notes on the New Testament* (Nashville: Publishing House of the M.E. Church, South, 1894).
8. Daniel Steele, *Love Enthroned* (Salem, OH: Schmul Publishing Co., 1961), p. 208.

9. Ibid., p. 208.
10. Richard S. Taylor, "Exploring Christian Holiness: The Theological Foundations," Vol. 3 (Kansas City, MO: Beacon Hill Press, 1985), 161. See also Acts 5:41 and Eph. 5:18-21.
11. Dayton, "Entire Sanctification: The Divine Purification and Perfection of Man," p. 536.
12. Nancy Ashcraft, "Holiness: Christ in Control and on Display," *Worldwide Thrust,* January/February 1988, p. 8.
13. A.M. Hills, *Holiness and Power* (Cincinnati: The Revivalist Office, 1897), pp. 312, 313.
14. Ibid., p. 314.
15. Samuel Logan Brengle, *Helps to Holiness* (London: Salvationist Publishing, 1896) pp. 38, 39.
16. Peter Cartwright, *The Autobiography of Peter Cartwright* (Nashville: Abingdon Press, 1956), p. 88.
17. Charles W. Ferguson, *Organizing to Beat the Devil,* (Garden City: Doubleday, 1971), p. 188.
18. Seth C. Rees, *The Ideal Pentecostal Church* (Cincinnati: The Revivalist Office, 1897). Bud Robinson, *My Life's Story* (Kansas City: Nazarene Publishing House, 1928).
19. Daniel Steele, *The Gospel of the Comforter* (Salem, OH: Schmul Publishing Co., 1960), p. 197.

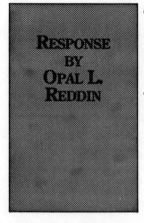

RESPONSE BY OPAL L. REDDIN

The Holy Spirit and Power: A Wesleyan Understanding

Dr. Hohensee has given us a lucid and concise statement of the Wesleyan understanding of "The Holy Spirit and Power." I appreciate his emphasis on the relationship of purity to power and his insistence that the primary purpose of the power of the Holy Spirit is "for use in evangelism." I agree with him that the infilling with the Holy Spirit should "result in holy living." All believers owe a sizeable debt to Wesleyan movements for their constant stress on holiness without which no one shall see the Lord (Heb. 10:14).

Pentecostals in particular are deeply indebted to Wesleyan Holiness movements. We are aware of many contributions made by Wesleyans to Pentecostals, including: emphasis on sanctification; enthusiastic worship; evangelical social concern; practice of divine healing; ordination of women preachers; emphasis on world missions, and even the term *Pentecostal*. In the decade preceding the rise of the Pentecostal movements, many Holiness groups had the term *Pentecostal* in their titles and spoke much of Pentecostal power.

As I have listened to Dr. Hohensee, I have rejoiced in

the knowledge that men such as he are teaching seminarians. The doctrine of holiness brings liberty to individuals and moral strength to a nation (Gal. 5:1). I have also noted some areas that I consider problematical. I shall list these briefly and then deal with them in order: the phrase "removal of the sin nature"; identification of sanctification with the baptism in the Holy Spirit; and, inadequate attention to the manifestation of the power of the Holy Spirit in evangelism and to the necessity of signs and wonders for full New Testament proclamation of the gospel.

Removal of the Sin Nature

Hohensee correctly sees Pentecost as the time when the disciples received the power of the Holy Spirit. He describes "the baptism in the Holy Spirit" as "both a cleansing and an empowering event." In his view, the believer is freed from the penalty of acts of sin in conversion and "freed from the sin nature" in the baptism of the Spirit. He maintains that "the person must be freed of both elements before one can enter a holy heaven." It seems that he is saying that one is not saved until he has received this baptism. If not, can one be saved and yet not go to heaven?

Most, if not all, Pentecostals would disagree. We have always recognized that believers are saved by the blood of Jesus and that being in Christ is the only *essential* for heaven. The statement that the baptism in the Holy Spirit "cleanses the heart" implies that the blood of Christ is efficacious for only partial cleansing.

Pentecostals agree with Wesleyans that man did not lose his power to choose. We do not see unconditional eternal security taught in the Word; it would seem, however, that the theory of removal of the sin nature would result in a belief in the absolute security of the believer against falling away from Christ.

The Assemblies of God view is that at conversion the believer is justified, regenerated, and sanctified (1 Cor. 1:30; 6:11). The sinful nature (flesh, old man, etc.) is not eradicated (Gal. 5:16-24; Rom. 6:11), but it must be kept "crucified with Christ." The instantaneous aspect is at conversion; the progressive aspect is described as perfecting holiness (already received) in the fear of God (2 Cor. 7:1). We grow *in*, not *into* sanctification.

Sanctification and the Baptism

Not all Pentecostals agree as to the time of sanctification. Some of them believe that one is saved, then sanctified, and then baptized in the Holy Spirit. All Pentecostals agree that the baptism in the Spirit follows sanctification.

There is no Scripture that equates the baptism in the Holy Spirit with sanctification. The only reference Hohensee cited is Acts 15:8,9. As we interpret in context, we can see why Peter mentioned the receiving of the Spirit first as unequivocal proof that Gentiles could be saved without keeping the Mosaic law. He cited the experience that is accompanied by an objective sign: the Holy Spirit fell and they heard them speak with tongues (Acts 10:44,46). It would not be doing violence to the meaning of verses 8 and 9 to paraphrase: *God proved to us that He had purified the hearts of the believing Gentiles by pouring out of the Spirit upon them, and we knew they had been baptized in the Holy Spirit because they spoke in tongues just as we did at Pentecost.*

This brings us to the matter of subjectivity in the Wesleyan understanding. How does the believer know that he has received the second cleansing? It seems that Wesley had problems with this. Melvin Dieter, in discussing Wesley's understanding of sanctification, says, "His distinctive contribution was his conviction that true biblical Christianity finds its highest expression and ultimate test of authenticity in the practical and ethical experience of the individual Christian and only secondarily in doctrinal and propositional definition."[1] According to Donald Dayton, Wesley even "vacillated as to whether Christian perfection was to be achieved in crisis or process."[2]

While Pentecostals may differ on some points regarding sanctification, all agree that the baptism in the Holy Spirit will be accompanied by the initial physical evidence of speaking in languages never studied but spontaneously given by the Holy Spirit. We base this belief on solid scriptural ground (Acts 2:4; 10:44-46; 19:6). Any other position is based either on human experience or on the silence of Scripture rather than objective biblical statement.

Manifestations of the Power

Having seen both the Wesleyan and the Pentecostal views on the baptism in the Holy Spirit, let us consider the power of the Holy Spirit as it is manifested in ministries and gifts. Hohensee has said that "this power will be manifested along the lines of spiritual giftedness." He then lists a number of gifts, including: teaching, living the Christian life "in an extraordinary way", overcoming temptation, testimony, courage, prayer and facing death. While no one could deny that these are all manifestations of God's grace to us, it seems to me that these are not extraordinary but the expected norm for genuine Christians. Brief mention is made of "signs and wonders," with illustrations of such phenomena as people trembling, falling, screaming aloud and deliverance from alcohol.

All of these are indeed examples of the Holy Spirit at work, but the list is incomplete. When Hohensee uses 1 Cor. 12:11 in connection with the dispensing of gifts by the Holy Spirit "dividing to every man severally as He will," he calls our attention to a listing of manifestations of the Holy Spirit that includes some gifts not usually accepted by non-Pentecostals, particularly those of tongues and interpretation. It would seem that this is an arbitrary application of the sovereignty of the Holy Spirit to only a partial listing of His manifestations.

The Holy Spirit's explicit purpose is to reproduce the ministry of Jesus in and through His Church (John 14:12) so that all the world may hear the gospel and witness the power of the Holy Spirit. Every record of the Great Commission is accompanied by the Lord's promise of power. It is God's will that *all* the gifts of the Holy Spirit be in operation in His Church. Those who say that some of the gifts ceased reveal their lack of knowledge of both Scripture and church history. They will cease (as such) when the Perfect comes and we no longer know in part (1 Cor. 13). It is true that they have waned and almost been lost at times. However, there is ample documentation of occurrences of everything described in the New Testament at various times as individuals and groups have received the fullness of Pentecostal power. Bernard Bresson has catalogued 24 charismatic movements appearing between late second and mid-nineteenth centuries, from Montanism to the Irvingite Catholic Apostolic Church.[3] John Wesley said that "the real cause why the extraordinary gifts of the Holy Spirit were no longer to be found in the Christian Church is that the love of many, almost all Christians was waxed cold."[4]

Pentecostals know that all the so-called extraordinary gifts of the Spirit are in evidence today because they have seen all of them and experienced some of them. The greatest need of Pentecostals is to stop being defensive about supernatural manifestations and to humbly seek God for a greater effusion of His power for this generation. Peter Wagner is correct when he says that the theology of some Pentecostals greatly exceeds their experience. Sincere Pentecostals join him in his prayer that "Pentecostal and charismatic flames that have died down" might be fanned into a new baptism of fire of the Holy Spirit.[5]

Since we are here concerned mainly with two kinds of demonstration of the power of the Holy Spirit, I will concentrate on the two subjects: divine healing and the exorcism of demons, as these gifts relate to power evangelism.

All Pentecostals believe in *divine healing* for the physical body. This belief and practice is one of the main reasons why they are the fastest growing group of evangelicals in the world today. They see healing as both a manifestation of the nature of our loving God and as provision in the atonement for man physically as well as spiritually. It was manifested in the Old Testament and in the New Covenant. Our theology and practice of healing could be called an inheritance from both the Wesleyan and the Keswickian Holiness movements. It is recorded that "the belief in and witness to miraculous divine healings attended the Holiness movements at every turn."[6] What was added by Pentecostals was a greater emphasis on and a higher incidence of actual healings.

It is clear in Scripture that one of the most characteristic displays of the power of the Holy Spirit is the *exorcism of demons*. I agree with Hohensee when he says that Jesus gave His disciples both power and authority to drive out demons. Pentecostals have preached that this same authority is necessary today for full New Testament evangelism. A survey of Pentecostal history in this century will yield many well-documented accounts of the exorcism of demons. Growing up in a classical Pentecostal church, I have witnessed many exorcisms and have had some personal experience in my own ministry.

We have said that the power of the Holy Spirit is given to believers so that the full-orbed ministry of Jesus can flow through His body here on earth. His ministry was marked by many accounts of exorcism. A brief listing of the persons so delivered includes: a man in the temple (Mark 1:21-28); Mary Magdalene (Mark 16:9); the epileptic boy (Matt. 17:14-21); a man with a dumb spirit (Matt. 12:22); Legion (Mark 5:1-20);and a Syrophoenician girl (Mark 7:24-30). He also delivered the woman bent double but it is not stated that this was exorcism; the demon may have been external in this case though afflicting her dreadfully (Luke 13:10-17).

Jesus attributed His exorcism of demons to the power of the Holy Spirit (Matt. 12:28). It was when He was accused of casting out demons by Beelzebub that He warned of the unforgivable sin of blasphemy of the Holy Spirit (Matt. 12:27-32). In God's sovereign plan, Jesus was anointed with the Holy Spirit and did signs. O.J. Sharp tells of a time when Martin Luther "laid hands on a girl and exorcised a demon on the basis of John 14:12."[7] One of the best-known instances of exorcism in this century is that of Clarita Villanueva's deliverance in Manila.[8] Under David Wilkerson's ministry in New York City, Nicky Cruz was delivered of demons, saved and filled with the Holy Spirit and is now instrumental in multitudes being saved.[9] This is power evangelism.

The Assemblies of God do not accept the premise that Christians can be inhabited by demons.[10] Though Hohensee does not state the Wesleyan understanding of exorcism for the contemporary Church, I believe on the basis of his statement of sanctification that Wesleyans would agree with us on that point.

It seems that all evangelicals are agreed that a demon cannot possess a believer's spirit. Some, however, are teaching that the believer's body, mind, will and emotions can be inhabited by one or more demons. While it is true that man is spirit, soul and body, the Bible does not teach such a radical separation that a demon could come into any part of a believer while his spirit is indwelt by the Holy Spirit. There is no scriptural basis for such teaching.

The Word is clear that believers' bodies are "members of Christ" and "the temple of the Holy Spirit" (1 Cor. 6:15-19). The Holy Spirit will not allow a demon to cohabit with Him! The only time a demon can enter a believer's body is when he finds it empty, without Christ inside (Luke 11:24-26).

There are only two kingdoms involved here: the kingdom of God and the kingdom of darkness. The Christian has been delivered from the power of darkness and "translated into the kingdom of God's dear Son" (see 1 Cor. 1:13). There are only two families, God's and Satan's. Jesus told a group of unbelievers, "Ye are of your father the devil" (John 8:44, *KJV*). Believers have the witness of the Spirit that they are sons of God (Rom. 8:16).

The term *demonized* is being used unscripturally by those who say that Christians can be demonized. It is a transliteration of *daimonidzomai* which in Scripture carries the meaning of *demon possessed*. It is never in any way used of a person who was right with God.

Hohensee's presentation of the power of the Holy Spirit to produce holiness in us is the biblical path to victory over sin and Satan and all his forces. The Christian's internal battles are with flesh (Gal. 5:16-24), not demons.

Jesus' message to the seven churches illustrates this

perfectly. When He spoke of awful wickedness in some of the believers, He never told them to get the demons out. Rather He told them to repent or else they would lose Him (Rev. 2:5,16,22; 3:3,19).

The person who claims to be a Christian but has a demon inhabiting him is in one of the following positions. First, he may be a nominal Christian (not a biblical term), one who has never been born again (John 3:3-5). Second, he may be calling a carnal habit a demon (Gal. 5:19-21). Third, he may have once been a true believer but has now lost his spiritual life. Rom. 8:13 tells Christians that if they continue to walk after the flesh they will die. Commenting on this verse John Murray writes:

> Paul is speaking here to believers and to them he says, "If ye live after the flesh, ye shall die." The death referred to here must be understood in its broadest scope and does not stop short of death in its ultimate manifestation, eternal separation from God. [11]

The power of the Holy Spirit gives Christians power to overcome the flesh, to resist demons (Eph. 6:12-18), and to cast them out of others (Mark 16:17). In approaching exorcism, they should follow scriptural principles and they should have no unconfessed sin. Some cases will require fasting with prayer (Matt. 17:21).

The *power* of the gospel cannot be separated from its *proclamation.* Jesus began to do and teach; the Word that is not confirmed by signs following will have little effect. If we are to evangelize our world we must, regardless of our denomination, be open to the full New Testament panoply of power (Acts 1:8).

In preparing to respond to the Wesleyan understanding

of "The Holy Spirit and Power," I have been challenged anew to contend for the faith (Jude 3), to humbly seek the Lord more earnestly and to teach more fervently than ever before that the power of the Holy Spirit is more than sufficient to overcome all the powers of the enemy.

Notes

1. Melvin E. Dieter, Anthony A. Hoekema, Stanley M. Horton, J. Robertson McQuilkin, and John F. Walvoord, *Five Views on Sanctification* (Grand Rapids: Zondervan Publishing House, 1987), p. 11.
2. Vinson Synan, ed. *Aspects of Pentecostal-Charismatic Origins* (Plainfield, NJ: Logos, International, 1975), p. 49.
3. Bernard Bresson, *Studies in Ecstasy* (New York: Vantage Press, 1966).
4. Donald Gee, *Concerning Spiritual Gifts* (Springfield, MO: Gospel Publishing House, 1972), p. 19.
5. C. Peter Wagner, *How to Have a Healing Ministry Without Making Your Church Sick* (Ventura: Regal Books, 1988) p. 9.
6. Vinson Synan, ed. *Aspects of Pentecostal-Charismatic Origins*, p. 68.
7. O. J. Sharp, "Did Charismata Cease with the Apostles' Death?" *Paraclete* 20 (Spring 1976): pp. 18-22.
8. Lester Sumrall, *Modern Manila Miracles* (Springfield, MO: Gospel Publishing House, 1954).
9. Nicky Cruz, *Satan on the Loose* (Old Tappan, NJ: Fleming H. Revell Company, 1973).
10. See an Assemblies of God Position Paper, "Can Born-Again Believers Be Demon-possessed?" (Springfield, MO: Gospel Publishing House, 1972).
11. John Murray, *Epistle to the Romans* (Grand Rapids: Eerdmans Publishing Co., 1965), pp. 293-4.

CHAPTER

7

Pentecostal/ Charismatic Under- standing of Exorcism*

L. GRANT McCLUNG, JR.

L. GRANT McCLUNG, JR., is assistant professor of missions and church growth at the Church of God School of Theology in Cleveland, Tennessee. He has also taught at West Coast Christian College in Fresno, California and at European Bible Seminary in West Germany. He is the author of *Azusa Street and Beyond*, an analysis of Pentecostal missions and church growth.

A review of the literature, history and oral stories of Pentecostalism reveal the centrality of the practice of exorcism in the expansion of the Pentecostal and charismatic movements. While there is some general agreement in theology and practice, a broad diversity remains in specific beliefs and ministries surrounding exorcism.

A clarified doctrinal statement on demonology and exorcism does not exist among major Pentecostal bodies. There are Pentecostal expositions such as Duffield and Van Cleave's *Foundations of Pentecostal Theology*.[1] Much of these discussions, however, are the reworking of earlier evangelical commentaries on the subject. Like many themes in Pentecostal/charismatic belief and practice, exorcism has been practiced but not formally theologized.

Though the *New International Dictionary of the Christian Church* describes exorcism as, "The practice of expelling evil spirits by means of prayer, divination, or magic,"[2] Pentecostal/charismatic theology would not understand the means of exorcism in any other source than the power of God. For them, exorcism would be, "The act of expelling evil spirits or demons by adjuration in the name of Jesus Christ and through His power."[3]

Scriptural Data

Since the Gospels are replete with the accounts of the liberating power of Jesus over demons, Pentecostals have seen the ministry of Jesus as the biblical paradigm for the practice of exorcism. This would also be true of the work of the Apostolic Church in the book of Acts. Almost every Pentecostal/charismatic writing on the subject will include a case study from the story of the Gerasene demoniac (Matt. 8:28-34; Mark 5:1-20; Luke 8:26-39).

In addition to the many general statements in the Gospels of Jesus' work against demonized persons (Matt. 4:24; 8:16; Mark 1:32-34,39; 3:11; 6:13; Luke 4:41; 6:18; 7:21), Michael Green has noted seven specific accounts of His work with individuals.

1. The man with the unclean spirit in the synagogue (Mark 1:21-28; Luke 4:31-37).
2. The blind and dumb demoniac (Matt. 12:22-29; Mark 3:22-27; Luke 11:14-22).
3. The Gerasene demoniac (Matt. 8:28-32; Mark 5:1-20; Luke 8:26-39).
4. The Syrophoenician woman's daughter (Matt. 15:21-28; Mark 7:24-30).
5. The epileptic boy (Matt. 17:14-21; Mark 9:14-29; Luke 9:37-43).
6. The woman with a spirit of infirmity (Luke 13:10-17).
7. The dumb demoniac (Matt. 9:32).

Along with this list, Green includes "with probability" the healing of Simon Peter's mother-in-law (Luke 4:39), whose fever Jesus "rebuked." He notes that three incidents were deemed important enough to appear in all three Synoptics—the Beelzebub controversy, the Gerasene demoniac, and the epileptic boy.[4]

One is impressed with the clear authority with which Jesus cast out demons. In terms of His own self-understanding of His authority and mission, Jesus most certainly believed that He was liberating the demonized person completely. In other words, it was not psychological transference or unfulfilled hope. This was also immediately visible by observers and witnesses. He made this fact of His ministry practices a proof of His divinity and authenticity. His language of exorcism exhibits expressions consistent with His divine authority: "He *commanded* the unclean spirit"; "Jesus *rebuked* the devil"; "He *cast out* many devils"; "He *suffered not* devils to speak".[5]

The deliverance ministry of exorcism continued in the Early Church as normative and expected. In fact, the disciples understood it as inclusive in the Great Commission of the Lord Jesus (Mark 16:15-17). Apostolic practices and subsequent correspondence to the newly-established churches evidenced exorcism as an ongoing practice (Acts 8:6-7; 16:16-18; 19:11-12; 26:18; Eph. 2:2; Col. 1:13; 2 Tim. 2:25,26; 1 John 5:18). A complete listing of Scripture references to Satan and evil spirits is found in Michael Scanlan and Randall J. Cirner's *Deliverance from Evil Spirits.*[6]

Nature and Origin of Demons

Demons are characterized as being individualistic with traits normally applied to personality: knowledge, emotion, speech, will (Mark 1:24; Acts 19:15, Jas. 2:19; Matt. 12:44). In Scripture they are seen as disembodied spirits with total control over the possessed.[7] In New Testament usage, along with *daimonion,* adjectives such as "unclean" (*akatharton,* Mark 1:24-27; 5:2-3; 7:25; 9:25; Acts 5:16; 8:7; Rev. 16:13) and "evil" (*ponera,* Acts 19:12-16) are used.[8] They are wicked, unclean, and vicious (Matt. 8:28; 10:1) and, based on Matt. 12:43-45, some feel that there are degrees of wickedness among them.[9]

Reflecting earlier conservative scholarship among evangelical scholars, there is not a clear-cut agreement in Pentecostal/charismatic literature regarding the origin of demons. Many sources, however, indicate a belief that demons are fallen angels. Relying upon the former foundational work by evangelical scholar Merrill F. Unger,[10] Duffield and Van Cleave discuss three principal theories for the origin of demons:

1. That demons are disembodied spirits of inhabitants

of a pre-Adamic earth (based upon interpretations of Gen. 1:1-2; Ezek. 28:14; Isa. 14:13-14).

2. That demons are the offspring of angels and antediluvian women (based upon interpretations of Gen. 6:1-4; Jude 6,7; Job 1:6; 2:1; 38:7).
3. That demons are fallen angels (based upon interpretations of Matt. 12:24; 24:41; Rev. 12:4,7,9; Jude 6; 2 Pet. 2:4).

Though preferring the third interpretation, they are, "forced to recognize difficulties in upholding any of these positions beyond controversy. We therefore conclude that God has not chosen to reveal the answer to the question of the origin of demons."[11]

Although he concedes that the origin of demons is not fully clear, Gordon Lindsay says, "The demons are not the same class of beings as fallen angels, although the evidence is strong that their fall is also associated with Satan's rebellion. There is a general belief among Bible scholars that demons had their origin in a pre-Adamite age. There is strong scriptural evidence, if not conclusive, to support this belief."[12] Other Pentecostal/charismatic sources, however, do not verify such a "general belief" or assurance of "strong scriptural evidence" as Lindsay believes.

As practitioners, Pentecostals and charismatics have not speculated on the origin of demons as much as they have advised on the surety and methodology of their expulsion. Better known discussions on spiritual warfare and demonization focus more on the practice of exorcism than on the origin of the exorcised spirits.[13]

Exorcism in the Christian Tradition

There is evidence for the practice of exorcism in the Christian tradition from the time of the apostles until the present day. Some writers would argue that it became common to exorcise catechumens from pagan and Jewish backgrounds before baptism, citing the mention of this practice at the Council of Carthage in 255 as evidence. Exorcism became part of the ceremony of infant baptism by the time of the Middle Ages. Reportedly, the service included the thrice-repeated breathing on the face of the infant with the accompanying command, "Depart from him, thou unclean spirit, and give place to the Holy Spirit."[14] A brief exorcism found its way into early Lutheran baptismal services and an exorcism prayer formula is recorded in the *First Prayer Book* of Edward VI (1549).

Peter Toon explains that the title of "exorcist" is a part of a minor order of the ministry in the Early Church, with tasks including laying hands on the insane, exorcising catechumens and helping at Holy Communion.[15] Today in the Roman Catholic Church the order is retained as an intermediate step toward full priesthood. The Eastern Church has no order of exorcists.[16] Michael Green reports that the Church of England published a report, *Exorcism*, in the early 1980s and at the same time recommended that every diocese appoint a "Diocesan Exorcist."[17] The reader may also consult the appendix of Michael Harper's *Spiritual Warfare* for samples of older forms and rituals of exorcism used in the historic churches.[18]

Charismatics, informed from the polity and theology of the traditional churches, have approached exorcism from a ritualistic and confined perspective. Scanlan and Cirner, for example, are very careful to explain the differences in the types of exorcism and who is allowed to perform them:

Solemn exorcism is for the purpose of driving out the

devil from a possessed person. The Church requires that such exorcism be public, that is, that it be done in the name of and with the authority of the Church. Canon Law requires that only a priest specifically approved by the local bishop can engage in public exorcism; therefore only such an authorized priest is approved for solemn exorcism.

Simple exorcism, however, is for the purpose of curbing the devil's power and can be executed through private exorcism . . . . The effectiveness of this exorcism is not derived from the authority of prayers of the Church, nor is it done with the name of the Church, but in virtue of the name of God and Jesus Christ.[19]

Mainline Pentecostals and Protestant charismatics would not separate the duties of clergy and laity in the performance of the exorcism ministry. All believers share equally in the power of exorcism according to the biblical teaching of the priesthood of all believers (1 Pet. 2:9; Mark 16:15-17). Philip, the deacon (Acts 6:5) was instrumental in the exorcism of demons (8:4-8). However, exorcism in Pentecostal ranks has been exhibited through missionaries, pastors and evangelists, especially those seen to have a special "deliverance" ministry. This may be more characteristic of North American and European Pentecostalism than in the Two-thirds World where, among those Pentecostals, everyone is a "preacher."

There has been a general skepticism in classical Pentecostalism toward those claiming to have a specialized ministry in this area. British Pentecostal George Canty expresses this attitude:

In this connection, nobody was ever given a special

gift for 'exorcism,' only for discernment, as part of
the protection of the Church, chiefly against false
teachers with lying and deceitful doctrines of
demons. Nobody manifested a ministry exclusively
for dealing with demons. This would draw attention
more to Satan than to Christ.[20]

Though some orders have been established in the historic churches for a special class of persons called "exorcists," this model was not incorporated into the classical
Pentecostal awakening or the charismatic revival.

Green points out that the church father Tertullian
claimed that any Christian who did not know how to exorcise deserved to be put to death! But he is quick to add a
word of caution:

But that certainly does not mean that every Christian
ought to be involved in this type of ministry. All can:
not all should. And never look for it. If God means to
use you in this ministry he will make it so painfully
obvious that you can scarcely avoid it without gross
disobedience.[21]

There is evidence to determine a symbiotic relationship of influence between Pentecostal/charismatic theology and traditional evangelical scholarship on the subject
of demonology and exorcism. Duffield and Van Cleave
(1983), Green (1981), and Harper (1970), for example,
show a familiarity with and dependence upon earlier foundational work by Unger and others. In turn, some evangelical writers have been informed by the practices of
Pentecostals and charismatics in the area of exorcism.
Mark Bubeck (a Baptist pastor), for example, shows a
familiarity with, and appreciation for, Pentecostal/

charismatic sources in his best-selling book, *The Adversary,* though he is quick to offer strong cautionary statements on the charismatic movement.[22]

The influence of Pentecostals upon evangelical thought is seen especially in the marketplace of missions and the extension of the Church. Missiologists have been among the first to recognize the Pentecostal contribution to world evangelization through a serious confrontation with Satan's power. This is the conclusion of Arthur F. Glasser, a respected Presbyterian missionary dean:

> Besides this, the Pentecostals were willing to tackle the "dark side of the soul" and challenge the growing phenomenon of occultism, Satan worship and demon possession. Whereas, IFMA people and other non-charismatic evangelicals (particularly the Baptists!) had found it relatively easy to expose the extravagance of the occasional charlatan, they were silenced in the presence of the Pentecostals' serious confrontation of the hard realities of the spirit world. Here was a spirituality which could not be ignored.[23]

The relationship between the Church Growth Movement and the Pentecostal Movement has been traced in my chapter on "Pentecostals and The Church Growth Movement" in *Azusa Street and Beyond.*[24]

Special Issues

A survey of the literature on exorcism reveals a wide variety of sub-topics and special issues. Three of the most common discussions relate to exorcism and healing, classifications and terminology, and the types and orders of demons.

1. *Exorcism and Healing*

The diversity of opinion regarding the source of disease (whether from demons or natural causes) and the connection (or separation) of exorcism to healing is as broad as the number of authors one wishes to consult. There is no monolithic agreement in doctrine and practice. Pentecostal and charismatic understandings of exorcism are diverse and complex.

For example, "There seems little doubt that every accident, misfortune, quarrel, sickness, disease, and unhappiness is the direct result of the individual work of one or more wicked spirits," says one Pentecostal writer.[25] Others, particularly from a North American middle-class perspective, would argue a distinction between sickness from natural causes and demon-related disorders (based upon an understanding of such references as Matt. 4:23,24; 8:16; Mark 1:32; Luke 7:21). Thus, as Longley believes, "We do not exorcise sickness itself, only demons who cause sickness. Prayer for the sick within various Christian ministries is totally different from casting out demons."[26]

Many Pentecostal writers are careful to point out that Jesus healed diseases and cast out devils, citing such examples as Matt. 8:16 and Luke 13:32. In addition, mention is made of examples of healing without the notation of any presence of demons, as in John 11:1 ff.[27] Canty would conclude that:

> Even in Mark 6, where healing and deliverance from demons are mentioned together, they are not confused as if they were both the same thing. The language is that some would be sick and need healing, and that some would be possessed and need spirits

to be cast out. Sheer lack of Scriptural suggestion
about demon possession and sickness being one and
the same thing obliges us to reject such a doctrine,
while recognizing that the one or two cases recorded
make it possible that violent possession will also (as
we might expect) have effect on the body.[28]

The practice of some, therefore, "who in ministering
to the sick always try to cast out a demon, is not biblical
procedure."[29] This would be Green's conclusion, who
points out that in His mission charge to the twelve, Jesus
empowered them,

> in two respects, not one: to have authority over
> demons and to heal diseases (Luke 9:1f). Demons
> are expelled: diseases are healed. In other words,
> the Gospel writers seem to indicate that illness may
> be caused by direct demonic invasion though it cer-
> tainly need not be. They are abundantly clear that
> there is a difference between healing and exorcism.[30]

While John Wimber would understand this view of an
"either or" distinction built upon Western dichotimization,
he argues for a more holistic approach in dealing with sickness, "Jesus frequently spoke the same way to fevers as
he did to demons, because he saw the connection between
sickness and Satan."[31] Because of Western secularization,
Wimber argues, modern Christians find it easier to com-
partmentalize faith and science away from each other:
"Often, of course, there are psychological or physical
explanations for illness. But more frequently than many
Christians realize, the cause is demonic."[32]

2. *Classifications and Terminology*

Classical Pentecostal writings have traditionally made a distinction between demon possession and demon influence. While allowing for demonic affliction, Pentecostal commentators have been adamant against any possibility of demon possession among believers.[33]

To differentiate types of demonic activity, Pentecostal/charismatic writers have used a trilogy of "states of demonic control": oppression, obsession, and possession.[34] These three words, "oppression, obsession, and possession" are typical in Pentecostal/charismatic literature. Lindsay sees them in a progression and adds a fourth in the series, "oppression, depression, obsession, and possession." He sees demonic activity in a number of ways with the terms, "attacking, harassing, and actually dominating" and includes "professing Christians" as objects of demonic offensives.[35]

Regarding Christians, Bubeck understands "oppression" as attacks from the outside in terms of spiritual warfare. "Obsession," he says, has traditionally meant the subject's "uncontrollable preoccupation" with demonic forces of phenomena:

> It is something less than total commitment or ownership, but is a step in that direction. A Christian who has of his own will developed overt curiosity about the occult, or in other ways has habitually given ground to Satan, may find himself demonically obsessed as traditionally defined.[36]

Possession, says Bubeck, is the total control by the evil spirit exhibited by the command of a person's will, and ownership by another. He claims that the word "possession," though an English expression, is not a word of the original language and agrees with classical Pentecostals that:

> No believer can be possessed by an evil spirit in the same sense that an unbeliever can. In fact, I reject this term altogether when talking about a believer's problem with the powers of darkness. A believer may be afflicted or even controlled in certain areas of his being, but he can never be owned or totally controlled as an unbeliever can. [37]

In terms of classifications and terminology, says Green, Jesus made no distinction between oppression or possession:

> The Greek word is *daimonizomai* "to be demonized" or sometimes *echein deimonion*, "to have a demon." The modern distinction between oppression and possession has no basis in the Greek New Testament. [38]

Wimber also prefers the broader term, "demonization." [39] In discussing "How Evil Spirits Affect Mankind" (chapter 3), Scanlan and Cirner prefer the threefold classifications of "temptation, opposition, and bondage" and make no mention of "oppression, obsession, and possession." [40]

3. *Types and Orders of Demons*

Pentecostal literature, especially from the ranks of evangelists, has asserted that all demons are not alike. Pentecostals have said that the Bible speaks of many kinds of evil spirits, discerned by their manifestations or effects they have in those they afflict. Richardson says the Bible refers to spirits of fear, unclean spirits, foul spirits, spirits of error, perverse spirits, lying spirits, deceiving spirits,

spirits of emulation, spirits of jealousy, spirits of whoredom, spirits of infirmity and familiar spirits.[41]

Others would add the spirit of bondage, deaf and dumb spirits, spirits of heaviness, whoredoms and haughtiness.[42] Lindsay devotes a chapter to this discussion (titled "Different Orders of Demons") and claims that certain demons are specifically adapted to afflict the bodies of people. He refers to "demons of the sense organs" (deaf and blind spirits, infirm spirits) and lying spirits which cause oppression in the brain.[43] In the popular preaching among groups taking a position of total abstinence from alcohol and tobacco, one also hears attacks against the "demon of alcohol" or the "demon of nicotine."

Methodology and Practices

Michael Green provides three points for the discussion of the "how" of exorcism: discernment, preparation and action.[44] Most of the literature will usually discuss approaches under these categories.

1. *Discernment.* Citing biblical support for supernatural insight (1 Cor. 12:10; 1 John 4:1), Pentecostal/charismatic writers have stressed the need for discernment. "We do not have to rely on a sensation or a hunch," says Green[45] and it would be dangerous to do so.[46] Lindsay devotes a special chapter to discernment, along with a four-fold test for discernment. He, along with most others, would assert that the discernment gift, "is particularly designed to detect the presence of demons."[47]

Various signs of demonization are suggested. Green, for example, lists such things as an irrational and violent reaction against the name of Jesus, unnatural bondage to sexual perversion, strange behavior or moodiness, and sudden changes of voice or emotions.[48]

2. *Preparation.* Some instances are immediate and there is no time for prolonged preparation. In these instances, the long-term maturity and preparedness in the Christian readies him for the confrontation. In cases where there is time for preparation, fasting and prayer has been held up as the primary way to ready oneself. [49]

Green provides a checklist of preparatory steps including confession, giving time to prayer, claiming the victory of Christ, Bible study, gathering the support of a team, etc. [50] Harper stresses the importance of personal holiness:

> We should never go lightly into this ministry. First we should seek personal cleansing, in the same way as a surgeon will wash before an operation. We should repent of any sin, and relinquish any trust or confidence in ourselves. We must confess, if necessary, any unbelief in the power of our Lord and the authority of His word. [51]

3. *Action.* To cast out demons "in the name of Jesus" would indicate that it is being done under His authority and by His power. In His commission, Jesus said that His followers would cast out devils in His name (Mark 16:17; Acts 16:18). This is not to be taken as a magic formula or special ritual. As Richardson notes, "Enunciating the name 'Jesus' or even claiming the protection of Christ's blood is meaningful only if the person has a genuine relationship with Jesus and exercises his position of authority that is in Christ." [52]

This should not mean, however, that we must constantly quote or repeat the name of Jesus with every act we do in His name. Duffield and Van Cleave point out that demons also left people when the name of Jesus was *not* uttered (Acts 5:15,16; 19:11,12). The casting out of demons, they insist:

> Does not require a barrage or words with voluminous repetitions of the word "Jesus" or "Christ." We have authority, and can use it, as "ambassadors" (2 Cor. 5:20), but we must avoid treating it as a magic incantation, like a piece of abracadabra or spell. When we utter "Lord Jesus Christ" it indicates that he is the Lord of the one who speaks, otherwise we are like the sons of Sceva, unknown to the spirits.[53]

Varieties of methodologies are recorded in Pentecostal/charismatic sources. In the New Testament, even aprons and handkerchiefs from the hand of Paul were instrumental in exorcism (Acts 19:11,12). Some may lay hands upon the demonized, others may not. There is no actual record in the Scriptures of deliverance from demons by the laying on of hands. Neither is there any data on coughing up or spitting out demons, though this is reported in some contemporary deliverances. In addition, the Scripture does not give us any encouragement to hold conversations with demons.[54]

Harper (and others) state that the name or nature of the demon may be revealed and, in that case, we name the spirit when we command it to leave the person. However, the practice followed by some of asking the demons for their names has no scriptural warrant.

> There is no instance of Jesus doing it; in Mark 5 he asked the man what his name was, and it is the man who answers, "my name is Legion," although the demons would seem to have added the words "for we are many" (Mark 5:9). As for carrying on a con-

versation with them, this is extremely dangerous and scripturally unwarranted. [55]

Harper also emphasizes the need for "after-care" in the life of the delivered person. He speaks of filling, healing, self-discipline, faith and praise. [56] Green also points out the need for encouragement and pastoral care after one has been delivered. [57]

Exorcism and the Mission of the Church

Green sees exorcism as a natural part of the growth and extension of the Church into new areas of darkness. He refers to the commission of Jesus to the 70 (Luke 10:19) and says that demonic opposition is to be expected when the kingdom of God is being advanced. [58] Paul Pomerville, a Pentecostal missiologist, says that the power encounter involved in exorcism has been an intentional Church growth strategy among Pentecostals. [59]

Church growth proponents have noted that seriously dealing with demonic opposition has been one of the distinctive marks of Pentecostal growth. McGavran cited exorcism as a part of the answer to his question, "What Makes Pentecostal Churches Grow?" Pentecostals, he said:

> Accept the fact that most men and women today believe that demons and evil spirits (varying forms of Satan and dark thoughts) do invade them, bind them, and rule over them. Pentecostals believe that the mighty name of Jesus drives out evil spirits and heals all manner of sickness. [60]

Wagner concluded that exorcism was a key factor in the exploding growth among Latin American Pentecostals[61] and De Wet believes that is the only way to success-fully deal with the world view of Animists and the unseen spiritual resistance in the Muslim world.[62]

Notes

1. Guy P. Duffield and Nathaniel M. Van Cleave, *Foundations of Pentecostal Theology* (Los Angeles, CA: LIFE Bible College, 1983).
2. Peter Toon, "Exorcism," *New International Dictionary of the Christian Church*, J. D. Douglas, Editor (Grand Rapids, MI: Zondervan Publishing, 1974), p. 365.
3. Carl Richardson, *Exorcism: New Testament Style* (Old Tappan, NJ: Fleming H. Revell, 1974), p. 5.
4. Michael Green, *I Believe in Satan's Downfall* (Grand Rapids, MI: William B. Eerdmans Publishing Company, 1981), pp. 127-130.
5. Duffield and Van Cleave, *Foundations of Pentecostal Theology*, 486; and Charles W. Conn, *The Anatomy of Evil* (Old Tappan, NJ: Fleming H. Revell Company, 1981), p. 104.
6. Michael Scanlan and Randall J. Cirner, *Deliverance from Evil Spirits* (Ann Arbor, MI: Servant Books, 1980).
7. Richardson, *Exorcism: New Testament Style*, 17; and Green, *I Believe in Satan's Downfall*, p. 126.
8. S. E. McClelland, "Demon, Demon Possession," *Evangelical Dictionary of Theology*, Walter A. Elwell, Editor (Grand Rapids, MI: Baker Book House, 1984), p. 307.
9. Duffield and Van Cleave, *Foundations of Pentecostal Theology*, p. 483.
10. Merrill F. Unger, *Biblical Demonology* (Wheaton, IL: Scripture Press, 1952).
11. Duffield and Van Cleave, *Foundations of Pentecostal Theology*, pp. 480-482.
12. Gordon Lindsay, *The Ministry of Casting Out Demons* (Dallas, TX: Christ for the Nations, 1977), p. 8.
13. Michael Harper, *Spiritual Warfare* (Plainfield, NJ: Logos International, 1970); Scanlan and Cirner, *Deliverance from Evil Spirits*; Green, *I Believe in Satan's Downfall*; John Wimber, *Power Evangelism* (San Francisco, CA: Harper and Row Publishers, 1986).
14. The Rite is found in the *Rituals Romanum*, 1614.
15. Toon, "Exorcism," *New International Dictionary of the Christian Church*, p. 365.
16. Ibid., p. 365.
17. Green, *I Believe in Satan's Downfall*, p. 114.
18. Harper, *Spiritual Warfare*, pp. 125-127.
19. Scanlan and Cirner, *Deliverance from Evil Spirits*, p. 66.
20. George Canty, "Demons and Casting Out Demons," *Pentecostal Doctrine*, Percy S. Brewster, Editor (Cheltenham, England: Grenehurst Press, 1976), p. 255.
21. Green, *I Believe in Satan's Downfall*, p. 132.

22. Mark I. Bubeck, *The Adversary* (Chicago, IL: Moody Press, 1975) pp. 129-130.
23. Arthur F. Glasser and Donald A. McGavran, *Contemporary Theologies of Mission* (Grand Rapids, MI: Baker Book House, 1983), pp. 119-120.
24. L. Grant McClung, Jr., *Azusa Street and Beyond: Pentecostal Missions and Church Growth in the Twentieth Century* (South Plainfield, NJ: Bridge Publishing, 1986), pp. 109-118.
25. H. A. Maxwell Whyte, *Dominion Over Demons* (Toronto, Canada: published by the author, 1972), p. 27.
26. Arthur Longley, *Christ Made Satan Useless* (Hull, England: Expositor Publications, n.d.), p. 93.
27. Duffield and Van Cleave, *Foundations of Pentecostal Theology*, 487; Conn, *The Anatomy of Evil*, 105; Canty, "Demons and Casting Out Demons," *Pentecostal Doctrine*, p. 250.
28. Canty, "Demons and Casting Out Demons," *Pentecostal Doctrine*, p. 251.
29. Duffield and Van Cleave, *Foundations of Pentecostal Theology*, p. 487.
30. Green, *I Believe in Satan's Downfall*, p. 127.
31. Wimber, *Power Evangelism*, p. 100.
32. Ibid., p. 98.
33. Duffield and Van Cleave, *Foundations of Pentecostal Theology*, pp. 487, 494-496; Conn, *The Anatomy of Evil*, pp. 105,132; Longley, *Christ Made Satan Useless*, pp. 86-90. See also the official statement of the General Presbytery of The Assemblies of God, "Can Born-Again Believers Be Demon Possessed?", May 1972 and a booklet by Church of God (Cleveland, TN) evangelist Dollas Messer, "Can a Demon Possess a Christian?" September 1975.
34. Whyte, *Dominion Over Demons*, p. 29; Lindsay, *The Ministry of Casting Out Demons*, pp. 26-32; Bubeck, *The Adversary*, pp. 83-85.
35. Gordon Lindsay, *Demon Manifestations and Delusion* (Dallas, TX: Christ for the Nations, 1972), p. 23.
36. Bubeck, *The Adversary*, p. 84.
37. Ibid., pp. 85, 87-88.
38. Green, *I Believe in Satan's Downfall*, p. 131.
39. Wimber, *Power Evangelism*, p. 187.
40. Scanlan and Cirner, *Deliverance from Evil Spirits*, pp. 27-36.
41. Richardson, *Exorcism: New Testament Style*, p. 39.
42. Thomas Lanier Lowery, *Demon Possession* (Cleveland, TN: T. L. Lowery Evangelistic Association, n.d.), pp. 33ff.; Mary Garrison, *How to Try a Spirit* (New Port Richey, FL: published by the author, 1976), p. 1.
43. Gordon Lindsay, *The Origin of Demons and Their Orders* (Dallas, TX: Christ for the Nations, 1972), pp. 14-21.
44. Green, *I Believe in Satan's Downfall*, p. 133.
45. Ibid., p. 134.
46. Richardson, *Exorcism: New Testament Style*, p. 20.
47. Lindsay, *Demon Manifestations and Delusion*, pp. 30-38.
48. Green, *I Believe in Satan's Downfall*, pp. 134-135.
49. Richardson, *Exorcism: New Testament Style*, p. 21; Green, *I Believe in Satan's Downfall*, p. 138; Gordon Lindsay, *Fallen Angels and Demons* (Dallas, TX: Christ for the Nations, 1972), p. 19.

214   *Wrestling with Dark Angels*

50. Green, *I Believe in Satan's Downfall*, pp. 137-139.
51. Harper, *Spiritual Warfare*, p. 111.
52. Richardson, *Exorcism: New Testament Style*, p. 25.
53. Duffield and Van Cleave, *Foundations of Pentecostal Theology*, p. 490.
54. Ibid., pp. 490-491.
55. Harper, *Spiritual Warfare*, p. 117.
56. Ibid., pp. 119-122.
57. Green, *I Believe in Satan's Downfall*, p. 145.
58. Ibid., p. 146-147.
59. Paul A. Pomerville, *The Third Force in Missions* (Peabody, MA: Hendrickson Publishers, 1985), p. 109.
60. Donald A. McGavran, "What Makes Pentecostal Churches Grow?" *Church Growth Bulletin*, Donald A. McGavran, Editor (Pasadena, CA: William Carey Library, 1977), pp. 97-99.
61. C. Peter Wagner, *Spiritual Power and Church Growth* (Altamonte Springs, FL: Strang Communications, 1986), pp. 126-129.
62. Christiaan DeWet, "The Challenge of Signs and Wonders in World Missions for the Twentieth Century," *Azusa Street and Beyond: Pentecostal Missions and Church Growth in the Twentieth Century*, L. Grant McClung, Jr., Editor (South Plainfield, NJ: Bridge Publishing, 1986), pp. 163-164.

Sickness and Suffering in the New Testament

PETER H. DAVIDS

PETER H. DAVIDS, associate professor of New Testament at Canadian Theological Seminary in British Columbia, has also taught at *Bibelschule Wiederest* in West Germany, Trinity Episcopal School for Ministry in Ambridge, Pennsylvania, and at New College in Berkeley, California. He has written two commentaries on the book of James, and numerous journal articles.

ANY evangelism that demonstrates the power of God will frequently express that power through either the expulsion of demons or through physical healing. That is the experience of many Christians today. However, while few Christians have doubts that God wants to expel demons, many Christians wonder if physical healing is really God's will. They may think that perhaps the illness is sent by God, and thus prayer is unwarranted. Or they may wonder if it is the experience of suffering that will bring a godly result, and feel that healing is a bypass of the divine will. While such questions are often asked about prayer for healing, they are rarely if ever asked about the medical treatment of illness. To be consistent the question should be asked of both.

Such doubts about the divine attitude will have a profound effect upon prayer for healing and therefore upon any power evangelism utilizing it. As Ken Blue has pointed out, belief that "God wills to heal the sick, that he desires wholeness rather than sickness for people," is one of the essential characteristics of all effective healing ministries.[1] But obviously for Christians there is no reason to believe what the Scripture does not teach, even if it is effective. Therefore it is necessary for us to examine the data of Scripture to see what it really does say about sickness and suffering.

The first point that can be established is that while illness and suffering have always been part of human life, they have strangely had little interest for biblical scholarship. An examination of the New Testament research of the past decade reveals several articles on the suffering of Jesus, another set of articles on specific suffering texts in James and 1 Peter, none of which refer to sickness, but only two exegetical articles on sickness, and those of limited scope. As a result of this vacuum Christians writing on healing, illness or suffering generally assume they know what the Scripture means by those terms, yet often display ignorance of biblical data.[2] While there have been some very helpful studies in this area, both practical and theoretical, most of them are flawed by the failure to have the relevant exegetical data in hand.[3] Our study will have to provide that data before discovering God's attitudes toward sickness and suffering.

Sickness in the New Testament

What does the New Testament speak of as sickness? Five general terms for sickness are used in the New Testament—104 times—although over half of these occurrences do not mean sickness. Besides these general terms, 16 specific terms are used 140 times for various physical and mental diseases.

The diseases mentioned, in descending order of frequency of the Greek terms used, are: blindness, lameness (crippled), dumbness and/or deafness (perhaps deaf-mutism), paralysis, leprosy (indicating a variety of skin disorders, not just Hansen's Disease), withered (stiff) limbs, fever, mania, deformity (crippled), dumbness (another term meaning "speechless"), moon-struck (perhaps meaning epilepsy), hemorrhage, speech impediment, dropsy, worm infestation and dysentery. What is notable here is that most of the diseases fall into three categories, namely sensory impairment, mobility impairment and skin disease, which is significant since it also made the person ritually impure. It is relatively less frequent that behavior disorders or infections are described. This observation probably reflects two things, that the Gospel writers remembered and recorded the more memorable, and thus physically outward cures; and that a society without modern medical technology focused on disease only after it manifested itself outwardly.

The Causes of Sickness

Before one prays for healing of a disease, it is helpful to know what caused it. One would not want to oppose God (Acts 5:39). On the other hand, removing symptoms without removing causation might lead to recurrence of the same or a worse disease. Although relatively little is said about the cause of disease in the New Testament, what is said is highly significant. Generally the causes fall into three categories.

1. *Sin*. A person's own sin can clearly be the cause of disease, according to Scripture. In 1 Cor. 11:30, Paul argues that some in Corinth are weak and sick because of their sin with respect to the unity of the Body at the Lord's Supper. James 5:14-16 notes that confession of sins will lead to healing, although the author stops short of tracing all sickness to sin, for, James states, "if he has committed any sins, he will be forgiven" (v. 15, *RSV*). Jesus, who can reject talk about connecting sin and sickness in John 9, can also say in John 5:14 (*RSV*), "See, you are well! Sin no more, that nothing worse befall you"—something worse than 38 years in bed. Again in Mark 2:5 Jesus forgives sins before going on to heal paralysis, which suggests that in this case He saw a connection. Further examples could be found, but these are enough to demonstrate that in all strands of the New Testament personal sin is seen as a common cause of sickness.[4]

2. *God*. If sin is a cause of sickness, does God ever cause sickness in the New Testament? He certainly does in the Old Testament; for example, "the Lord smote the king, so that he was a leper to the day of his death" (2

Kings 15:5, *RSV*).[5] However, many things that are said in the Old Testament, to have been directly caused by God, are given a more differentiated explanation in the New Testament. That something similar happens in the case of sickness, is indicated by the fact that the New Testament has very few passages in which sickness is traced to God. We will examine each of the four possible times this may have been the case.

First, *Ananias and Sapphira* (Acts 5:1-11). When Ananias and his wife lie to the Holy Spirit, they die. There is no indication as to what caused the deaths. Peter does not seem to anticipate Ananias' death, although after Ananias dies Peter is aware that Sapphira will also die (Acts 5:9). Probably the author's explanation, if he had given one, would have been that God or an angel visited the results of their sin upon them; but the text as it stands is not explicit about the causal agent.

Second, *Herod Agrippa* (Acts 12:20-23). Herod, after an oration, was acclaimed by his audience with the words, it is "The voice of a god, and not of a man!" Then "the angel of the Lord" struck him because "he did not give God the glory" (*RSV*). Here again a specific sin is mentioned. Presumably the close proximity to his murder of John is not accidental, although it is not named as a causal sin. The text does name the angel of the Lord, familiar from the Old Testament, as the ultimate cause, and worm damage as the proximate cause of death.

Third, *Elymas* (Acts 13:6-12). When Paul is explaining his message to the proconsul Sergius Paulus, a Jewish sorcerer, Elymas Bar-Jesus, attempts to discredit the message. Paul, under the power of the Holy Spirit, denounces him and prophesies his temporary blindness, which begins immediately. Here the disease and its connection to sin are clear. It is probable that the Holy Spirit is viewed as the agent causing the blindness. One cannot be certain, for it is possible that the prophetic word merely announces the event about to take place rather than causing the event.

Fourth, *the Corinthians* (1 Cor. 11). The 1 Cor. 11 passage has already been mentioned as an instance of sin as the reason for illness. But Paul goes on to say, "If we should examine ourselves we would not be judged. For the one who is judged by the Lord is disciplined" (see 1 Cor. 11:31-32). The implication of this passage, along with 1 Cor. 10 and its warnings, is that the Christians who have sinned are being disciplined by God through sickness "in order that [they] might not be condemned with the world." Here God is probably the cause of a number of sicknesses, and the reason for His action is to turn these people from sin and prevent their damnation.

We can summarize this data, then, by stating that there are some rare instances in the New Testament in which God is seen as the cause of disease. But in each of these few instances there is a specific sin involved. The purpose of the sickness is to stop further sin or to warn others away from sin. Therefore, God's sending disease is a minor sub-division of sin causing disease. Disease is never seen as something that God sends for our character development or growth. Disease is never said to develop such Christian virtues as patience, longsuffering, trust or faith, but rather something that in extreme cases God may use to stop our descent into further sin.

Viewed from the New Testament perspective then, if one has to ask, "Why did God send this disease?" and one is not suppressing awareness of sins, then God did not send it. Discipline only makes sense if those being disciplined know what their fault is (for example, what sin to repent of). Any other form of discipline is not only senseless, but is in fact a form of child abuse. Nor is God ever said in the New Testament to send sickness upon a family member for someone else's sin.

3. *Demonic forces.* In the New Testament demonic forces are connected to disease more frequently than God is. In 1 Cor. 5:5 Paul commands the church to turn a flagrant sinner over to Satan for the purpose of "the destruction of the flesh." This passage, as well as 1 Tim. 1:20, probably indicates an expectation that a person put out of the church, and thus away from the sphere of the protection of Christ, would be made ill by Satan. Luke 13:10-17 presents a woman bent over for 18 years by the "spirit of sickness" and describes her as one whom "Satan has bound." Furthermore, there are a number of cases like Mark 9 in which a dysfunction like mutism, or a disease like epilepsy, is attributed to a demon.

Yet, given that demons do cause illness in the New Testament, we cannot say that this is the normal cause. Most illness, in the New Testament period as today, was probably traced to "natural" causes. Many of the natural causes could be accidents. Others could be obvious inflammations. In some cases people surely traced them rightly or wrongly to diet and similar influences. But in the New Testament causation is only important if it must be removed before healing takes place. Cure, not cause, is its concern.

The Cure of Sickness

Except in cases in which illness is a judgment and the person either dies or otherwise disappears from the narrative, the treatment of illness and its outcome are also reported in the New Testament.

1. *Human care of the ill.* The fact of divine healing of sick people does not negate human care for health, or of

the sick. There are two types of such care. First, Paul can advise Timothy to drink a little wine for his stomach and his frequent sicknesses (1 Tim. 5:23). Paul recognizes that Timothy is frequently sick. He traces it to poor diet, perhaps abstinence from wine due to the ascetic teaching in Ephesus.

The ancients normally drank wine mixed two-thirds parts wine and one-third water. Their belief was that both water and wine alone were unhealthy. This view was held partly because it was more difficult to drink enough pure wine to quench thirst without getting drunk. Unscrupulous dealers watered their wine before sale, which means that when Jesus turned water into wine, the master of ceremonies' statement about its quality means in part that it was unwatered—it was the pure, strong stuff. Many ancients would have given Timothy the same advice Paul did.

Whatever Timothy's reasons for being sick, Paul advises the correction of diet rather than some other means of cure such as *pray harder, have more faith, live a more righteous life, cast out the demon who is harassing you.* Apparently, for Paul, divine healing did not negate the need for healthy living or exclude the use of medical treatments.

A second type of care for the sick is seen in Paul's advice in 1 Thess. 5:14, "Care for the *asthenon.*" We have left this term in Greek because it is often interpreted as spiritual weakness—for example, "help the weak" (*NIV*). The context, however, suggests that these are likely the physically sick, for people have been dying in Thessalonica (1 Thess. 4:13-18). It could be that the Christians were withdrawing from the sick, feeling that they were in some way being judged, in which case they are instructed instead to care for them. Or, it is possible that the Christians are simply being exhorted to care for those who are sick and perhaps about to die, by encouraging them with the hope of the Resurrection.[6] In either case, neither divine healing nor a possible connection of sickness to sin means that sympathetic care of the sick may be neglected. Examination of the *astheneo* (ill, sick) word group supports this conclusion. It appears 84 times in the New Testament. All uses in the Gospels, the prison and Pastoral Epistles, and the Catholic Epistles (except 1 Pet. 3:7, where *asthenes* indicates relative physical weakness) are for physical illness. In all but one case healing is accomplished or attempted. The exception, 2 Tim. 4:20, is inconclusive as to final outcome. In contrast, all uses in the Pauline writings are metaphorical. They indicate moral, personal or other weakness normally carefully qualified by a dative expression indicating what type of weakness is involved. Some forms of this type of weakness in others or in oneself may be endured, for it can lead to God's glory. In 2 Cor. 10-13, there are 14 occurrences in all. One should not mix physical with moral or spiritual meanings of *asthenes*, transferring proper attitudes toward one circumstance to the other.

2. *Divine healing of the sick.* Most references to sickness in the New Testament have to do with healing. Jesus was well known for His healings and expulsions of demons; Acts contains numerous examples of healing. In fact, in most of the places where sickness is mentioned, it is mentioned because someone is about to be healed, by one form or another, of divine intervention. In Matt. 10:8 healing is part of the commission of the 12. Healing also appears in the parallel passages in Mark and Luke, and in Luke's sending of the 70 (Luke 9:1; 10:9). Most significantly, Jas. 5:14-18 focuses on prayer for the sick. This passage is important for several reasons. First, it is in the final section of James, where the author of a letter usually

included a health wish. It is not in a section in which new material would normally be introduced. James, then, refers to prayer for healing by way of reminding them of the standard activity of the Church, in place of the customary pagan health wish. Pagans may wish for health or pray to their gods, but the prayer of faith in Christ or God really heals. Second, as noted above, sin is seen as a possible cause of illness, but not as its necessary cause. Third, God appears interested only in healing. If there is sin, get it confessed and forgiven so that healing may take place (Jas. 5:16); if there is no sin, pray immediately for healing. There is no implication that God would wish anything else than health for the Christian.[7]

3. *Uncured illness.* Having said that there is no implication that God would not will health, there are instances in the New Testament in which people are not well. For example, 2 Tim. 4:20 states that Paul left Trophimus sick in Miletus. Presumably Paul had prayed for him, and yet he was not well enough to travel when Paul had to move on. Or take Epaphroditus in Phil. 2:25-30, who was so sick he almost died. It is obvious that he had not been healed immediately, for Paul knew that the Philippians had heard of his sickness and had not yet heard of his healing. Paul attributes Epaphroditus' present health to God's having had mercy on him and on Paul as well. In other words, God had healed him. Whether in a sudden wonder or in a gradual progress we are not told, but He did not intervene before Epaphroditus came to the very door of death, and Paul came to the point of deep sorrow. Paul takes the restoration of Epaphroditus as a mercy from God, not as something that God had to do, sooner or later.

What strikes the reader in both of these passages is the somewhat casual attitude of Paul toward disease. He is unapologetic about leaving a colleague ill. His concern with

Epaphroditus does not include any sense of failure, in that his prayers were not answered immediately. When people are healed, Paul is thankful to God. If they are not, he does not appear to feel guilty, although he does seem sad. Instead, he is able to leave the results with God.

4. *Two problem cases.* We have deliberately not discussed two passages that may relate to sickness and healing, yet are problematic because of exegetical uncertainties involved in them. In order to explain the reasons for this, and because they are often dragged out as a type of red herring in any discussion of healing, it is necessary to make a detour to look at them.

First, *Paul's sickness in Galatia.* Paul reports that he preached in Galatia "due to fleshly weakness" (*NIV*: "illness," Gal. 4:13). He later notes that if they had been able they would have "dug [their] eyes out and given them to [him]" (v. 15). Unfortunately that is all we know about this incident. The "weakness" looks like a sickness, although alternative explanations are possible, for example, being depressed by the loss of John Mark. But assuming it is a sickness, we do not know what type it was, for the digging out of the eyes may be an idiom such as "I would have given my right leg to have him well again."

We also do not know why it was such a trial to the Galatians (4:14). Did it make him hard to understand or repulsive? Or was he unavailable due to his weakness and frequent need of rest? Or was it that his fleshly weakness seemed to contradict his proclamation of the reign of Christ? Finally, if he was sick, we do not know when or if Paul was healed, nor how it came about, if it did. What we can say is that assuming this was a sickness, Paul is as unapologetic about it as he is about Epaphroditus. It does not seem to have been a major issue for Paul how God eventually took care of the problem.

Second, *Paul's thorn.* Paul's thorn in the flesh (2 Cor. 12:7), which many people automatically connect to his problem in Galatia, is often assumed to be a sickness. Unfortunately for those who assume this, it is more likely that the thorn is the type of thing he mentions in 2 Cor. 12:10, that is human opposition, for that is the way the idiom is used in the Old Testament and that is what best fits the context in 2 Corinthians.

The only term in 2 Cor. 12 that might refer to sickness is *weakness* in 12:10. In 2 Cor. 10-13 Paul uses weakness 14 times; but in none of these uses is he referring to physical sickness, nor does he, unlike other New Testament authors, normally use this term elsewhere in his writings to refer to sickness. In other words, there are no terms in the context of 2 Cor. 12 that would normally mean sickness in a Pauline context; but there are a number of words that indicate types of social weakness or powerlessness.

When we turn to the phrase *thorn in the flesh* itself, we discover that in the Old Testament the only close equivalents refer to enemies who persecute or otherwise harass the Israelites.[8] While there are no terms in the context in 2 Corinthians that refer to sickness, there are plenty of references to false apostles who harassed Paul. In fact, 2 Cor. 10-13 is one long apologetic against these false apostles. It therefore seems logical to conclude that this ongoing persecution is what Paul refers to as his *thorn in the flesh.* Even if one does not accept this explanation, a study of the major commentaries would show it is still far from certain that sickness is intended; and if so, which illness. Thus, it would be unwise to attempt to build any generalization about sickness on this uncertain passage.[9]

We conclude, then, that if Paul was sick, he does not seem overly concerned about it. He has prayed for healing. Nor is God directly responsible for any sickness he may have, for even if 2 Corinthians refers to sickness, it is due to a *messenger of Satan* who afflicts Paul with God's permission. Thus it is sickness from an external, demonic cause, which brings us to suffering, the second major topic of our study.

Suffering in the New Testament

The English word suffering, and its equivalent in French and German, includes all causes of emotional and physical pain within its range of meanings and thus includes sickness. It is normally assumed that the New Testament concept of suffering is closely connected to that of sickness. But in the New Testament we are dealing with a Greek term and concept which overlap only part of the meanings of the English term. In fact, we will discover that we are dealing with quite a different complex of ideas than we were in discussing sickness. [10]

The first place to begin observing the differences between suffering and sickness is in the vocabulary of suffering. In the New Testament this terminology involves only one Greek word group, or two at most, along with a few other related terms. There are two advantages to this situation. First, there is a single Greek root translated by the English word "suffer"; and second, this root is an abstract term like its English counterpart. But this is also a confusing situation because there is not a complete semantic overlap between the English and Greek counterparts. This situation is made easier because of a very limited set of terms. [11]

We discover our first hint of the difference between suffering and sickness when we observe that the terms for suffering are never applied to physical disease. The one apparent exception is Matt. 17:15, and there the symptoms are ascribed not to physical causes but to a demon, an external force. This should not surprise us, for it is totally in line with the meaning of the terms in pre-New Testament Greek.

Likewise in Mark 5:26, the woman is not said to suffer from the disease, but to have suffered from physicians. One may be sick due to disease, but suffer due to external agency. In 1 Cor. 12:26 we have a problematic passage in that it is not clear at which level the Body/Church comparison is functioning. Is Paul applying the suffering vocabulary to physical pain and thus metaphorically to the Church? Or has he already made the mental shift to the members of the Church and thus applies the suffering vocabulary? Is he thinking of illness in the members of the Body, or of externally caused pain since the contrast is honor? In spite of the problematic passage and possible exceptions, it is clear that for the Greek speaking world suffering was something that came from outside a person. It is to these external causes that we now turn.

The Causes of Suffering

The causes of suffering in the New Testament can be divided into three groups. They look similar to the groups noted under sickness, but even here differences appear.

1. *Evil persons.* Persecution by evil persons can be a cause of suffering in the New Testament. For example, Jesus suffered at the hands of the elders and chief priests and scribes (Matt. 16:21). The Thessalonians suffer at the hands of their own fellow-citizens (1 Thess. 2:14). Christians, of course, are not the only ones to suffer; for example, certain Galileans suffered at the hands of Pilate (Luke 13:2).

2. *Demonic forces and Satan.* Behind the human forces

are the forces of Satan. A man's son is said to have suffered at the hands of a demon, which caused physical symptoms (Matt. 17:15). More commonly Satan appears as the ultimate cause of human persecution. For example, in Rev. 2:10 the Church is about to suffer because the devil will throw some of them into prison. This places much suffering, whether by direct demonic agency or through the use of human agents, into the context of the eschatological tension of the end of the age in which Christ reigns in heaven. But the earth is yet a scene of warfare between His Kingdom and that of the evil one.

3. *God.* The question arises, does God ever cause suffering. God does inflict pain upon individuals, but here the references are all to his eschatological judgment at the end of the age.[12] In each case the text does not use the term for suffering, but the term for affliction or tribulation. This drives a wedge between tribulation and the persecution or suffering which Christ and the Church experience. But even this affliction is part of the eschatological tension of the end of the age, for it is part of the preparation for the final consummation of the kingdom of God.

The Purpose of Suffering

While God is not said to be the cause of suffering, He does have a purpose for it. This is in contrast with sickness, which only once, in John 5:3 , is said to have a purpose. Indeed, what makes sickness so hard to bear for many people is that it comes without any apparent reason and serves no clear purpose. This is not to deny that in Christian experience there are cases in which God has used sickness, whatever its cause, to bring about some good result in a person's life. But this is not a teaching found in either Testament.

The purpose of suffering can be described in terms of *education* (Heb. 5:8) or *testing* (Heb. 2:18). While the reference in both of these passages is to Jesus, they are important in that they link suffering to the testing theme in Scripture. Here again God is not the subject. In fact, Jas. 1:13 denies that God tests anyone, but the results of testing are the development of character, especially patient endurance and longsuffering.[13] Thus, while suffering is not pleasant, it can have a good result, even a reward (1 Pet. 2:19, 20).

The question arises, then, whether the "various tests" of Jas. 1:2 and 1 Pet. 1:6 might include sickness. We must answer this in the negative. Tests in the New Testament arise from desire within (Jas. 1:14) or Satan and his agents including human agents (Luke 22:31). They come in connection with challenges to obey God, even when it may seem that obedience will mean failure and death, as is the case of the testing of Jesus in Matt. 4. But tests are not said to come from sickness, and they are explicitly said not to come from God (Jas. 1:13).

Another reason for suffering is that it is part of the imitation of Christ. Peter refers to this theme in several passages, all of which suggest that because Christ suffered Christians are called to suffer. They will be like their Lord.[14]

The rewards of suffering for the sake of Christ and its development of character explain why it is to some extent in God's will. We say "to some extent" because Peter implies in his grammatical constructions that suffering *might* be the will of God, although it is not necessarily so. In fact, the whole thrust of 1 Pet. 2-4 is to minimize the causes of suffering in the Christian life.

Thus, the Christian prays, "Do not lead us to the test, but deliver us from the evil one." At the same time he or she knows that Christ was not always delivered; and, if the test is properly controlled as 1 Cor. 10:13 states and 1 Pet. 4:19 implies, the suffering can be for their good.

This explains, in part, why Jesus and His followers can speak of the necessity of suffering. Paul could say that entering the kingdom of God involved much tribulation (Acts 14:22). Even if God could remove all of this suffering, He would not, for it is good for us.

Yet, this is only a partial explanation. The other explanation is found in such passages as John 16:33, where suffering is an expression of the eschatological conflict between Christ and the world. Until Christ returns to consummate His Kingdom and fully express His victory, there will be suffering for those who are identified with Him and yet live in the world.

The Response to Suffering

If the above is true, then there are proper responses to suffering. The first is to *recognize that it is a privilege to suffer.* Phil. 1:29 expresses this sense of privilege that one is granted not only to believe on Christ but also to suffer for Him.

Here again we see a difference between sickness and suffering. While God may use sickness to His glory, and the one recorded instance in John 9 is through healing the sickness not through enduring it, it is never said that one can be sick for Christ. Sickness is part of the curse of death and comes to Christians and non-Christians alike, for we have not yet received the redemption of the body in its fullness (Rom. 8). But the suffering with which the New Testament is concerned is the unique privilege of Christians; for only they can suffer for Christ.

The second response is to *realize that suffering is the*

doorway to blessing. Paul experiences this as an identification with Christ (Phil. 3:10). Furthermore, suffering is the means to experiencing the comfort of God (2 Cor 1:5-7). Finally, this brings favor with God, or blessedness (1 Pet. 2:20; 3:14).

It may be because of this sense of blessing attached to suffering that Peter makes it clear that all suffering is not blessed. Christians are not to invite suffering through doing wrong (1 Pet. 4:15), nor to consider punishment for their failures to be blessed (1 Pet. 2:20). The danger in the Early Church was that to which the Post-Apostolic Church succumbed, that of seeking suffering to convince oneself of one's special relationship to God, rather than simply serving God and allowing to come whatever suffering may come. Peter also saw the danger that people who were simply disagreeable or sinful might label the suffering they experienced godly suffering rather than admitting that it was well-deserved.

Third, one should *meet suffering with patient endurance.* This is the message of Jas. 5:7-11 and similar passages.

Fourth, one should *rejoice in suffering.* This is not pleasure in pain, but an eschatological joy in anticipation of the eventual reward. One tastes the blessedness in advance, so to speak.[15]

Conclusion

Our survey of the data on *suffering* and *sickness* has been brief, but it is fair to draw several general conclusions from our observations.

1. *There is a distinction between the two categories.* The vocabulary of suffering is not applied to sickness and the sickness vocabulary is not applied to suffering.

2. *There is a difference in the valuation of suffering and sickness.* Sickness in the New Testament is viewed negatively. It is not sent by God, except for punishment of sin, and that is a rare occurrence. Naturally, God can use anything in our lives for His own good purposes (Rom. 8:28), but sickness by itself is viewed as an enemy, like death—part of the Fall and the curse. It does not bring a blessing nor is it the mark of a pious life.

Suffering is viewed positively. It can be part of an identification with Christ and can lead to positive benefits for the Christian. At the same time, God does not send suffering upon the Christian, but allows a Christian to enter into it. Its sources are in the eschatological tension between the kingdom of God, to which Christians belong, and the forces in control of this present age.

3. *The response to suffering and sickness differs in the New Testament.* Sickness is to be healed. It is never welcomed, but always prayed against. Full redemption means the removal of all sickness (Rom. 8:23). If it is due to sin and thus perhaps discipline from God, the sin is to be confessed so the healing can take place (Jas. 5:14-16). There is no hint that continuing in sickness is in itself beneficial, although, as mentioned above, God is quite capable of turning any situation to our benefit, from our sins to our sicknesses.

At the same time, there is no sense of guilt among New Testament authors when a person is not healed. Healing is not automatic, but is a gift of God and thus at God's disposal, not the Christian's. Thus, when people are not healed, or are healed slowly, there is no apologetic needed (nor are there any cautions in passages like Jas. 5, to indicate that lack of effectiveness in prayer was a problem for that age). And, every healing is viewed as mercy.

On the other hand, suffering is to be endured. While it

is not to be sought, it is part of the eschatological tension inherent in following Christ in a world in rebellion against God. The contrast becomes especially clear in Matt. 10 and Jas. 5. In both passages there are commands to pray for the sick and demonized with the expectation of healing. In both passages suffering is presented as a separate issue and the call is to endure it. The non-acceptance of sickness and the acceptance of suffering stand in stark contrast.

4. *Both suffering and sickness can be attributed to evil.* Sickness is due to human and demonic evil. It is part of the Fall and comes upon people due to sin (either their own or the general fallenness of the world) or to demonic attack.

Suffering is likewise due to human and demonic evil. It comes upon people due either to the sinfulness of other human beings or to demonic/Satanic attack, often through human beings.

5. *God is the source of healing.* On rare occasions God is said to send sickness as a punishment for sin, but the implication is that repentance brings healing. God finds no good in the sickness itself, but in the repentance it may produce.

Normally, God is presented as healing illness. Jesus, the full revelation of God, heals all He meets. The disciples, the trained representatives of Jesus, likewise heal. Paul knows of gifts of healing and attributes them to the Spirit sent by God. James gives no indication that a true prayer of faith will result in anything but healing. There is no indication that sickness is good for a person or that God takes any pleasure in it.

6. *God is sovereign over suffering.* While God does not normally send suffering, He is the one who protects the Christian from the evil one. Thus, God is sovereign over suffering.

God's will does allow for the suffering of Christians,

because it produces present character and future blessedness. Thus, patient endurance of suffering receives a reward.

The fact that God allows Satan and evil persons to persecute Christians does not rule out His deliverance. Jas. 5:11 points to the deliverance that Job received, and Jas. 5:13 indicates that the sufferer should pray. While the content of the prayer is not stated, prayer for endurance and deliverance such as Paul writes about in 2 Cor. 1:8-11 seems implied by the context.

It is clear that we are dealing with two categories of thought in the New Testament when we speak of sickness and suffering. Each of these must be handled separately. It is when this happens that the Church will be in the best position to clearly announce the proper comfort of God to both the sick and the suffering, without confusing the categories and applying comfort to the wrong human situation. It is when this happens that the Church will be in the best position to demonstrate the power of God, often through healing, in a world in rebellion against God, and to accept the suffering for Christ which will likely come as a consequence.

Notes

1. Ken Blue, *Authority to Heal* (Downers Grove, IL: InterVarsity Press, 1987), p. 122. Note that all of his chapter 5 is given to arguing this point.
2. E. G. Dobson, "Suffering and Sickness," *Fundamentalist Journal*, 1987, 6: pp. 16-17, 54, 63, shows absolutely no awareness of the differences among the terms he lumps together.
3. Ken Blue, *Authority to Heal* is the biblically best informed of these, as well as being soundly practical. It is the published version of his DMin. thesis from Fuller Theological Seminary. J. H. Ellens, "Toward a Theology of Illness," *Journal of Psychology and Christianity* Vol. 3, 1981, pp. 61-73 is a fine theoretical discussion. D. Amundsen's article in R. L. Numbers and D. W. Amundsen, eds., *Caring and Curing: Health and Medicine in Western Religious Traditions* (New York: Macmillan, 1988) mixes the concepts of

sickness and suffering as if the New Testament overlapped to two in either vocabulary or approach.

4. In other words, the more absolute sin-sickness equation of the Old Testament, which is never absolute and has already been rejected in Job, is viewed as a totally inadequate explanation of illness in the New Testament, although it is admitted that the equation is based on a truth, i.e. that sin as a cause of *some* disease. See Peter H. Davids, *Themes in the Epistle of James that are Judaistic in Character* (University of Manchester, Unpublished Ph.D. thesis, 1974), pp. 94-183, although this was written at a time when the author did not recognize the distinction between sickness and suffering in the New Testament.

5. Compare 2 Kings 15:5 with 2 Chron. 26:20.

6. This interpretation was suggested to this author by Gordon Fee from his work on Thessalonians. It is possible that this "weakness" is a result of persecution, but if this term refers to physical disability, that is unlikely, for one would expect the support of such people to have been less of a problem and would also expect to find suffering vocabulary used.

7. See Peter H. Davids, *Commentary on James: New International Greek Testament Commentary* (Grand Rapids: Eerdmans, 1982), for further discussion of this passage. Likewise, in the Gospels there is no example of Jesus refusing to extend healing to people approaching Him, nor do we read of any deliberation in Acts as to whether or not it is God's will to heal.

8. Num. 33:55; Josh. 23:13; Ezek. 2:6; 28:24; and Judg. 2:3 has the term in some English translations, but has no Hebrew equivalent of "thorn." Paul, of course, was steeped in the Old Testament and its imagery.

9. See F. F. Bruce, *1 and 2 Corinthians* (London: Paternoster Press, 1971), p. 248, for the variety in the interpretation of this phrase. Charles K. Barrett, *The Second Epistle to the Corinthians* (New York: Harper & Row, 1973) pp. 314-316, is even more doubtful about the thorn being physical. So also Victor P. Furnish, *Corinthians II* (New York: Doubleday, 1984) pp. 528-529, 547-550. See also Phillip E. Hughes *Commentary on the Second Epistle to the Corinthians* (Grand Rapids: Eerdmans, 1962), pp. 442-448.

10. Much of this material in this section of this paper was published as "Suffering: Endurance, and Relief," in *First Fruits* (July/August, 1986), pp. 7-11.

11. Virtually every time the word suffer or suffering appears in an English translation it translates the *pascho* ("suffer") word group, which includes *pascho, propascho, sumpascho, pathema, kakopatheo;* See W. Michaelis, *"pascho,"* Theological Dictionary of the New Testament V: 904-939; B. Gartner, "Suffer," *Dictionary of New Testament Theology* III: 719-725.

   The *thlipsis* ("oppression, affliction") word group, while not translated "suffer," does include ideas which are common to it and the *Pascho* word group. This word group includes *thlipsis, thlibo;* cf. H. Schlier, *"thlibo, thlipsis,"* Theological Dictionary of the New Testament III: 139-148; G. Ebel and R. Schippers, *"Persecution,"* Dictionary of New Testament Theology II: 805-809.

   In the LXX *pascho* appears with a Hebrew equivalent only in Amos 6:6. Otherwise it appears almost exclusively in the intertestamental literature, especially 1 and 2 Maccabees, which are concerned with the persecution of the Jews by Seleucid rulers. The *thlipsis* word group does appear frequently in the Old Testament, mostly for the *tsar* ("pressure" or "weight") word group and mostly in the Psalms. It also is focused on situations of persecution.

"Test," *peirasmos,* "persecute," *dioko,* "lack," *hustereo,* "experience loss," *zemioo,* "evil situation," *kakosis* are all related to the idea of "suffering."

12. Rom. 2:9; 2 Thess. 1:6; and Rev. 2:22.
13. Peter H. Davids, *Commentary on James* (Grand Rapids: Eerdmans, 1982), pp. 35-38 and in the literature cited there.
14. 1 Pet. 2:21; 3:17, 18; 4:1.
15. 1 Pet. 1:6-7; Jas. 1:2-4; Rom. 5:3; 1 Pet. 4:13. See also Paul's underlying meaning in passages like Rom. 8:18.

RESPONSE
BY
WALTER R.
BODINE

Sickness and Suffering in the New Testament

I count it a privilege to respond to the paper by Peter Davids. I had heard of this research some months previously from George Mallone. When George briefly summarized Peter's argument for me, I was both encouraged and hesitant. I sensed, in what I understood to be the basic thrust of the argument, a long needed corrective for the Church's attitude toward sickness. At the same time, I responded with discomfort to some of the specific interpretations and some of the distinctions. When I received the paper and worked my way through it, both reactions emerged again.

Let me begin in the affirmative with a couple of specifics and then move to the broader questions that are raised. The point is well taken that objections to healing prayer based on the view that sickness is sent by God should be equally applied to the use of medical treatment. If one does not wish to receive prayer for healing because of the potential spiritual value of sickness, neither should one visit a doctor. If one calls upon medical assistance with the anticipation of accepting the sickness as God's will if the treatment is not effective, then the same approach can be followed with respect to prayer.

The observation that the Gospel writers focused on memorable outward cures is helpful and probably explains why there is not more notice of emotional healings. They are, in any case, clearly a part of God's provision for His people and explicit in the Messiah's agenda (Ps. 147:3; Isa. 61:1).[1]

I also want to acknowledge my agreement with Peter's exegesis of 2 Cor. 12:7-10. I have wrestled at length with his treatment of Paul's "thorn in the flesh." I have done my best to find weaknesses in his explanation that would enable me to continue to believe that the thorn was a physical illness. I have failed to find them and changed my mind. My turning point came in recognizing the usage of weakness (*astheneia*) in 2 Cor. 11:30-33, clearly in the sense of "social weakness or powerlessness." With the connection of 2 Cor. 12:5 with *boasting in weaknesses* forming the link, this is surely the meaning in chapter 12:9, 10, especially in light of the other uses of astheneia in chapters 10-13.

Now, for some larger issues. I believe that this paper offers a fundamental corrective to the view of sickness that many evangelicals grew up with, including myself. Apart from Pentecostal and charismatic circles, sickness has been viewed primarily as something to be endured. The possibility of divine healing has not been denied outright, though the operation of healing gifts has, and sometimes it has been prayed for.[2] Still, it has been seen a remote possibility for the most part. Prayer has been focused on wisdom and skill for the doctor and grace for the patient. The redeeming benefits of enduring sickness have been emphasized, and where there has been hope of recovery, it has centered in medical science at the practical level. As Christians, we have trusted God to use our doctors and their technology for our healing.

Modern medicine and doctors are a gift of God, and God does indeed work through these means. It was so even in Paul's day, as Peter Davids has shown.[3] Prayer and faith along these lines are quite proper. Our problem has not been that these things have been wrong, but that other gifts of God for our healing, specifically His healing gifts distributed in the Church and His healing power released through believing prayer, have been more or less non-functional. Because these avenues were understood to be limited to the first century, they have not been freely practiced. At best, we have had little or no experience in such things and consequently have shied away from them, or we have attempted to practice them only with reticence.[4] At worst, they have been forbidden and, as a result, ruled out as a possibility.[5]

Yet, from a New Testament perspective, the primary response of the Church to sickness should be an expectant looking to God for His divine healing through prayer and the operation of the gifts of the Spirit. The paper sets forth some of this evidence, and the overall argument calls for this posture toward sickness. One of the precious results of the movement that C. Peter Wagner has called the "Third Wave" is that evangelicals are now joining their charismatic brothers and sisters in receiving the healing work of the Spirit, both for their own benefit and for the benefit of others to whom they minister.[6] The papers in this symposium, including the one by Peter Davids, should be a help along these lines.

This movement is a gracious gesture of the heavenly Father toward His evangelical children in the West. The genuine work of the Holy Spirit has been manifested throughout church history, though unevenly, and more extensively among Pentecostals and charismatics in this century. These believers deserve our appreciation for their willingness to pioneer the way in the recovery of many of the gifts of the Spirit. Evangelicals have no valid excuse for not having participated with them. Admittedly, there have been distortions in their movements in both theology and practice.[7] One of the leading criticisms from evangelicals has been their lack of theological underpinnings based on sound exegesis. Yet, if this criticism were serious and we had been practicing the unity our Lord calls for in His Body, we should have responded by getting involved and helping work out that needed theology. We did not. But the Lord has extended His forgiveness and is now coming to us on our own turf, so to speak, pouring out His Spirit on evangelicals, as such. He is truly a merciful Father. As a result, we have another chance to join in the task of theologizing about the work of the Holy Spirit.

Having said these things in support of what I understand to be one of the primary points of the paper, I must now raise a question about the main distinction that is drawn, that between suffering and illness, at least as it is presently set forth. The distinction seems questionable to me.

My fundamental concern is that we not allow the task of elaborating an adequate view of healing to so absorb us that we overlook or misconstrue other truth. Let me phrase it as a question. In trying to restore God's primary disposition toward healing,[8] are we in danger of negating the positive role that sickness can play for people whom God does not will to heal?

As an example of a comparable tactical mistake, I believe that an unfortunate move was made in Pentecostal theology when speaking in tongues was designated as the "initial physical evidence" of Spirit baptism.[9] This gift did, in fact, serve as evidence of the reception of the Spirit on several occasions (Acts 2:4; 10:44-47; 19:6; and 8:15-18).

Granting the inference that it was tongues that Simon saw, no Scripture identifies tongues, or any other specific gift, as a necessary evidence of Spirit baptism. The teaching to this effect goes beyond the biblical text and has done considerable harm to believers who sincerely seek the fullness of the Spirit, but do not receive tongues. They are shut up by this teaching to several alternatives, none of which is desirable.

One could imagine the same kind of mistake with respect to the role of dreams in a believer's life. In Matt. 1-2 there is indication of a concerted use of dreams, in the life of Joseph especially, as a means of guidance (1:20; 2:12, 13, 19, 22). By a reasoning process similar to the above mentioned view of tongues, one could infer and teach on the basis of these passages that dreams are essential to guidance. This would, however, be going beyond the Scripture, which only records that dreams were so employed at that time. It does teach elsewhere that dreams have a function in the life of believers (Acts 2:17), but never that they are essential.

So it is with tongues. We can observe from the record in Acts that God did use tongues as an evidence of Spirit baptism on several occasions. On the other hand, there is no biblical statement that tongues must be present when Spirit baptism occurs. In an enthusiasm to recover something valuable that had been lost, a step was taken beyond the biblical text, with hurtful consequences. If they who affirm all of the gifts of the Spirit are concerned to hold forth a convincing witness to Christian brothers and sisters, then they must be willing to do what they want to see others do: to change doctrinal positions when such change is indicated. This is a case in point.[10]

I am raising the question here of whether in the present discussion we may be in danger of going beyond the biblical text in the subject of healing and ending up with a position which would be hurtful to another group of sincere believers. This would be those who are sick and pursue, but do not receive, the Lord's healing. If we end up saying, "There is not a hint that continuing in sickness is in itself beneficial," where will this leave such people?

The primary question, of course, is what the Bible actually teaches. Let me then address the issue with some particulars. In Davids' paper he states that, "Disease is never seen as something that God sends for our character development or growth." Yet, in 1 Cor. 11:30-32 it is acknowledged that God sends sickness to retrieve sinning Christians. Since the verb for discipline in the passage is *paideuo* (v. 32), this is an indication of character development. While the believers at Corinth were involved to a serious degree of sin, all sanctification includes dealing with sin, among other things; and the Corinthians who benefited from this discipline surely grew in their character.

In reference to the *asthenes* word group, Davids states that "all uses in the Pauline writings are metaphorical." Yet, 1 Cor. 11:30 and Gal. 4:13 both seem to clearly refer to physical illness.[11] Again we read that "the terms for suffering are never applied to physical disease." But the term for testing, *peirasmos,* is applied to Paul's sickness in Gal. 4:14. While the pronoun is perhaps second person plural and there is a textual problem with the majority text having the first singular, and that pronoun refers to the Galatians, shall we assume that Paul did not feel the testing they felt? He was sufficiently conscious of their feelings to speak to them about how they felt. In any case, *suffering* terminology is applied to sickness, at least insofar as Paul's sickness was a testing to the Galatians.

This is perhaps a good place for a broader comment on

methodology. I am not comfortable with conclusions drawn on the basis of what vocabulary is or is not applied to a given subject. There are other possible reasons as to why a given set of terms may not be used of a given subject, including the limited corpus of our literature in the New Testament or, for that matter, the entire Bible; the fact that a writer may have simply not needed the terminology in question to make his point and, mere happenstance. The absence of terminology in reference to a subject may or may not be significant. It is, at most, an argument from silence.

Overall, I wonder if it might be helpful to view sickness as a subclass of suffering, along with persecution, satanic attack and accidents and to make the same observations about them both. It is already acknowledged that they are both due to evil and that the statement of God's direct agency in sending them is relatively rare. Should we not also say that they are both viewed negatively in that God is sometimes pleased to deliver people from them? This view is in contrast to statements in this paper, where sickness is viewed negatively, but suffering is viewed positively. In support of this, it can be observed that the New Testament authors acknowledge deliverance from suffering due to persecution (Acts 12:3-17; 2 Tim. 3:11; 4:17); and Paul urged others to pray for his deliverance from persecution (Rom. 15:31; 2 Cor. 1:8-11; 2 Thess. 3:2). The author of the Pastoral Epistles speaks once rather comprehensively of deliverance from all persecutions and sufferings while, in the same breath, putting his readers on notice that all who pursue godliness will be persecuted (2 Tim. 3:11, 12).[12] I should have thought that prayer for deliverance would be prominent in the section dealing with response to suffering in light of such Scriptures as these.[13] On the other hand, could all that is said positively about our response to suffering be said of sickness as well, in cases where healing may not be God's will?

The point of arguing for sickness to be regarded as a subclass of suffering is to recognize that the same responses to both are called for in biblical texts. I have just shown that prayer for deliverance from persecution is called for. Such prayers, of course, were not always answered in the affirmative (Heb. 11:32-40). It is also true that occasions appear in which healing of sickness has not been forthcoming, although prayer for healing may be assumed to have been offered (Gal. 4:13-15; Phil. 2:25-30; 1 Tim. 5:23; 2 Tim 4:20).[14]

Furthermore, the text does recognize, at least implicitly, the potential benefit of sickness when healing is not God's will. I have already pointed out the uses of the word *paideuo* in 1 Cor. 11:32 with reference to the sickness of some of the believers at Corinth. This verb would relate their sickness to the larger context of discipline in such a passage as Heb. 12:4-11, where the aim of such experiences is character development in the believer (Heb. 12:10, 11). One of the key words used to describe the results of suffering in a believer's life when properly received is *hupomone* (Rom. 5:3, 4; Jas. 1:3, 4). The same word is used by James of the results in the life of Job of his response to suffering, which included the illness he suffered at the hands of Satan (Jas. 5:11).

Having said this, I want to recognize that Peter has correctly observed a difference in the treatment of sickness and suffering due to persecution. It is true that in Matt. 10, for example, the call is for ministry to the sick with a view to healing, while the emphasis with regard to persecution is on endurance. I would not, however, want to leave this as a "stark contrast" which indicates "two categories of thought."

I hope that my comments have established a broader picture so that we should, rather, see a different emphasis in the treatment of two common experiences in the life of the followers of Christ. Both sickness and suffering due to persecution are undesirable and, when experienced, may be prayed about in the hope of deliverance. Such deliverance may be more often God's will in case of sickness, but He may, on occasion, will that sickness continue for the greater ultimate good of the believers. While persecution will perhaps more often need to be endured, it is sometimes God's will to deliver; and this may be prayed for expectantly.[15]

Before closing I want to reaffirm my appreciation for both the spirit and the expertise evident in Peter Davids' paper. It was a beneficial experience to work on it, and I appreciate the light it has brought to me.

Notes
1. There undoubtedly are objectionable practices employed in some forms of what is often called "inner healing." This does not warrant the wholesale rejection of the term, however, since it is clear from the biblical text that the Lord desires to heal people emotionally as well as physically.
2. I refer here to the cessationist teaching, which affirms that some of the gifts of the Spirit passed from use with the closing of the New Testament canon, or the death of the apostles. Those gifts most often designated as temporary in this sense include healing, miracles, prophecy, tongues and interpretation of tongues. While dispensational theology is often identified with the cessationist viewpoint, this position is equally at home in reformed circles, as witnessed by the influential book *Counterfeit Miracles* by the well-known reformed theologian B.B. Warfield (Edinburgh: The Banner of Truth Trust, 1972, [first edition 1918].) The cessationist viewpoint is a part of the larger theological heritage of many Western evangelicals. I will argue that it is an unfortunate part of this heritage.
3. Further indications of Paul's favorable attitude toward the medical profession can be inferred from his taking Luke along in his traveling company and referring to him as "the beloved physician" (Col. 4:14).
4. Of course there are exceptions among evangelicals to these generalizations. God in His graciousness comes as far as He can to meet us wherever we are.
5. An unbiased and straightforward reading of the New Testament reveals, it

seems to me, continuity in the operation of all of the gifts of the Spirit from Pentecost until the return of Christ. The present age is to be characterized by the supernatural operation of the Spirit in all believers (Acts 2:16-21). Paul taught the use of all of the gifts to the churches, with never a hint of any distinction between some that would be permanent and some that would be temporary (Rom. 12:6-8; 1 Cor. 12:4-11, 28-30; Eph. 4:11). He indicated, in fact, that the gifts would operate until the Second Coming. (1 Cor. 13:8-10, speaking specifically of prophecy, tongues and knowledge, with "the perfect" obviously referring to the Lord's return in light of verse 12). All efforts to find teaching of the cessation of certain gifts during this age are strained and unconvincing.

6. C. Peter Wagner, "A Third Wave? An Interview with C. Peter Wagner," *Pastoral Renewal* 8:1, July/August 1983: 1-5.

7. I hasten to add that Western evangelical theology and practice have by no means been without flaws. There will be no immaculate theology as long as theologies are constructed by humans. Regardless of one's view of the nature of Scripture, every elaboration on the meaning of Scripture must be regarded as an approximation and always remain open to the need of change for the sake of improvement.

8. This is, I believe, the proper conclusion to draw from the significant data briefly summarized by Davids in his paper.

9. Carl Brumback, *What Meaneth This?* (Springfield: The Gospel Publishing House, 1947), pp. 184-88, is a clear statement of this understanding.

10. I do not want the spirit of this paragraph and the preceding one to be misunderstood. I delight to be one in the Body of Christ with Pentecostal and charismatic believers. I relish opportunities to learn from them. But if we are going to be all the Lord wants us to, we must be open to mutual critique.

11. While I recognize that the Pastoral Epistles are not generally attributed to Paul by New Testament scholars (otherwise 1 Tim. 5:23 and 2 Tim. 4:20 should be included), I was under the impression that Philippians is (although its integrity is often questioned). Unless Davids does not accept Pauline authorship for the passage, Phil. 2:26-27 should also be included in the list. I believe, in any case, that 1 Corinthians and Galatians are generally accepted as Pauline.

12. I take no position on the authorship of the Pastoral Epistles for the purpose of this response, but I do cite them freely, assuming that whatever Davids' position on the question may be, he would regard them as canonical Scripture.

13. The possibility of deliverance from persecution is acknowledged.

14. Davids also assumes that prayer for healing had been offered on such occasions.

15. This would in no way minimize the validity and urgency of prayer for healing, but it would leave open the possibility of a believer accepting sickness as a dignified option with redeeming possibilities when God has given a negative indication with regard to healing. On the other hand, it would encourage prayer for deliverance in the face of persecution, while preserving the helpful teaching which Peter has assembled for those who are not to be delivered, but must endure their persecution.

CHAPTER
9

In Dark Dungeons of Collective Captivity

F. DOUGLAS PENNOYER

F. DOUGLAS PENNOYER, coeditor of these lectures, is director of the Intercultural Institute of Missions at Seattle Pacific University. He is an anthropologist, church planter, two-time Fulbright scholar and former corporate executive. Dr. Pennoyer teaches courses in anthropology and missiology, and conducts seminars on spiritual warfare.

DEMONIZATION is a personal relationship, the imposition of an evil spirit into the life of a human being. The Bible contains numerous accounts of demonization, and personal case histories on the subject can be found in bookstores around the world. Much less attention has focused on the collective impact of demonized individuals in their society or subculture. We may be somewhat familiar with the classic manifestation of extreme individual demonization, such as unusual strength, other voices and disclosure of private information. But what are some of the features of a society or subculture where the majority of individuals are demonized? To begin to explore this topic, I've chosen to tell some of my personal encounters with an isolated society, the Tawbuid of Mindoro, Philippines. This will provide us with the background to discuss the concept of collective captivity, the idea that demons working through individuals can control the society to some extent and actively use the system to prevent the gospel light from penetrating into members' lives. Once the good news arrives, demonic strategies flow with the changing culture. The demonic goal is to keep the captives in the devil's dark dungeon, in a kind of collective captivity that discourages the individual from breaking out and into the kingdom of light.

Power to Cross the River and Landslide

I had been hiking in the Philippine forest for five hours. My legs ached from yesterday's long journey and my back felt the heavy weight of a 60-pound pack. It was refreshing to see the cool waters of a highland river. Swollen to twice its normal size, the muddy waters churned and flowed swiftly. I wanted to cross it right now for we had to reach the Tawbuid village tonight.

"It's too high," my Buhid guide said. "We'll wait until tomorrow and maybe it will go down." The strains of a song drifted into my mind, "Got any rivers you think are uncrossable . . . He can do what no other power can do." Across the wide river I saw faces peering from the bushes. They were watching and wondering if the tall white stranger would attempt to cross the river. If I did, I knew they would disappear, because the Tawbuid always ran on sight of strangers.

I unstrapped my pack and put it on top of my head. It was heavy but manageable. Would I lose it if I stumbled? Would I be swept downstream or drowned? "When you pass through the waters, I will be with you; and when you pass through the rivers, they will not sweep over you" (Isa. 43:2, *NIV*). That is the promise I needed. My feet groped for steady rocks as I began to cross, and my confidence increased as the distance to the other side became shorter and shorter. The imaginary cheers of the silent audience on the other shore rang in my ears as I saw them start to leave. They were gone when I arrived, exhausted, on the other side.

"Lunaw! Come over here!" I shouted across the river. He ignored me and sat down on a log. No amount of argument would persuade him. I had to go get him. I had to cross the river three times that day.

It was a surrealistic scene. A young American anthropologist with a rope around his chest leading a short Buhid tribesman through the flood waters. The water reached Lunaw's neck but he held tightly onto the lifeline and we both made it safely to the other side.

Our clothes dried as we ate lunch in the hot, noontime sun. Hiking away from the river, we climbed up onto a high mountain ridge. Two hours later, the trail ended at a landslide. An unstable side of the mountain had given way, sending rocks and earth down on the thin ridge trail, leaving a 300-foot gap filled only with loose soil. Six hundred feet below, the bottom of the landslide was filled with large boulders. There were no footprints in the soil; no one had attempted to go across the landslide.

I surveyed it carefully. "How many hours to hike down, around and up to the other side?" I asked Lunaw.

"About one hour only," he replied.

Actually two real hours, I thought; *I just don't have the strength to do that.*

As if he were reading my mind, Lunaw simply said, "Don't, don't do it. Come with me."

I started onto the landslide very slowly. Each footstep sent showers of little rocks rolling down to the boulders below. "Oh, God, you got me through the river this morning, get me across this landslide now," I prayed. "Got any mountains you can't tunnel through, God specializes in things thought impossible." Halfway across, I determined it was impossible. I felt like Peter who began walking on water with confidence and then began to sink. I, too, cried out, "Lord, save me," and proceeded ahead, but only because it was the same distance back to where I had started.

My hands were shaking as I stepped off the landslide onto the firm trail. "Lunaw, you go around! I'll wait for you here," I shouted. I was not going back and bring him across the landslide. I had hauled him through the floodwaters but I didn't have the faith or strength to bring him across the landslide. I realized that I had foolishly cast myself on God's grace twice that day. However, I had no way of knowing that my divine deliverance at the river and at the landslide would brand me as a person with unusual power and contribute to my eviction from two highland villages and a lowland Buhid settlement. I would learn later that such displays of power or mastery over nature simply signified that the individual could also control people and animals through potent curses. Unknowingly, I had demonstrated to the Tawbuid that I was a powerful person and one who should be greatly feared.

Thrice Evicted

In 1973, I was able to penetrate into the interior villages of the Buhid and Tawbuid in the highlands of Mindoro, Central Philippines. I failed, however, to set up a research base for anthropological studies among the fearful Tawbuid. Using Buhid guides like Lunaw, I wandered into their villages, and was given overnight lodging. Each time I was asked to leave by two or three men, the only villagers who did not run away. Twice they evicted me from interior Tawbuid villages.

The standard eviction notice became a familiar refrain: "Your presence causes great fear among our women and children," they lamented. "They are so afraid of you that they run with great speed through the jungle, cutting themselves on thorns. They cannot work in the sweet potato fields while you are here." As I attempted to sleep at night they would bring in men from surrounding hamlets to perform ritual ceremonies to curse the unwanted stranger. I was escorted out over seldom used trails that bypassed all their other settlements and added an extra day to the trip.

Discouraged, I retreated to study a neighboring tribe, the Buhid, in a settlement only a two-hour trip from the coastal lowlands. After several weeks of ethnobotanical research with local informants, I was informed that they could no longer tell me any information about their culture and the plant world. I discovered later that the interior

Tawbuid, who work in the rice fields of the Buhid and constitute a cheap labor force, had threatened to strike if I were allowed to gather cultural data in the area. Furthermore, they would abandon their work in their own rice fields near the Buhid through denying the Buhid a share of their crop. And, finally, they threatened to curse the Buhid if they continued to work with me. Threats of economic and spiritual sanctions by a fearful, interior people stopped my research among the Buhid. I had been evicted for the third time by the Tawbuid![1]

Discovering the Tawbuid World View

Rejected by the non-Christian Buhid and Tawbuid, I went to live with a group of Christianized Tawbuid who lived north of the Buhid. This small group had experienced an amazing conversion. Russ and Barbara Reed, missionaries with Overseas Missionary Fellowship, were the fulfillment to a 16-generation, 350-year-old prophecy that white teachers would come speaking Tawbuid. The people were to listen and obey the new teaching. Unaware of the legend, the Reeds learned a dialect of Tawbuid on the other side of the island, then moved to be with this group of eastern Tawbuid when they began coming to meetings held by other OMF missionaries ministering in a neighboring tribe.[2]

In nine months of intensive study with the Safa Christian Tawbuid, I began to unravel the reasons for my previous evictions. The interior Tawbuid are in a closed culture dominated by an awesome fear of strangers and even each other. Strangers are assumed to be kidnappers, disease carriers or evil spirits. The people take elaborate precautions to avoid contact with anyone they do not recognize. Entrances to house trails are camouflaged. Guards may be posted, and cultivation plots are seldom in sight from the river trails. Hiding places, complete with emergency foods, are maintained, and discovered hamlets may be deserted.

Fear of spirits drives the people to these intensive ritual actions, some daily, some dependent on special circumstances, and some correlated with the seasonal cultivation cycles. They are also fearful of each other and of spirit power residing in individuals who may curse them, causing loss of possessions, bodily harm or death.[3] Supernatural displays of power by spiritual leaders are common, and reinforce the power of dictator-type "big men" who keep control over people in their territory.

Every facet of life is so integrated with the spirit world that they seldom offer a natural cause-and-effect reason for any life situation. Solving problems for non-Christian Tawbuid consists of marshaling the right spirits to fight other spirits who precipitated the problem. Individuals possess a tremendous storehouse of oral literature, including protective rituals and curses, and other spirit summonses.

As my study of the Christian Tawbuid's former religion progressed, I uncovered a pervasive, systematic organization of traditional knowledge in their oral literature. Associational sets or complexes of plant and non-plant members are embedded in their ritual chants. These ritual complexes are governed by culture heroes who were responsible for the creation or initial growth of their associated plant or non-plant members. Thus, in a ritual to cure snake bite the culture hero Siyanga is credited with the growth of the associated plant, the fungus, as well as the creation of the original *tagrara* or *libaga* snakes. The fungus and the snakes are considered siblings. The fungus is masticated and applied to the snake bite.[4]

While on the surface this is simply a convenient way of organizing traditional knowledge, Tawbuid are instructed as young people to practice the ritual chant whether they see one of the plant or non-plant members. Given the number of ritual complexes, following this admonition places the Tawbuid mind in an exercise that supplants the Creator with culture heroes. In many cases this exercise brings to mind the names of powerful spirits who are also mentioned within the context of the larger ritual performance.

Walking through the forest for many Tawbuid is like stepping on the keys of a giant computer keyboard. A conditioned response occurs when a ritual complex member is sighted, bringing up to the mind's screen the entire set, the culture hero and associated members. This conceptual organization is applied not only in a crisis reaction but in everyday-life situations. It is clear then, that demons working through individuals not only permeate the subsystems of Tawbuid culture; they may also penetrate the conceptual organization of traditional knowledge to disguise the true Creator's role and promote themselves.

Collective Captivity

Demons seek to gain an increasing influence and mastery over individuals through attacks on the mind, the thoughts, the emotions and the will. Individuals are members of societies who live according to a prescribed set of cultural rules and institutions. In some societies like the Tawbuid all social, political, economic, religious and even artistic subsystems of culture are actively manipulated and controlled by demons acting through individuals. Individuals within these societies live in a kind of collective captivity in which all transitions in the life cycle—for example birth, puberty, marriage, and death—are surrounded with evil spirit rituals. Spirit guides are acquired or inherited at specific stages in the life cycle. All annual steps in the food production system are linked with either praise, appeasement or blockage of spirits. Health care preventions and remedies involve spiritual rituals. Most social problems, for example theft, may be treated as spiritual interference in a person's life, causing the abnormal behavior.

The individual is the member of social groupings such as a household or family managed by the head of the house; a village dominated by a hereditary leader and a shaman; and, a larger territorial group of villages controlled by a big man dictator. Each of these leaders, as well as a variety of specialists, may be demonized. To effectively maintain their position, they must continually interact with demons, sometimes performing supernatural feats.

Cultural systems are not inherently evil, but the combined activity of demonized individuals, leading others in traditionally demonic focused activities, creates collective captivity. Individuals sit in collective captivity in their dungeons in the common societal prison surrounded by the collective darkness created by this demonic permeation of their cultural systems.

Captivity and Darkness:
Biblical Word Pictures

Captivity and darkness are vivid biblical word pictures often used in the Scriptures to describe the interaction between humans, the divine and the demonic. Unregenerates are portrayed as captives in dark dungeons in a kingdom ruled by the devil. A series of binary oppositions play out this theme: God versus Satan; light against darkness;

a state of being alive or dead, sighted or blind, captive or free.

Isaiah's Messianic prophecies spoke of Christ as "a light for the Gentiles, to open eyes that are blind, to free captives from prison and to release from the dungeon those who sit in darkness" (Isa. 42:6, 7, *NIV*). Matt. 4:16 and Luke 1:78, 79; 2:32 echo Isaiah's captivity and darkness themes. Christ announces Himself as the proclaimer of freedom for the prisoners, the recoverer of sight for the blind in Luke 4:18, and the light of the world in John 8:12; 9:5. Even Peter uses this popular binary opposition of light and darkness (1 Pet. 2:9). But it is Paul who brings all the elements of the captivity and darkness themes together.

In Acts, Paul testifies of his Damascus road commission, "to open their eyes and turn them from darkness to light, and from the power of Satan to God, so that they may receive forgiveness of sins" (Acts 26:18, *NIV*). In Corinthians, he states that the devil is responsible for linking minds and preventing the penetration of the light of Christ (2 Cor. 4:4). The church at Colosse was "in the kingdom of light" and "rescued . . . from the dominion of darkness" (Col. 1:12, 13, *NIV*).

The Ephesians were once "dead in . . . transgressions and sins" and "followed . . . the ruler of the kingdom of the air" (Eph. 2:1, 2, *NIV*). Paul exhorts them to "no longer live as the Gentiles do, in the futility of their thinking. They are darkened in their understanding and separated from the life of God" (Eph. 4:17, 18, *NIV*). He challenges them by reminding them that "you were once darkness, but . . . are light in the Lord. Live as children of light" (Eph. 5:8, *NIV*). They are admonished to "put on the full armor of God so that you can take your stand against the devil's schemes." The battle is a struggle "against the rulers . . . the authorities . . . the powers of this dark world" (Eph. 6:11, 12, *NIV*).

These vivid word pictures of captivity and darkness describe a condition or state. But how does the devil blind minds and prevent the penetration of the gospel light? How does Satan use his power to keep people in collective captivity? Let's look at some of the features of collective captivity.

Features of Collective Captivity

The following is not an exhaustive list; it is a series of observations on the key features. The schemes of the devil are numerous and varied, and he has been in business a long time. He existed at the dawn of human history and he has the advantage of living in each succeeding generation. Here are some of the tactics he employs to keep groups in the dark dungeons of collective captivity:

1. *Demonization of the leadership.* Household, village and larger territorial group leaders may all be demonized, as well as a variety of specialists, in societies like the Tawbuid. This means that the social, religious and political leadership of everyday events is effectively manipulated by demons. Individuals may also be demonized at differing levels, so that both leaders and followers are demonized. Strong territorial spirits may attach themselves to the bigmen leaders in their territory (see Wagner's "Territorial Spirits").

2. *Demonic bonding.* Another feature of collective captivity is that many individuals in the society or subculture are not only demonized but they have bonded with their demons. This bond of friendship may be especially strong

with generational or kin spirits who are passed along family lines. The demon can reinforce this bond by acting as a family historian and reciting real or fabricated facts concerning the individual's ancestors. In some societies the people with powerful demonic gifts are feared and even avoided by the ordinary people. These specialists, who may be lonely for human companionship, develop strong friendship and dependency ties with their evil spirits. They bond with their demons and breaking these well-established friendship bonds can be extremely difficult.

A missionary working among an upland Southeast Asian tribe began a women's Bible study. Every day a wild-looking woman came and stood outside listening through the open windows. She made the women inside very nervous.

"Mama," they begged, "make her go away. She is evil and we are afraid of her."

The missionary told the women, "Let her listen. Maybe she will learn about Jesus."

One day this wild woman came and said, "Mama, I want to have Jesus as my Savior, too."

So the missionary went to the woman's little hut near a riverbank. She walked up the pole ladder, stepped over a log in the doorway, and entered the darkened room. Seated on the floor with the woman and her husband, the missionary taught them about salvation in Christ. Her eyes focused on the log in the doorway. Its color and markings were remarkable and it seemed to join with other logs around the tiny room. Suddenly she realized the log was a giant snake. It surrounded the room. She was seated in the snake's coil!

"Why do you have this snake in your house?" the missionary asked. Lowering her voice, the woman replied, "Mama, it tells me things."

"What kind of things?" queried the missionary.

"Oh, Mama, it tells me who is sick, and who is going to die, and things like that."

"Well, if you want Jesus to come into your life, you must get rid of this snake because it belongs to Satan. You cannot follow both Jesus and Satan."

"Oh, no, Mama! This snake is my friend. I cannot get rid of it!" the woman cried.

The woman's husband spoke up. "Mama," he said, "if you can convince her to get rid of this snake, I'll receive your Jesus, too."

After much arguing back and forth, the woman finally allowed her husband to haul the snake outside. He took it to the riverbank, cut it in pieces, and threw it into the river.

Then the missionary asked, "Do you have anything else in the house that tells you things?"

The woman hesitated, and the missionary again warned her that these things were of Satan and he would take her to hell, if she didn't have Jesus as her Savior. Finally, the woman brought out a small wooden box, and the missionary asked her to open it. To her horror, the missionary saw that it was a dead baby covered with green mold.

"Mama, this baby is my friend. It tells me things. I will not let it go."

"Well then, I must go," the missionary replied. "This baby belongs to Satan, and you cannot serve both Jesus and Satan." And she went down the pole ladder and started walking away from the hut.

"Wait, Mama, wait! I do want to receive Jesus!" the woman called, running after the missionary.

"Well, you can't have Jesus and that dead baby, too.

I'm not coming back unless you get rid of it." The woman was crying, but she agreed, and gave it to her husband who took the dead baby away and buried it.

The missionary returned to the hut. Once inside, she felt the Holy Spirit warning her that this woman was demon possessed. The missionary had never dealt with this problem before. She looked directly at the woman, asking protection for herself in Jesus' name through His shed blood on Calvary, and then said commandingly, "You evil spirit, come out of her in the name of the Lord Jesus Christ." To her great surprise, the woman fell to the floor, foaming at the mouth. She lay quite still, and the man cried, "You've killed my wife! You've killed my wife!"

"Maybe I have," thought the missionary.

Then, suddenly, the woman opened her eyes and sat up. Her eyes were no longer wild. She was calm, and said, "Oh, Mama! Thank you! It's gone, Mama." Then the woman received Jesus as her Savior. There was such a change in this woman's life. She went everywhere among her tribal people, witnessing how Jesus set her free. The people were astounded, as they knew her well and had feared her power. Because of the testimony and changed life of this woman, many of her tribe put their faith in Jesus.[5]

Demonic bonding is the development of friendship and dependency bonds with demons and their associated objects, such as the snake and the dead baby in this story. In a society with many individuals who have bonded with their demons, these bonds are in effect the bars in the dungeon that help hold the society in collective captivity.

3. *Cognitive captivity.* This can also be called the *busy mind syndrome.* There are two main ways demons keep the individual mind or thoughts captive. First, demons may monopolize the individual's time with intensive rituals

and lengthy interaction with the spirit world. Memorization of long passages that must be repeated verbatim, and
meditation or chanting of repetitious phrases, are techniques that keep the mind busy and focused on the spirit
world. Second, demons may work to a deeper depth of
perception in the thought processes through elaborate
symbolic systems. These tactics may trigger both conscious and subconscious responses of worship to demons.

4. *Demonic counteraction against divine intervention.*
Throughout history the divine and the demonic have
waged battles over the human mind, will and emotions.
Yahweh is a jealous God who demands worship with all our
heart, soul and mind (Matt. 22:37)—that is total concen-
tration. The Old Testament sacrifice and worship systems
were designed to keep the people's thoughts focused on
Yahweh. Idolatry, promoted and energized by demons,
was and is a counterattack to capture people's thoughts
away from the one true God to a multiplicity of false gods
(Ps. 106:35-37; Deut. 32:16, 17; 1 Cor. 10:19-22).

The coming of the God-Man Christ as the true light in
the world was not understood by Jews, who were concen-
trating on their ethnic heritage through Abraham and their
legalistic religious system for salvation. John the Baptist
warned the Pharisees and Sadducees, whom he called a
brood of vipers, that repentance and its fruits were more
important than their claim of Abraham as their father
(Matt. 3:8, 9). But it was Christ who very clearly defined
the source and energy of their empty religious reliance on
being descendants of Abraham. He acknowledged they
were Abraham's descendants, yet they needed to know
the truth and be set free (John 8:36, 37). Who is responsible for their captivity, their spiritual blindness? "You
belong to your father, the devil, and you want to carry out
your father's desire" (John 8:44, *NIV*).

The completed canon of Scripture is a marvelous example of divine intervention in human history. The living Word of God penetrates our minds and the Spirit of God interacts with our thoughts and attitudes. To counteract this, and to call into question the primacy and exclusivity of God's Word, demons are active in the creation of oral literature, such as written religious dogma and worship liturgy. Christians often wonder why the cults have endured and their followers tenaciously hold on in spite of irrational beliefs or contradictory philosophies. One plausible explanation is that some of their literature, their "bibles" were written under demonic inspiration. Just as the Word of God is inspired and energized by the Holy Spirit, their demonic inspired literature is energized by demons in the dark dungeon of the unregenerate mind.

The Spirit gives spiritual gifts to each believer, empowering and equipping the believer for ministry in the Body of Christ and ministry to the world. In a similar fashion, demons may work with individuals providing them with counterfeit gifts and power. Paul's encounter with the demonic fortune-teller at Philippi made the girl's owners so angry they had him arrested and beaten. By casting out the girl's demon in the name of Jesus, Paul caused the loss of her demonic abilities, and her owners then lost a great deal of money (Acts 16:16-24). Apparently people recognized her spiritual abilities and paid for her services.

An Old Testament example of a godly gift versus demonic abilities is seen in Moses and Aaron's empowerment to perform miracles before Pharaoh (Exod. 4:7, 8). Aaron threw down the staff in front of Pharaoh's court and it became a snake. The sorcerers and magicians did the same thing, except that Aaron's staff swallowed up their staffs. The magicians were able to duplicate the plagues of blood and frogs, but could not produce gnats. Their demonic power released through their secret arts was not as powerful as God's, prompting them to say, "This is the finger of God" (Exod. 8:19, *NIV*).

Whenever God has intervened and interacted with humans, the devil and demons have worked in opposition, counteracting God's institutions or gifts. Demons working through human minds have inspired or promoted major counter offensives against God's strategies. These demonic counterattacks are designed to keep people in collective captivity.

5. *Dominant societal characteristics.* At the risk of recycling well-worn and sometimes discarded anthropological theories that some cultures can be described in terms of a set of distinct characteristics or themes,[6] I want to cautiously open the possibility that demons may tighten collective captivity by initiating or reinforcing certain societal characteristics. The Tawbuid are characterized by a dominant theme of fear. It is the single most powerful motivation in Tawbuid society. Children are taught fear in lullabies and adults daily act out their real fear of each other, spirits and strangers.[7] This all-pervasive fear kept the gospel light out of the highlands of Mindoro for years. Doubtless the demons preyed on this societal characteristic by intensifying individuals' emotional reactions and by compounding this paranoia of strangers.

In other societies demons may strive to accentuate illicit sex, deceit or other sinful activity. These may be the dominant societal characteristics that emerge as the result of individual acceptance of this demonic prodding. Do these shared traits reflect the specialty or emphases of powerful demons in the area? It is possible. Whatever the reason for the emergence of particular themes, it is evident that demonic empowerment of dominant societal characteristics certainly contributes to collective captivity.

Transferring Dungeons: A Captivity Cycle

Closed societies like the Tawbuid exhibit evidence of intense collective captivity. There are three ways to change collective captivity: *first* death, the termination of the individual's earthly existence; *second* transferring kingdoms, or moving from darkness to light through salvation in Christ; and, *third* transferring dungeons, or simply modifying or exchanging one belief system for another.

What happens when the traditional religious system begins to break down and the people's dependency on the system lessens? I propose a *captivity cycle* as a working hypothesis to illustrate that demons respond to cultural dynamics and shift their strategies as a culture changes.

The captivity cycle is based on four stages found in the Fall (Gen. 3:1-7). Satan *distracted* Eve by questioning God's commandment not to eat of the tree in the middle of the garden. Eve began to believe Satan's *deception* then she demonstrated her *dependency* on Satan's opinion when she desired wisdom and took the fruit. Eve and Adam were *dominated* by Satan when by an act of their will they ate of the fruit.

Distraction, deception, dependency and domination are all stages in the captivity cycle. The demons' ultimate goal is to keep the society and individuals in the cycle by rotating around to domination of the society's cultural systems (see figure 1). Levels of increasing darkness represent the degree of time spent in spiritual interaction.

The following is an example of stage-by-stage movement through time keyed to figure 1, starting and ending with Domination (D4):

1. *Domination (Level 4—D4).* The penetration and control of the cultural subsystems through the integration

of time intensive worship and appeasement rituals, as in the case of religions like the Tawbuid.

2. *Dependency (Level 3—D5)*. The highest level of dependency is domination. As a modern society interacts with religion like the Tawbuids, the level of dependency may decrease, if, for example, technology and modern medicine supplant the time intensive ritual systems.

3. *Deception (Level 2—D6)*. As dependency decreases, the demons try to advance a major deception such as syncretism, to convince the people that both the new and the old are needed to survive.

4. *Distraction (Level 1—D1)*. When the old system fades, demons may work on merely distracting people through the details of life, and their desire for power and prestige. At this level people may not even believe in spirits, or spend any time interacting with the supernatural but still may be under their influence.

5. *Deception (Level 2—D2)*. When people become dissatisfied with the emptiness of materialism, prestige and power, demons may deceive them into believing that spiritual satisfaction can be found again in their systems, cults or philosophies (as in the New Age Movement). Their influence may be disguised as "information sharing" or supernatural power demonstrations such as channeling.

6. *Dependency (Level 3—D3)*. A growing dependency develops as people buy the deception, and invest more and more time into the system. This leads to domination.

7. *Domination (Level 4—D4)*. Demons desire to dominate people's thinking processes and the society or subculture. In a modern multi-cultural society with numerous subcultures, individuals and people groups will be at all levels and stages of the cycle; nevertheless, the demonic strategy is to raise the level of captivity and shift around to this evil domination.

CAPTIVITY CYCLE

Levels   **Strategy Stages**

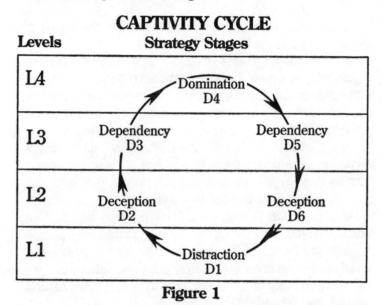

Figure 1

The individual who moves from stage to stage and level to level in the cycle is merely transferring dungeons as the societal prison scene keeps changing. Certainly other combinations of examples could be processed through the cycle. Indeed, movement back to domination (D4) in the face of decreasing dependency (D5) might be accomplished by individuals seeking to revitalize the changing state by returning to the old ways.[8]

Breaking out of the Dungeon

Since the Fall, unbelievers have been in the kingdom of darkness, in dungeons that become progressively darker as the blinds of the will continue to close out the light of the gospel. The ruler of the kingdom is the devil and demons carry out strategies to keep people in darkness. They attack the individual's mind, will and emotions, plying on the desires of the old sin nature, the lusts of the flesh.

It is easy to transfer dungeons within the kingdom of darkness. It takes power to break out. The purpose of evangelism is to help captives break out of the dark dungeon of collective captivity. Christ came as the light, the way out of the dungeon. In the first commission (Matt. 10:1) He gave the 12 disciples the authority to drive out the dungeon guards, if they are resident.

The Holy Spirit is given to all of us as the power source to assist in the breakout. The Spirit also convicts the world of the guilt of sin (John 16:8). We must learn to work with the Spirit's power, for no other power will break the captives out of the dungeon.

To effectively participate in the great breakout, believers need to live as children of light, exhibiting daily the qualities of holy, righteous living. This is the living sacrifice that transforms and renews the mind (Rom. 12:1, 2). It is a disciplined way of life that willingly submits to captivity in the kingdom of light, for Paul reminds us to take every thought captive in obedience to Christ (2 Cor. 10:5).

David, in Psalm 51, expresses these truths. He had committed adultery and murder, but he repented and asked for a pure heart and steadfast spirit. He recognized he needed the Holy Spirit and requested that the Spirit remain with him. Out of this joy of salvation and a willing spirit to continue in righteous living, world evangelism takes place: "Then I will teach transgressors your ways, and sinners will turn back to you" (Ps. 51:13, *NIV*). Under the power of the Holy Spirit, and through a life committed to disciplined holy living, the children of light can help the captives out of the dungeon of collective captivity.

Now it is time for the children of light around the world to shout a message that reverberates against the dirty walls of every dark dungeon. With the living Word in hand and our armor in place (Eph. 6), we boldly echo the words of the prophet, Isaiah, quoted by our ruler of the kingdom of light:

> The Spirit of the Lord is on me, [us]. because he has anointed me to preach good news to the poor. He has sent me to proclaim freedom for the prisoners and recovery of sight for the blind, to release the oppressed, to proclaim the year of the Lord's favor (Luke 4:18, 19, *NIV*).

Notes

1. F. Douglas Pennoyer, "Leadership and Control in a Samagui River Bangon Settlement," *Philippine Sociological Review*, January 1978, 26 (1): 49-55.
2. Barbara Flory Reed, Beyond the Great Darkness (Singapore: Overseas Missionary Fellowship, 1987).
3. F. Douglas Pennoyer, "Shifting Cultivation and Shifting Subsistence Patterns Among the Tawbuid of Mindoro," *Adaptive Strategies and Change in Philippine Swidden-based Societies*, ed. Harold Olofson (Laguna, P.I.: Forest Research Institute, 1981), pp. 43-54.
4. F. Douglas Pennoyer, *Tawbuid Plants and Ritual Complexes* (Pullman: Washington State University, 1975, unpublished Ph.D. dissertation), pp. 184-202.
5. Source unknown; retold by Virginia Pennoyer.
6. Ruth Benedict, Patterns of Culture (New York: New American Library, Mentor Books, 1934). Morris E. Opler, *An Apache Life Way* (Chicago: University of Chicago Press).
7. F. Douglas Pennoyer, "Ritual in Tawbuid Life," *Anthropos, International Review of Ethnology and Linguistics*, 1980, 75: pp. 703-709.
8. Anthony F.C. Wallace, "Revitalization Movements: Some Theoretical Considerations for Their Comparative Study," *American Anthropologist*, 1956, 58 (2): pp. 264-281.

In Dark Dungeons of Collective Captivity

First, I want to compliment Dr. Pennoyer on a very thought-provoking paper. We all have a lot to learn concerning how Satan runs his kingdom and what to do in response to demonic influences. The more we share our experiences and analyses, the more we can learn. So I'm pleased that we can benefit from Dr. Pennoyer's experiences and analysis. He raises a number of very interesting issues.

A number of excellent changes have been made since the paper was originally written, including the addition of the section on Features of Collective Captivity. I appreciate this section very much and will not comment on it directly except for a small comment in the third section following. Also, I will not comment on the intriguing analysis of what was called a "Captivity Cycle," which seems a bit extraneous to the main point, but is so original and thought-provoking that I am glad it was included. My comments on other issues raised by the paper follow:

1. The story about Dr. Pennoyer being perceived by the Tawbuid as a person of power is, I think, a good starting point. If we looked at mission history down through the ages with our minds alerted to the question of spiritual

power, we would find an interesting discovery. I believe we would discover that in almost every case throughout the Two-thirds World, the people to whom we came interpreted us as people of spiritual power.

We, of course, have usually seen ourselves as people of power also, but primarily of material power, since we carefully categorize material things and spiritual things in different compartments. Most of the people to whom we have gone, however, would not make that distinction in the same way we do and would, therefore, have seen our power over the material universe as demonstrating our closeness to God (or other powerful spiritual beings).

If we as Western Christians could understand the intense concern for spiritual power on the part of the people to whom we go and with that understanding come to more accurately see how they perceive who we are and what we do, we would be much less likely to fall into the kinds of misunderstanding Dr. Pennoyer fell into.

2. I'm pleased to see that my suggestion to drop "Cognitive" out of the title was followed in the revision of the paper. (The original title of the paper and of the third section included the phrase "Collective Cognitive Captivity.") My problem with the term "cognitive" in that phrase is that, in my experience, the process of bringing demonized people to freedom in Christ is usually more a problem of releasing them from the demon's grip on their emotions than on their minds.

I think, then, that what we are dealing with throughout the paper (originally referred to as "cognitive captivity") is really much more pervasive than the term allows. The ultimate aim of the enemy is not simply to control people's minds but to get at our wills. So he uses whatever channels are available to him to gain whatever control he can over the will. The emotions, then, seem to be much more fertile ground for his attacks. In my ministry, so far, I've dealt with over 50 demonized people but cannot recall any for whom the enemy's primary channel was the mind. It seems to always be emotions and/or, perhaps, the human spirit.

My sample is, or course, limited. Perhaps Satan uses different channels in different societies. In any event, I feel it was appropriate to broaden the concept to "collective captivity," rather than using the original phrase "collective cognitive captivity."

3. The use of terms like "cognitive" in such contexts betrays, I believe, a problem we all struggle with, from the perspective of our Western world view, as we look at data such as that presented here. We have learned to focus primarily on the cognitive, rational aspects of a subject such as this one and of the people affected by the enemy of our "souls" (soul = total being), rather than on a more comprehensive, holistic view, either of Satan's work, or of people in general.

As mentioned above, Satan's attack is much broader than any analysis of purely cognitive things will reveal. It is holistic, dealing with emotions and mind as channels to the will. Thus, the series of steps presented (distraction, deception, dependency and domination) should be seen as much more totally captivating than a simple focus on the cognitive dimension would allow. Indeed, I suspect that the majority of the demonic-human interaction that results in people following these steps would be in the emotional rather than in the cognitive area. For, as we learn in communication theory, meanings are primarily felt rather than reasoned.

In this regard, I think even the small section (No. 3 under "Features of Collective Captivity") entitled "Cognitive captivity" is mistitled. Though memorization is cognitive, rituals, meditation and even symbolization are more pervasive in human life than portraying them as cognitive would suggest.

4. To me, the most interesting part of the paper is the theory that in certain societies "all social, political, economic, religious and even artistic subsystems of culture are actively manipulated and controlled by demons acting through individuals." Such a theory is a good challenge and, hopefully, a helpful resolution to the problem posed by the conflict between those who see demonization totally in individualistic terms and those who insist on using what I believe to be misguided concepts such as "demonic structures," as if structures themselves can contain personal beings such as demons.

Just as God does not save structures but is eager to guide persons in the way they use them, so Satan seeks to influence groups of people through influencing those who operate the structures. I have found it very helpful in this regard to clearly separate between people and the systems by which people conduct their lives. (And I am happy to see that this distinction was incorporated into the paper.) We use the term "society" to refer to people organized in groups. The term "culture," then, should be reserved for the systems and patterns by which people govern their lives. We are taught these patterns as we grow up and follow most of them habitually for the rest of our lives. There is, however, no power and no personality in the pattern, only in the person who follows it. What keeps us following cultural patterns, then, is habit.

When we talk about the possibility of demonic control over cultural behavior, therefore, we are talking about control over the people and their habits, not some mystical infestation of systems and patterns. People may be invaded and controlled, but patterns may not—at least as

I see it. If the structures themselves were under demonic control, there would be no possibility for people to get released from them. The people would be totally determined by the evil system. If, however, as Dr. Pennoyer suggests, it is the people who become demonized and use their structures in anti-God ways, these people can be moved by the power of God out of the dungeon of captivity to Satan into the control of God. They can then be free to use almost all of these same structures to serve God, even as we see biblical peoples doing.

Satanic control is, therefore, over a society, a people. It is not over a culture, a structured system. When a cultural subsystem seems to be controlled by Satan, it is really the group that operate that subsystem that is controlled. It is the people, not the subsystem itself, that need to be delivered from the demons.

5. Demonic control is, therefore, always personal (even when the persons are in groups). We may speak of demonic control of, say, a kinship group such as an extended family or even perhaps of a whole tribal group—though I suspect that even when a large group of people are under such demonic control, not every person in the group is demonized.

And even when persons are demonized, demonic control over the person is never total. There is always some part of the human will that can be exerted and empowered by the Holy Spirit to throw off the control of the enemy. My own experience with demonized people has taught me that there are times when a person is totally submitted to the demon; there are other times when the individual is out from under that control, either by an act of the will or because in the name of Jesus the demon has been "shut down." An attack on the kind of collective demonization in view here, then, should seek to discover and bring about times—through the power of the Holy Spirit—when God's power and human will are brought together to bring freedom. This can certainly be done with individuals. Perhaps in cases of group demonization, deliverance can be done with whole groups if the proper preparation is done—in prayer—and the appropriate authority is given by the Holy Spirit.

6. To help my understanding of demonization, I have made two important changes in the way I think and talk about the subject. I believe these changes will be helpful to all of us. The first change is to refuse to use such imprecise and unscriptural terms as "influence," "affliction," "oppression" and "possession" to designate various degrees of demonic invasion of a person. I am pleased to see that such terms have been dropped from the revision of the paper. In place of these terms, I think we should use the single term used in the New Testament— demonization to refer to any degree of demonic activity from inside a person.

The second change, then, is to recognize that there are differing levels of demonic influence over a person. That is, the strength of the grip of a demon will vary from person to person in accordance with the amount of "garbage" they have in their lives to which the demons can attach themselves. Demons are like rats who have infested a house. They have to have garbage to feed on if they are to survive. If a person has a lot of emotional and/or spiritual "garbage" in his/her life, the grip of any demons resident there will be stronger. If those emotional and spiritual problems are dealt with and healed, the strength of the demons is lessened.

If this strength of attachment is estimated on a scale of 1 to 10 (as suggested some time ago by John Wimber), strong demonization such as that portrayed in the New

Testament may be seen at levels 9 and 10. I deal, however, with many who are weakly demonized (levels 1-3) and others who are demonized at an intermediate level (levels 4-6).

To date, I have found that demonized Christians who are actively growing in their relationship with Christ (and thus dealing with their emotional and spiritual "garbage") are seldom demonized at levels above 5 (though I am presently working with three or four who are at level 8 or above). Their Christian commitment, furthermore, usually makes them more open to inviting Jesus to use His power to assist them in getting rid of the intruders. Those who work with non-Christians tell me, however, that they find many who are demonized at the higher levels.

Having developed such a scale for dealing with demonization in individuals, we may use the same idea for evaluating the grip of demons on groups. We could thus estimate the overall grip of demons on the Tawbuid at, say, a 7, 8, or 9 level with the probability being that individuals within the group would vary from 0 to 10. If, in addition, we attempt to plot demonic influence from outside of individuals and groups in the same way, we could come up with a research instrument such as the following by which to evaluate situations of various kinds.

INSTRUMENT FOR PLOTTING
DEMONIC ACTIVITY

FROM OUTSIDE

I   INDIVIDUAL INFLUENCE
N
D   (e.g. Temptation, Affliction,
I   Besetting Sins)
V

I
D
U
A
L
                1-2-3-4-5-6-7-8-9-10

G   COLLECTIVE INFLUENCE
R
O   (e.g. Social Propensities and Sins)
U
P   1-2-3-4-5-6-7-8-9-10

                FROM INSIDE
I   INDIVIDUAL CONTROL
N
D   (Demonization)
I
V   1-2-3-4-5-6-7-8-9-10
I
D
U
A
L

G   COLLECTIVE CONTROL
R
O   (e.g. Social demonization)
U
P   1-2-3-4-5-6-7-8-9-10

The Tawbuid situation probably involves a good bit of demonic activity both from within and outside of individuals and groups. Given individuals, especially those in leadership, might be influenced from outside at high levels, since demonic activity is apparently so pervasive and so little hindered by Christian activity. In addition, many individuals are subject to internal demonization. This combination, then, would result in high levels of collective influence (from outside) and collective control (the collective effect of demonic influence from inside Tawbuid persons). To attack a demonization problem of this extent, it will be necessary for a group of committed Christians to seek God's specific directions and, depending on what they are, probably to go on the offensive to first crack the power of the territorial spirits and then to bring freedom to individuals and groups with much prayer, fasting and frontal challenges to the demonic forces presently in control.

I pray that these comments may be helpful to all of us as we ponder the issues Dr. Pennoyer has raised, and those that spin off from the ones that were dealt with.

CHAPTER 10

Power Evangelism in Pioneer Mission Strategy

JOHN LOUWERSE

JOHN LOUWERSE is professor of anthropology and world mission at Life Bible College in Los Angeles and adjunct professor in linguistics and Bible translation at Biola College. A native of Holland, he has degrees in mechanical engineering, cross-cultural communication, missiology and intercultural studies as well as theology.

DIVINE discernment always has been and still is a crucial ingredient in ministering to people. The reality of spiritual warfare cannot be overemphasized. Genuine supernatural manifestations of the awesome presence and intervention of God do occur. Research of those manifestations should not become an end in itself. Signs and wonders should contribute to the extension of the kingdom of God and glorify the name which is above every name—the name of Jesus.

Both inside and outside the Church of Jesus Christ today, there is a definite need for people to recognize the divine intervention of God in the lives of people through the miraculous. This is a biblical topic witnessed to in both the Old and New Testaments and never terminated in post-apostolic times. Throughout church history we read about signs and wonders clearly revealing God's awesome grace and judgment in the lives of individuals, families, people groups and nations. This divine intervention will continue until the time that every knee shall bow and every tongue shall confess that Jesus Christ is Lord.

Today, too, we are witnesses to the fact that a war is going on in the heavenlies. King Jesus is gathering His people from around the world, and this is frequently accompanied by impacting demonstrations of His undeniable presence. Personally, I see this happening here in the Western hemisphere just as well as I did in the Eastern "uttermost parts of the earth."

A Quest and a Filling

Having been raised in a Dutch Reformed family in Holland, I recall from early childhood the hundreds of hours spent in what Spurgeon called "hyper-Calvinist" services of one of the Dutch Reformed churches. With great sincerity and oratory, the doom-worthy nature of a sinner was spelled out from the pulpit. People in our church were always reflecting upon their fallen state and the righteous God we had to meet one day. Not many of us came to freedom in Christ and few perceived any demonstrations of God's mighty power. The hearts of many were crying out to encounter, in a personal way, more of the living reality of God. The regular expository discourses on the "right doctrines" and defense of our theological correctness was insufficient to stop the craving desire to experience all that God has for us.

One day one of my friends was miraculously and instantly healed, upon prayer, from a terminal stage of leukemia. This undeniable demonstration of God's merciful healing power created quite a ripple effect in our doctrinally well-organized church life; and it urged me on in a decade-long quest to know in a personal way the wonderful reality of forgiveness of sins through Jesus' sacrifice and the assurance of a loving and caring heavenly Father.

Finally, after years of religious exposure, the Lord entered my life. In an intense, life-changing conversion experience in a Baptist church in Illinois, all things became new. In a sovereign and powerful way the core of my world view was completely changed. Jesus now took His rightful position there. The first three days following this radical conversion experience it seemed like I was being elevated from earth and living in heaven. While witnessing anywhere I could about this new-found reality, I sensed an urgent call to missionary work to go "where Christ was not known" (Rom 15:20).

While preparing at a mission college to go to a hidden people, the Lord, in an awe-inspiring encounter on a Sunday afternoon in January, 1971, overwhelmingly assured me that all things are possible to them that believe.

Encountering what the Bible calls "a filling with the Holy
Spirit" (Acts 2:4), the Lord assured me that "he who
raised Christ from the dead [would] also give life to [my]
mortal bod[y] through his Spirit, who lives in [me]." (Rom.
8:11, *NIV*).

Regular "word checks"—that is, the extraordinary
divine communication from the Scriptures—are crucial in
pioneer missionary strategy. They provide the necessary
personal assurance that almighty God is right there with
you while obeying His command. The Lord knew that I
desired to hear from Him clearly before entering New
Guinea's *terra incognita*. Just before I left the first time for
the mission field He wonderfully encouraged me with the
words of Deut. 31:6, 8 (*NIV*):

> Be strong and courageous. Do not be afraid or
> terrified because of them, for the Lord your
> God goes with you; he will never leave you nor
> forsake you .... The Lord himself goes
> before you and will be with you; he will never
> leave you nor forsake you. Do not be afraid; do
> not be discouraged.

Mission in Irian Jaya

In 1971 I stepped off the plane in the interior of Irian Jaya
as a 23-year-old missionary having just finished training at
the Hendrik Kraemer Mission College in Holland. I felt a
tremendous burden from the Lord to see the eyes of people opened and to witness their turning "from darkness to
light, and from the power of Satan to God" (Acts 26:18).

But what kind of effective missionary strategy was I to
follow? As a green rookie missionary a few things were
clear to me. First and foremost I recognized my own

inability and therefore my need to go continually to the Source of all wisdom—my Savior and Lord. Every night until one or two in the morning was spent near the kerosene lamp in Bible study, meditation and prayer. This drawing from the Spring of Living Water provided vigor and freshness during the long days of ministry. Teaching spiritually hungry tribal chiefs, their wives and children every morning was a real blessing, followed by afternoons consulting the Yali Bible translation team and multiple other tasks that needed to be done at the isolated mission station. It was a daily blessing to teach and be taught by those dear brothers and sisters who had recently denounced their animistic practices and received Jesus as their Lord and Savior, and who were eager to share their new-found faith.

During the five months of apprenticeship training, the Lord provided me with an invaluable life companion and co-worker. Now, as a couple, we continued to minister to the needs of the people while the resident missionaries left on furlough. For the next year-and-a-half my wife and I pastored a congregation of 350 people, and acted as district supervisors of nine churches that consisted of 1500 young believers. Two years of expanding ministry responsibilities in the Yali region provided many practical hands-on experiences. A people movement among the Yalis swept through their valleys. Church buildings were erected in all villages and were filled to capacity daily.

While the Lord was building His Church, Satan with his demonic forces was active, too. Satan does not easily give up territory he has had under control for centuries. The young Christian leaders of my daily Bible study class, and their wives, were frequently beaten up or wounded with machetes and axes for sharing Jesus Christ with the people in surrounding villages. But after bandaging their wounds and committing themselves to their cause, and the people who hurt them to the Lord, they would continue to go back and witness to them.

As equippers of those church and community leaders, we were prime objects of the attacks of the evil one. During the first two years I was down with 10 rather severe malaria attacks. Finally, I lay in a coma for three days with malaria tropica (cerebral malaria). The symptoms were clear to the people. Traditionally, comatose conditions were reason to begin the wailing dirges, but the Christian community did not want to accept any spiritual defeat. They prayed their earnest child-like prayers for their *tuan,* and the Lord answered them by restoring me back to complete health.

We rejoiced in seeing multitudes of Yalis being added daily to those who were being saved. Teaching and translating the Scriptures and caring for those young Christians was the delight of my heart; but we knew this was not what the Lord had in mind when He called me to go "where Christ was not known" (Rom. 15:20). So we asked the Lord to open doors for us to go to the regions beyond.

Just two years previously, in 1969, two missionary colleagues, Stan Dale, Phil Masters and some of the indigenous evangelists had been savagely murdered and consumed in the eastern highlands. Don Richardson, in his well-known book *Lords of the Earth,* relates this episode in detail. Upon arrival in Irian Jaya, Phyllis Masters showed us the pictures of the arrow-pierced Bible and some of the memorabilia of her late husband. Then and there I felt drawn by the Spirit of the living God to go beyond those regions to share the good news of Jesus Christ.

The Pass Valley Yali Christians witnessed with great boldness and effectiveness to anyone about their new-found faith in the Lord Jesus Christ. They soon exhausted all target groups within their own community. It did not take long for them to respond to the Lord's call to reach out beyond their own people group.

They requested us to give leadership to their team. It definitely was a challenge to lead those young barefoot evangelists into cannibal territory. If possible, it would take us at least one month of hard and hazardous trekking to reach our destination overland from the late Phil Masters' mission station, Koruppun. It was clear to me that we needed a helicopter to reach our target group who were living in one of the world's most rugged terrains amidst towering mountain peaks topping 15,500 feet.

Realizing that the enemy did not want us to enter another domain of his absolute reign since time immemorial, we, like Gideon of old, needed a double confirmation from the Lord. Who was I—a 25-year-old upstart—to take my wife of a few months and give leadership to a group of young Yali Christians in such a dangerous area? I became even more aware of the need for God's approval when several old-time, senior missionaries called our plan a suicide mission and strongly advised against entering this isolated terrain without escape possibilities.

The Lord who says that when we call upon His name He will answer gave us His divine approval with a word check. He told me, "you will not leave in haste or go in flight; for [I] the LORD will go before you, the God of Israel will be your rear guard" (Isa. 52:12, *NIV*). Now, I knew that this plan was the Lord's will but also that we would run into quite a few formidable obstacles before we would see the first converts in this area. It would take quite some time and much engagement in spiritual warfare.

Following the old adage of the Christian Church *opa et*

labora, "pray and work," we requested and received permission for this new outreach from the Regions Beyond Missionary Union (RBMU) mission who had claimed the area for 12 years and from the Mission Aviation Fellowship (MAF) who had to fly in and drop all supplies. Next, we heard of an Australian outfit that temporarily operated two helicopters in Irian Jaya. We requested one helicopter for a morning of shuttle flights. Only one pilot was willing to help us, but told us that it would take quite some time before they were able to work it into their busy schedule. So, by faith, we started ordering and packing all the supplies in burlap sacks with grass filling to cushion them upon impact when dropped from MAF Cessnas. Next, we requested an MAF survey flight to locate the villages and airstrip site and estimate the population.

One morning our friend, Bob Donald, came to pick us up for the four-hour survey flight. Ten minutes after take-off, while crossing the high mountain ranges into the Balim Valley, the engine of the single-engine Cessna suddenly died. We looked at the propellor standing vertically before our eyes, while we began to fall down on a short crash course toward the ragged mountain peaks. The pilot transmitted a distress call and his location, while feverishly trying to find the cause and solution to the trouble and looking for a spot to land with a chance of survival. There was none! While the mountain came ever more rapidly toward us I held my wife and said, "This cannot be it! The Lord wants us to go to the people in the eastern highlands!" As soon as I spoke these words the engine started coughing and came to life again. A few seconds from impact the pilot was able to bypass the carburetor and inject fuel directly from the tank into the engine. The engine roared with maximum power, and though our ascent was agonizingly slow we pulled up out of the bowl-shaped valley away from those razor-sharp peaks and boulders.

We finally made it out of the valley but now had to find the longest airstrip on the island since the engine could not be slowed down upon landing. The tower put all flights on a holding pattern while giving us permission for an emergency landing. In order to descend and avoid overshooting the runway the engine had to be shut off completely and then restarted again when we began stalling. It was a rough landing with a sequence of a dead engine fall and a full power blast forward. Finally, we came to a shaky but safe stop at the ultimate end of the longest runway of the island.

The weather deteriorated quickly. Unable either to continue the survey flight or return home, we fought the weather all week in prayer and action. Finally, a week later, we were able to survey the area known as the Tri River Valley with its 35 villages, hundreds of round huts and an estimated 3,500 people living in the darkness of animism. Oh, how our hearts longed to share the good news of Jesus' saving grace with them!

Upon our return home we were informed that the sole helicopter pilot who was favorable toward mission work and our request was called back to Australia. The two other pilots made it clear that they did not want to cooperate. After weeks of prayer and repeated contact, they finally indicated their willingness to make a few shuttles for the outrageous price of 15,000 U.S. dollars! But prayer moves mountains! The Lord changed their hearts, they became cooperative and later completely annulled the bill!

Working Among the Una

On July 22, 1973, we entered the Una society as its first

outsiders and took up residence among 3,500 cannibals. We did not know their language or culture, but this was where the Lord wanted us to be. We started communicating with hands and feet. All the women and children fled to the bush, taking along all their valuable possessions; only heavily armed warriors stayed around at a safe distance. We were not aware that during our first night in their midst the chiefs were deliberating whether to kill all of us immediately or to wait awhile longer. They decided to wait until more goods arrived and then wipe us out, roast us, put us in cooking pits and devour us. They were not aware that the Lord of hosts protected us! It was much later, after we had mastered the Una language monolingually, that they told us about these plans. They perceived me to be their long-lost ancestor spirit who had finally returned from enemy territory in the far West tumbling out of the belly of a noisy dragonfly (helicopter). Only the bravest of these brave pigmies finally came closer and showed their goodwill by offering us sugarcane, and sticking one of their home-grown cigars in my mouth! Next, they started pinching us and found out that we, unlike ghosts, had some substance to us somewhat similar to their flesh.

Later on, we found out that for years they had been waiting for their long-lost ancestor who, according to their mythology, had left for the West. They were not aware that it was the Lord who had prepared their hearts for this intrusion into their community. In 1932, one of their dying shaman had prophesied that at the time when one of the young boys by the name of Memer would be a grey-haired chief, the long-lost ancestor of the Malyo clan would return. He would descend out of the western sky bringing a bundle of carved banana leaves along with a message from the spirit world. He told them to listen carefully and to act upon this message. It would stop the endless cycle of revenge killings, sorcery and hatred, and bring genuine peace.

The Lord prepared and continually intervened on our behalf. The battle for souls was on! One day I noticed a group of shaman digging in the airstrip site, inserting sacrifices of marsupials, pork and lard from a sacred white pig into the hole, while placing a curse upon us and endlessly repeating their incantations to the spirits. I simply came against it in the name of Jesus. Since the helicopters had left for Australia we continued working long days on the airstrip construction, eager to open up a connection to the outside world.

One morning I left the Yalis working at the airstrip to order supplies over the radio for the drop the following day. The valley was completely filled with heavy fog. While I was talking on the radio in our grass hut a group of some 30 fearsome fighters suddenly came out of the grey fog. We noticed their war vests, war paint, bows and bundles of arrows. These were the feared Laji warriors who had sneaked up on us! They were the archenemies of the Langda people, who by now had accepted us. Only two of us were around. We went outside the hut trying to talk to them and give them some salt (a very precious commodity in the area). They did not want to accept any, and stood there looking fiercely at us. No one sat down to accept our gift as a sign of peaceful intentions.

This was another tense situation. They clearly came to eradicate all of us! We intensified our prayers. Suddenly we heard a mighty crashing sound in the invisible mountains nearby. The warriors immediately sat down with great fear in their eyes. They quickly accepted our salt and shared sugarcane and sweet potatoes as a sign that they had changed their mind and had decided upon friendly cooperation. After they left we called the MAF area pilot and asked him if he heard about a crash of a big airliner in the foggy mountains of our area. But he assured us that he had heard nothing from the tower. The Lord, at the right time, had intervened again, placing fear in hearts like in Old Testament times, clearly showing His protection over His people.

A Miraculous Healing

By now we had been in the Langda area one month. I had started losing weight at an alarming rate, due to hepatitis. The evil one once again tried to wipe me out! Now, while completely isolated from the outside world, not only was the fight for spiritual life of the Unas on but also the fight for my own physical life. After a month of hard physical labor and spiritual warfare with the geopolitical spiritual forces of the area, I had lost 32 pounds of weight. I could keep down no food, and orange blood seeped through my skin everywhere. It became clear that I had to leave for a hospital soon. The evangelists worked long days to finish the minimum length of the strip. I was flown out on the first plane that landed. Five percent of my liver still functioned, the doctors told me. I had to be tube-fed for a whole month, and nothing improved. We clearly recognized this as another frontal attack of the enemy to avoid penetration of the gospel among the Una people.

Finally, I felt the anointing of the Lord coming upon me in a mighty way. I again affirmed that I belonged to the Lord, both in life and in death, and that I refused to give up the pioneer work He had called me to. I trusted God, ordered an airplane and pulled the intravenous tubes out of my arm. My MAF friend and pilot wheeled me to the Cessna airplane, wondering if that was the last time he would fly with me. I was still so sick that during a one-hour layover one of my missionary colleagues contracted the hepatitis and became ill for three months.

Upon my return among the Unas, I found our grass hut completely wet from all the rain. Exhausted, I went to sleep upon a wet bed, trusting the Lord to reveal the evidence of my healing provided for me at Calvary. In the middle of the night I awoke, knowing that I was healed miraculously. I started eating day and night. After a few days I was carried outside to catch the warm rays of the sun while the Una people were placating their spirits to avoid revenge from my supernatural source of healing, whom they had to admit had already won the battle. After three weeks I was able to cross the canyon to evangelize in a village on the opposite slopes. It involved a day of hard trekking, ascending and descending a total of 4,000 feet along 70 percent slopes.

A Providential Rescue

On the other side of the high mountain ranges one of our colleagues was opening up the Nipsan area. Our Yali evangelists had quite a few relatives working there. One day, Bob Donald, the pilot of our Langda survey flight, took off in the dark at 3:30 A.M. from the coastal airstrip in Sentani, planning to arrive at dawn in the interior and to be home early to play some tennis. He finished all his flying around noon.

On his way back to the coast the Lord told Bob to turn east and to land at the Nipsan station. He landed there and asked the missionary if there was something unusual going on. He was told that they had not seen the people in a long time and that they did not seem to be making any progress. After they chatted a while, Bob decided to take off before the clouds would fill the valley. While they walked

to the plane out of nowhere, hundreds of fully-armed warriors descended upon the mission station in an all-out
assault. Bob grabbed the missionary wife and her toddlers
and strapped them in the plane with seatbelts. Gerrit, my
colleague, stayed behind with the evangelists while Bob
took off, with a roaring engine, scattering the assaulting
warriors off the airstrip, from where they shot volleys of
arrows at the "hard-skinned bird."

Bob, an old Korea fighter pilot, now really got into
action. He pulled his Cessna—with the scared missionary
family—into unbelievable curves and loops between the
mountain walls, descending over and over again upon the
hundreds of attacking warriors to "give them a haircut"
with his propellor, as he put it. The warriors decided that
their spirits, whom they had placated, were afraid of the
"pale-skinned" people's God and did not want to cooperate; therefore, they quickly vanished behind the mountains.

At the same time, we continued giving leadership to
the Yali evangelists on outreaches to surrounding villages
and valleys. One Saturday we approached one of the villages. We were at the bottom of a narrow canyon ready to
cross a suspension bridge of bush vines high above a raging mountain stream. Suddenly, some 40 heavily-armed
warriors appeared out of nowhere on the other side of the
stream, attacking us. We called upon the Lord to intervene. And there, at that exact moment, an MAF airplane
roared a few feet overhead, wriggling its way through the
narrow canyon! The fearsome warriors stopped dead in
their assault and disappeared into nowhere as fast as they
had come. The Lord's timing was perfect. His awesome
presence was clearly felt by those animists as well as by
us. We met the pilot at the airstrip. He told us that his
parents-in-law from the U.S. wanted to see "real pioneer-

ing work among primitive savages." So he had decided to take them on this Saturday, when no MAF flying was being done, to the Langda area. He made a low swoop far down into the narrow canyon to give them a good exposure of the rough terrain. When we told them how the Lord had orchestrated this unexpected visit we all rejoiced, and mixed praise with prayer for the salvation of the Kerabuk people. The Lord answered that prayer, and the whole village turned to Him and became one of the strongest churches in the area.

From Death to New Life

The reality of pioneer missionary work was pressed home in 1975, when we received word that the Nipsan mission station was attacked again, burned down, and that 13 of our friends, their wives and children were killed and devoured by an uprising of the local people. I arrived in Nipsan one day after this happened and saw the bones of my friends who gave up their lives while serving their master. That Sunday I led a funeral service for the devastated Yali evangelists in Langda, several of whom lost their brothers or sisters. For weeks some of them were terrified, fearing the same fate from the 3,500 cannibals surrounding us. But the Lord strengthened their faith and they continued witnessing. For two years we saw the Unas going on raiding parties and heard them proudly recount the number of enemies they had killed and eaten. At other times they were defeated and we saw them placing their dead in treetops. They let us excise the arrows from their bodies. Living among those cannibals, loving them in the Lord, we prayed for their salvation and looked in faith toward the day when they would find new life in Christ.

The Lord holds His promises. We witnessed Satan's strongholds being torn down one after another. The open-ended expansion of the book of Acts unfolded before our eyes. The Lord gathered in a great harvest among the Una people of Irian Jaya. Our eyes saw it happen, our ears heard it and we were amazed.

It is a wonderful, humbling experience to be used of God to reach a hidden neolithic tribe in the jungles of Irian Jaya and to see in a multi-individual Christward movement approximately 98 percent of a tribe of 3,500 members change allegiance, acknowledging the lordship of Christ over their lives. We have seen multiple thousands healed and freed from demonic forces who had sway over their lives. The Lord chose to use human vessels in the ministry of healing and deliverance to bring honor to His name and to leave a deep impact upon our lives. We witnessed how the results of power evangelism drastically changed the core of their world view and subsequently every sub-system of their culture.

While actively involved in outreach, training 66 pastors, planting 27 churches and translating the Scriptures into Una vernacular, we were regularly reminded that there is no reason for easy triumphalism. The victorious outcome of power encounters are just the beginning of a continuous, raging battle. But they are the obvious, undeniable proof of the numinous—the awesome presence of God—and they show us clearly that the Lord is in charge and is gathering His Church. *Vicit Agnus Noster Eum Sequamur.* The Lamb has won the battle and we may follow Him! *Soli Deo Gloria!*

RESPONSE
BY
EDGAR J.
ELLISTON

Power Evangelism in Pioneer Mission Strategy

I praise God for His faithful and powerful vindication of His message and messengers described in Dr. Louwerse's paper.

I was raised in a Christian family in a small Kansas community of wheat farmers. I do not remember a time when I did not go to church regularly. However, I never saw any demonstration of the kinds of power that I would have interpreted as God's direct intervention in power.

After attending a Christian college and serving as a pastor in a small rural church in Kansas, I still had not seen any dramatic acts of power that related to spiritual warfare, although I had seen some dramatic answers to prayer. While theologically ready to see God at work in powerful ways, it was not until I lived and worked in a pioneer situation in western Ethiopia that I saw His hand at work in powerful ways that related to both the message of the gospel and to the messengers who were carrying that message.

I am persuaded that God's acts of power provided events that gained a hearing for the message of the gospel and, repeatedly confirmed both the messengers and the message in the context where I was privileged to work in

Ethiopia. The power was demonstrated in hundreds of cases of deliverance from personal or geographical spirit possession, healings, unexpected deliverances from imminent physical danger, power encounters and answer to prayers in situations of persecution or spiritual warfare. I have personally witnessed or experienced all of these kinds of demonstrations of power.

I am also convinced that *miraculous* powers are not only available to the Christian, but are used by Satan to thwart, frustrate, discredit, discourage or otherwise stop the expansion of the Kingdom. I can also describe specific instances where such instances were used against me, my missionary colleagues and the new Christians with whom we worked.

In my response to Dr. Louwerse's presentation I would like to draw your attention to some of the issues that he has raised, some cautions I would note and then close with a suggestion or two.

Issues to Be Considered

1. The reality of the "spiritual" nature of the task of pioneer missions.
2. The "sovereign" way that God acts in power in the situation.
3. The importance of personal commitment, recognizing the risk but trusting in the ultimate victory.
4. That casualties may well result in the conflict, especially if the people involved are not aware of the spiritual character of the conflict.
5. That, while spiritual power is available and often used through us or for our personal benefit, it is often employed in ways other than we might choose.
6. That discernment, undergirded by one's own prayer

and others' intercession, coupled with regular input from the Word of God, is important.

7. That retaliation from the evil one may come in a variety of ways—spiritual, emotional, physical, circumstantial, social, etc.

8. Whether God works in a different way in a "pioneer" situation than in more established situations.

9. Whether the working of God in powerful ways is limited by our Western world view and Western theologies.

10. The relation between our faith and the working of God in power.

11. The qualities of the kind of faith that God honors with His working in powerful ways.

12. The place of the demonstration of God's power in strategic planning in a pioneer mission, beyond one's faithful obedience and care, in maintaining one's relationship with the Lord. Or, to put forward a somewhat different question, to what extent should a person in a pioneer situation seek or "provoke" demonstrations of power in issues such as power encounters, deliverance from demonization or other such issues?

13. Whether there are levels, types or degrees of power that are available to Christians. If we are engaged in a spiritual conflict, is not the power to be used primarily spiritual? How does one access this spiritual power? How does the issue of spiritual maturity relate to the use of power?

14. If we would accept the idea from management theory that authority is the "right to use power," and that authority is both delegated from above by the one who has the power, in what ways does the Lord delegate spiritual power to us? How would you relate the use of spiritual gifts to the use of power?

15. Whether a "pioneer situation" is different from an established church situation in terms of the uses of power that may be available. If so, why? If not, why not?
16. That demonstrations of God's power affect. evangelism, Christian fellowship and nurture in very positive ways.
17. That seeing the power of God demonstrated requires obedience, and often obedience that demonstrates both our vulnerability and weakness.

Cautions to Consider

1. One should be careful about being too glib about not accepting the reality of spiritual warfare.
2. We should be careful about being overly confident that we have all of the answers or that we are above the conflict.
3. Research into signs, wonders and demonstrations of power should not become an end in itself.
4. We must be careful not to think we are sovereignly in control of God's power, or that we can always predict what He will do. We are given authority—the right to exercise power, but it is a delegated right.
5. One must be alert because Satan seeks to devour (1 Pet. 5:8, 9).
6. One should avoid pride in the availability of the spiritual; rather, rejoicing in the salvation God has granted us (Luke 10:17-20).

Recommendations

I suggest that in the arenas of faith and teaching we continue to look at the biblical examples, especially Jesus

Christ, for models of instruction, as in Heb. 13:7. We should also be careful of our company because "Bad company corrupts good morals." Here in the West we tend to deny God's normal activities of power and place them in the abnormal, paranormal, supernatural or miraculous categories rather than seeing His acting daily in powerful ways.

In conclusion, I would also call for research or further study.

CHAPTER 11

Out of Africa: Evangelism and Spiritual Warfare

DONALD R. JACOBS

DONALD R. JACOBS is executive director of the Mennonite Christian Leadership Foundation in Landisville, Pennsylvania. An anthropologist and theologian, he was a missionary in East Africa for 20 years and has written widely on missions and demonology in this region.

As a missionary in East Africa for 20 years, first in Tanzania and then in Kenya, I passed through two major crises. The first was when I discovered that, even though I had been converted years before, my heart was filled with pride, prejudice, fear, envy, jealousy and the entire nest of attitudinal sins. I struggled for months, not willing to accept my sinnerhood. But finally, surrounded by loving brothers and sisters, the dam broke and I found myself at the foot of the Cross once again, just as when I first believed, pleading the blood of Christ for my cleansing. That opened my life to a great inflooding of the Spirit of the Lord. As I kept my heart open to Jesus, a new power and joy surged through my life. The pride of my heart was broken. (I emphasize that it was broken, not eliminated!)

The second crisis occurred a few years later. Having been educated in the Western world view I had slowly, through a study of modern theologians, developed persisting doubts about many of the supernatural aspects of the Scriptures. But my belief in the ethical teachings of the Scriptures, particularly the teachings of Jesus, was never shaken.

As a young missionary I was not sure how to solve this problem. Then I felt a persistent question which I now believe was from the Lord Jesus: "Do you believe that the statements attributed to me in the Gospels are in fact my statements?" This was just as much a crisis for me as the earlier one. After a season of mental anguish I finally answered yes. This sent me into a seismic shock because by accepting Jesus' words as true, I knew that I had a new world view, *His*! And I discovered that His world view was nearer to the African world view than to the Western one. The pride of my intellect was broken.

Defeating Satan in East Africa

In Western circles we are studying the experiences of the spiritual movements with which we have become familiar: the Classical Pentecostal Movement, the Charismatic Renewal and the more newly coined *Third Wave*. I believe it would be helpful to go a bit further afield and at least briefly examine how another movement somewhere else in the world deals with the demonic. I suggest we give attention to the East African Revival which is now almost 60 years old.

The East African Revival has probably been the most substantial movement of the Holy Spirit to the life of the Protestant churches in East Africa to date. The appeal in this movement was not and is not what some call *signs and wonders*. Rather, when the people find Jesus Christ as their personal Savior and Lord they are released from Satanic bondage—not necessarily all at once, but conversion does definitely break the devil's power.

They reject the use of medicines that are prepared and prescribed by the traditional spiritual doctors. And they have no use for the curse or the oath. When threatened by an ancestral spirit or a demon they simply flee to Jesus Christ who they know is their only true protection from Satan. In cultures that are conscious of spiritual power, the new surging power of the Holy Spirit which is released by their newly-found salvation gives them extraordinary vitality.

Overcoming the Power of Satan

Having lived in this setting for many years I learned slowly how the born-again believers care for those who are being accosted by Satan. I was highly impressed. I shall try to list a few of my learnings. I will state them in declaratory sentences.

1. *Do not be taken with demonic taxonomy.* I was once told, "We find help, not in learning more of Satan's tricks, but by learning more of Jesus Christ's marvelous grace." I sense that there is a subtle temptation to try to gain some control over Satan and his forces by studying their activity. Paul set a good pattern for us. He said that he was no stranger to the tricks of the devil, yet he did not major on the subject (2 Cor. 2:11). Among East African believers, it matters little whether the spirit is a demon, a nature spirit or an ancestral spirit. Each and all must go when ordered by Jesus Christ to leave.

When we in the West approach an issue we find it helpful to hone every term to an edge. When it comes to the realm of the demonic I wonder how wise it is to concentrate great energies on definitions. As I reflect on my learnings as a missionary in East Africa I recall that the demon cults and the ancestral spirit cults put phenomenal energies into cataloging the demons. They had elaborate ways of finding out the precise name, nature and power of each demon. They were identified by means of color, smell, area of origin, fine tastes such as whether the demon prefers Lifebouy soap over Lux or cotton clothes over synthetics. In that culture when a person becomes demonized the experts can, within minutes, describe the demon in great detail. Perhaps by so doing they increase their power over these forces. It struck me strangely at first that when people in that culture become believers in Jesus Christ they abandon the need to classify spirits in this way. All evil spirits, they know, are subservient to Christ.

In our culture we have a compulsion to describe and delineate. This is understandable. It only becomes a problem when by so doing we are unconsciously pursuing power over spirits without the power of Jesus Christ. Maybe the East Africans have something to teach us on that aspect of our search.

Having said that, one good reason to seek common definitions is that if we have the same spiritual lexicon we will then at least communicate with one another. Often our semantics and substantive theological differences vex our fellowship.

Also, for the purposes of teaching we must have some frames of reference. That is legitimate, but my guess is that no two teachers come up with the same notes and diagrams. I, too, for example, make a distinction between normal temptation, persistent temptation, oppression and possession; but as I reflect, I realize that these categories are made by people. The Bible provides little definitive help in some of the sticky areas of difference.

2. *Dramatize and highlight Jesus Christ and Him crucified.* I have been told that from the inception of this revival in East Africa all of the manifestations of the power of the Holy Spirit were present. Through living and sensitive leadership, the gifts were utilized to lift up Jesus Christ. Emphasis on gifts, however, never took precedence over the hard sayings of Christ to repent of sin and follow Him with a daily cross.

3. *Seek cleansing from sin and the spiritual gifts will be released.* The one definitive sign that a person is being yielded to the Holy Spirit is a penitent heart. When it comes to the spiritual gifts, they simply assume that these gifts will find normal expression when the heart is right before the Lord.

I learned that one of the reasons for downplaying the dramatic aspects of the spiritual gifts is that in East Africa many of those gifts find expression in the traditional cults and worship. There they are displayed dramatically.

4. *Walk in the light of Christian fellowship and new power over the enemy is available to you.* Ongoing fellowships of light create the context for a continual breaking of Satan's power. As people come to Christ they form little fellowships of light where they pray for one another for all their needs, from physical distress to joblessness. The power of the Lord is released by the Holy Spirit in these little groups just as it has happened in every authentic spiritual awakening.

By coming to Christ for cleansing and forgiveness, they discover that the demonic powers which earlier had binding power over them are, in Christ, broken. Persons who relied on traditional practitioners to correct their maladies shift their hope instead to Jesus Christ. The fellowship groups pray for believers who are in especially vulnerable states, such as being the objects of witchcraft. They are encouraged to live only and entirely on the grace of the Lord Jesus Christ.

5. *Exercise the gifts primarily in the context of living fellowship.* The gifts are exercised in the context of face-to-face, blood-cleansed relationships. Spiritual, physical and even relational healing is experienced and enforced in the fellowship groups. And each group discovers the gifts of the Spirit which enable them to minister to one another.

But the point upon which all things turn is the truly repentant spirit. The believers are keenly aware that the big block to the flow of spiritual power is sin in some form or other. Thus, repentance, which includes a desire to leave a sinful way and follow Jesus, remains a prerequisite for the fullness of the Spirit.

There is only one sign of the receiving of the Spirit among them, and that is that the person is broken before God and before the brothers and sisters. Even though all of the gifts are desired and exercised, the broken spirit is the authentic sign that a person is walking in the Spirit.

6. *Christian fellowship is crucial for post-deliverance care.* In the West I have seen that one of the areas of weakness in deliverance ministries is post-deliverance care. In East Africa these fellowships of God's grace and love become the healing communities in which some of the most distraught people find acceptance and love.

7. *Refuse to tap sources of power that do not originate in Jesus Christ.* Staying free from Satan's power requires a complete denunciation of all non-Christian spiritual sources of well-being. In the Revival fellowship, Christians feel free to take chemical medicines as needed, together with prayer, of course; but they denounce taking local medicines that are prescribed by the traditional doctors. They know that the context in which those medicines are prepared are demonic.

8. *Pursue evangelism, and the necessary power will be available.* It is assumed that Jesus Christ will enable all of His followers to engage in life-changing evangelism and helpful ministries. As they live the life of Christ and seek to bring others to Him, they know that the Lord will empower them for any exigencies that they might meet. The important thing is to be out doing witnessing and evangelizing.

They expect the signs to happen so that the authenticity of the witness concerning Jesus Christ is strengthened. Signs accompany the proclamation of the gospel of salvation. The goal is not to see mighty acts but to increase the number of those who are robed in white robes made clean by the blood of the Lamb.

I might add that as the brethren in East Africa love their Muslim neighbors in the name of Jesus Christ they often pray for them. They have discovered that Muslims have no problem in allowing Jesus to heal them; they get stuck when Jesus reveals Himself as the sin-bearer and the unique Son of God.

The World View Issue

One reason there is such a wide divergence in our comprehension of the work of the demonic is that we have a great variety of world views. Most main-line Western denominations have embraced the major world view of their society, the enlightenment world view or, we might say, the secular humanist world view. This is not amazing because the enlightened world view forms the basis of Western epistemology. If Christians in this culture are to witness effectively they must come to terms with this prevailing world view. But not everyone holds to this world view. Some may do so publicly but in their heart of hearts they believe in the reality of a God who intervenes and makes Himself known, in nature as well as in history.

This raises a question in my mind. Let us say that a person who is educated in the context of Western or scientific world view receives an overwhelming infilling of the Holy Spirit. Does that person then automatically experience an immediate shift in world view, a gradual shift, or none at all? Must there be a shift in world view before a person can fully enter into a relationship with the Holy Spirit of God?

There is an additional aspect of this problem that concerns me. Do I carry the proper impression that when we think of the demonic in our culture we largely limit its activity to the individual? This may be due to the fact that Western cultures focus on the individual personality rather than on the activity of spiritual powers, spatially or in groups. The demonic surely encourages institutions or groups to do evil things such as exploiting or harming other people. If this is true, then how do Christian evangelists destroy the works of the devil at those levels? Is there not a social context in which the demonic operates? How do we go about frustrating Satan in that?

Is it possible that the experience of the Holy Spirit changes but slightly the world view of Western believers? I suspect that this might be true. For some, the experience of the Holy Spirit might not challenge the Western world view at all. It is simply a very meaningful, private, spiritual experience. The world view in its cosmic dimensions remains as it was before the experience of the Holy Spirit.

It is my contention that when we fully accept the world view espoused by Jesus Christ, we then cooperate most naturally with the Holy Spirit. I speak of a world view that comprehends the cosmic drama as a clash of loyalties between the kingdom of God and the kingdoms of this world.

Sometimes I launch little crusades to convince Westerners to allow their world views to broaden to include the world of the spirit. But then I am reminded that we are not saved by changing our views of the world; we are saved by the loving grace of Jesus Christ. Yet my own experience points to the fact that when our view of reality keys with that of Jesus, marvelous things can and do happen.

A final word. If I am not mistaken, Western culture is undergoing some sort of a pronounced world view shift. One evidence of this is the astounding growth of the New Age Movement. My generation believed only that which could be proved by an empirical method. The new winds that are blowing encourage a person to believe almost anything as though there were something dreadfully wrong with the scientific methodology. I fear that we are entering an era when a neo-Platonist world view is becoming more and more possible.

I also foresee masses of young people being swept into the New Age experience which will ultimately place them under spiritual bondage similar to the bondage of the occult and the demonic. About the time we identify the dangers of secular humanism, a new cosmic humanism has taken hold among us, and it may be some time before we really take this one as seriously. In the meanwhile, the number of casualties will mount. Often New Age thought looks less harmful because it encourages religious belief; but I believe it is a hundred times more devastating to Christocentric faith than secular humanism.

CHAPTER

12

The Relevance of Power Ministries for Folk Muslims

J. Dudley Woodberry

J. DUDLEY WOODBERRY, associate professor of Islamic studies at the School of World Mission at Fuller Theological Seminary, served for 13 years in missions in Lebanon, Pakistan, Afghanistan and Saudi Arabia. He has also consulted with the U. S. government and several corporations on Middle Eastern affairs, and served as editor of *Muslims and Christians on the Emmaus Road: Crucial Issues in Muslim Evangelism.*

ALL morning we had watched the people trickle into the city from the surrounding villages, waving flags. Like fallen rain pouring out of little crevices into ever larger gullies, they combined with similar streams of people until they poured into a hollow by some shrines of Muslim holy men.

We had joined the resultant flood and were now waiting in line to file through the tomb of a saint. As we passed by the grave, people pressed their hands or bodies against the sides to draw power or blessing from the spirit of the deceased saint. Some wore amulets to protect them from the evil eye or the spirits. Outside, cloth, hair and replicas of cradles were hung on a tree as people had prayed for healing or made vows. Then we climbed a hill to a shrine where a holy man surrounded by Hindu-type pictures dispensed his power or blessing to the needy who clustered around him.

I sat down to reflect. Here we were in the outskirts of Islamabad or *the place of Islam,* the capital of Pakistan or *the pure land,* in a nation created so Muslims could live according to the Law of God as they understood it. Yet the felt need of at least those who had gathered for religious purposes was power—the capacity to produce results. They had come at a *time* of power, a birthday or holy day of one or more saints. They wore *objects* of power, their amulets. The people came to visit a *place* of power, a shrine, and a *person* of power, a holy man. They wanted to offer a *prayer* for power, or receive a power incantation to ward off the power of the spirits.

How different all this was from the Islam I was prepared to meet. I had just finished a dissertation on contemporary creeds in Islam at the suggestion of Sir Hamilton Gibb, who felt I would profit from research on the system of doctrine in Islam. In this study, the focus was *truth*

rather than power. Prior to that I had studied the most cel-
ebrated Muslim theological treatise, the *Ihya* of al-Ghazali.
Here he dealt with the concepts of theology and the experience of God in worship—truth and mystery. I had written a thesis on the quranic vocabulary for sin, a focus on
sin and righteousness, which I had perceived to be a major
felt need. I had also wandered through Palestinian refugee
camps, even been arrested and questioned as a spy, and
experienced the concern for justice.

In all these cases I had studied and experienced ideal
or formal Islam. Today I was experiencing folk Islam with
its mixture of animism. Yet, most of these people participated in both forms of faith. They went to the mosque on
Friday with its focus on truth, righteousness and mystery;
and they went to the holy man during the week, if their
child was sick, to get power to ward off harm. Obviously, if
the presentation of the gospel was to meet them where
they were, more attention had to be paid to power along
with the other religious concerns.

Formal and Folk Islam

Formal, in contrast to folk, Islam may be called *high* as
opposed to *low*, *ideal* instead of *popular* or *orthodox/
orthoprax* versus *animistic*. The high form centers on the
obedience and the worship of God (the word *islam* means
submission). Conversely, the low form seeks to manipulate what is divine for human purposes, while the orthoprax Muslims will try to use those names to accomplish
their own ends. One book, *Ninety-Nine Names of Allah* by
Shems Friedlander, published in a number of languages in
Nigeria and Pakistan, tells how many times and in what
context to repeat each name to get, for example, power,
health and protection from harm, hunger, bad habits,

disaster, sickness, fear, danger, miscarriage, enemies, childlessness and sin.[1]

Folk Muslims may feel a certain uneasiness about associating traditional beliefs and practices with God; but they see in them a source of power, so they try to integrate the two systems. In a rice ritual of the Maranaos of the Philippines the leader enjoins: "Praise to Allah! Pray that we will not sin in inviting the *tonong* [spirits]. He created the *tonong.*" The devotees then ask the *tonong* to be intermediaries and "Pray to Allah that all farmers will have a bountiful harvest." Finally, the leader again admonishes the farmers to pray to God that they might not sin in inviting the *tonong;* but God created them and, the leader adds, "gave them power."[2] This need for power leads them to risk an offense against God.

In high Islam the mosque is the place for submission; while in low Islam the shrine is the place of power or blessing. In ideal Islam the Quran and Traditions of Muhammad are the primary sources of authority; whereas in popular Islam the Quran itself, or selected portions of it, serve as power objects to ward off harm, and books on magic serve as guides.

In high Islam the practitioners are *imams* or *ulema,* recognized for their training or intellectual knowledge; but in low Islam the practitioner is a *pirl* or *wali* who has prepared by such means as 40 days and nights of fasting and is recognized for his or her power or blessing.

Interaction Between High and Low Islam

The interaction of the ideal and popular has taken place since the rise of Islam. The new faith was both reacted against and colored by the animism that existed in Arabia. Stone fetishes, sacred trees and sacred wells were rejected as power objects, but Muslims treated the Black Stone and the Zam Zam water in the sanctuary of Mecca as sources of power or blessing.

Power people such as sorcerers and soothsayers were rejected;[3] yet some of the first utterances of Muhammad took the form of soothsaying and, by demanding obedience to God and His Prophet, the Arabian Prophet laid a foundation from which Muhammad veneration and then saint veneration would rise. Likewise the spirits or *jinn* and personal spirits or *qarina* were incorporated into the Quran.

Finally, the power ritual of the pilgrimage was included in the orthoprax cult. Even though its pagan origins were radically reinterpreted, it still included the Black Stone and the Zam Zam water, which continued to be treated as sources of power or blessing.

The Quran condemned sorcery, and the authoritative traditions of Muhammad condemned such magical practices as divination but allowed certain forms of it.[4] Thus, what we see repeatedly is the camel's nose in the tent.

The spread of Islam was frequently carried on by mystics or sufis who already were syncretistic in beliefs and practices. This further facilitated the incorporation of local animistic beliefs and practices into local manifestations of Islam. Fundamentalists decried this as the major sin of associating other power or administration with that which is God's alone. But the fusion of animistic with the formal faith became widespread, and with it the concern for power. The more the mix included folk elements, the greater the focus on power.

High Islam, of course, also includes a concern for power, though the source of that power shifts more to God. For example, tribal West Africans pray *to* the ancestors as sources of power. As they became more Islamized, they may pray *through* the ancestors to God. As they become still more fully Islamized, they pray to God *for* the ancestors, who need power or blessing.

Power in the Folk-Islamic World View

The felt need for power is so great among folk Muslims that their entire world view is seen through the spectacles of power—one lens is power through living beings; the other is power through forces. These two categories can be divided into those that are helpful and those that are harmful. Although the two-dimensional limitations of a page restrict us to listing these helpful and harmful beings and forces in four columns (see figure 1), we might illustrate them on four different pages of a book, all connected through the common spine.[5] This might better express that many of the beings and forces can slip back and forth between being helpful and harmful; that the helpful beings and forces are in conflict with their harmful counterparts; and, that the beings are not rigid divisions. Angels, for example, may pass from the other world to this world.

From the array of helpful and harmful beings and forces pitted against each other, it is evident that the folk Muslim wants to acquire the aid of helpful beings and forces and avoid those that are harmful. The confrontation is evident in the rites of passage.

Attempts to Acquire Helpful Power

At birth, helpful power is acquired by reciting the call to prayer in the infant's right ear and the confession of faith in God and Muhammad in the left ear. An amulet is attached to the body to guard against the evil eye and incense burned to drive away the spirits. Among the Tausug

Power Confrontation in Folk-Islamic World View

	HELPFUL		HARMFUL	
	Powers(Beings)	*Powers*(Forces)	*Powers*(Forces)	*Powers*(Beings)
Other-worldly	God Angels	qadr(divine decree) Heavenly Tablet	bad fate	Shaytan(Iblis)
This-worldly	good spirits(*jinn*)	*baraka*(power, blessing)	evil eye	shaytans(*jinn*)
	fairies	vows	cursings	qarina(personal spirit)
(extra-ordinary)		*dhikr*(reciting divine names)	omens	
	apostles	*haram*(sacred locations)	*haram*(taboo)	dews(powerful spirits)
	prophets	good magic	evil magic	als(spirit witches)
	dead saints	amulets		Zar(divining spirit)
	ancestors	sacred objects		*balbalang*(spirit with human trunk and wings)
	recently dead	magic numbers designs		
	walis, pir(saints) Secret Societies "bush devils"		Secret Societies "bush devils"	
		<visions/dreams>		
(ordinary)	pious Muslims other Muslims	herbs, drugs alchemy natural forces	disbelievers	natural forces

Figure 1

of the Philippines noise will be made to frighten away the *balbalan* spirits who are believed to have trunks of men and wings. Also, anyone suspected of having an evil eye is kept away. In Mindanao, the placenta is buried or put in an amulet to guard the relationship between the child and his or her spirit twin. In Iran, the mother is protected from various spiritual beings by an onion over her head and quenching red-hot iron in her drinking water.

Naming is done on an auspicious day such as the birth-day of Muhammad or one determined by astrology. A derogatory name may be chosen so as not to attract the spirits, and any compliment is accompanied by the excla-mation *mashalla* ("what God wills") to show there is no jealousy that might attract the evil eye. A substitutionary sacrifice of a lamb may be made so that the child will be preserved.

Circumcision, likewise, would be performed on similar auspicious days by a person with power at a place such as a shrine oriented toward Mecca. The Samal of the Philip-pines, likewise, will not walk over a rice pestle at such times.

Marriages, similarly, will be held on auspicious days at places of power. Also the couple's birth dates will be checked by astrology and their names by alchemy to make sure that the two will be compatible. When the wife is pregnant she may tie amulets or strings above and below the fetus to ward off spirits and the evil eye, and those believed to have an evil eye or to be jealous will be kept away.

Finally, at death, people are made to face Mecca in their final moments as they will later in burial. Those ritu-ally unclean are kept away. Messages to the archangels may be buried, too. Friends and relatives acquire merit by sewing the shroud, carrying the bier and digging the grave. On the fortieth day after death, when the spirit is believed to leave the body, the merit is transferred to the deceased.

These rites of passage demonstrate the constant power confrontation in their world view and the resultant fear in which they live. Since much of their faith and practice expresses the kingdom of darkness, there is still another confrontation with which the Christian is concerned and that is with the kingdom of light.

Christian Power Ministries Among Folk Muslims

In the light of folk Muslims' felt need for power, it is noteworthy that the rise of Christianity in southwestern Arabia is attributed to power ministries by the oldest extant biography of Muhammad Ibn Hisham's recension of a work by Ibn Ishaq. It tells of a Christian construction worker who cursed a snake which died, prayed for a blind boy who was healed, and then in God's name cursed the local sacred palm tree which was uprooted by a wind. [6] The last account fits the original restricted definition of a "power encounter."

Today, the major movements to Christ in the Muslim world are among folk Muslims. With their felt need for power, it is not surprising that all of them are associated with power ministries—exorcisms, healings and ever reports of the dead being raised. These accounts range from such widely separated countries as Burkina Faso in Africa, Bangladesh in South Asia and Indonesia in Southeast Asia.

Because of the relevance of power ministries to folk Muslims and the fact that God is using them, we need biblical models. Therefore, we might ask how Jesus and Paul would encounter power in folk Islam. Illustrations will be drawn from contemporary experiences.

How Jesus Would Encounter Power in Folk Islam

Jesus lived in a world concerned with power similar to the world of folk Islam that we have observed. There were *spirit* powers which He exorcised (Luke 9:37-43). The woman with an issue of blood treated the hem of His garment as a power *object* (Luke 8:41-56). The pool of Bethesda was a power *place,* and when the water was stirred it was a power *time* (John 5:1-47). Anointing the sick with oil (Mark 6:13) or exorcising by believing prayer and command (Mark 9:14-29) might be seen as power rituals. Our Lord Himself was a power *person* (Luke 5:17-26).

Jesus' sending out of the disciples in a power ministry in Luke 10 suggests what He would do with similar folk Muslims. We read that the Lord sent them out "two by two" (v.1). The *first* principle we see is that He would go in partnership. Although He originally faced His adversary alone, He developed an approach of partnership. The powers are real, and discernment is needed. The most significant work among folk Muslims in South Asia has placed a couple in each village.

The passage goes on to say that the Lord sent them ahead of Him into every place prior to His arrival (v.1). *Second,* He would have the way prepared for Himself. Every major advance of the Church has had a period of preparation, of preevangelism. A man named Inayat, who has an effective power ministry in Pakistan, finds that healing and salvation usually come gradually after preparation in teaching.[7]

Jesus continues, "Pray . . . the Lord of the harvest to send out laborers" (v. 2). *Thirdly,* He would pray for reinforcement as He entered the spiritual warfare. The most effective power ministries among folk Muslims in South Asia are team ministries. One team is made up of 15 believers from Brethren, Roman Catholic, Pentecostal and Episcopal backgrounds.[8] This is spiritual warfare so prayer is essential. In another country in which there was flooding and erosion of the river bank, a naked madman called for five Christian couples to pray that the erosion would stop. They waded into the river and prayed from 8:30 A.M. until noon with villagers watching and jeering. Then the wind changed, the water calmed and the erosion stopped. Two villagers accepted Christ, and others still point to the place on the bank where the erosion stopped.

"I send you out as lambs in the midst of wolves," Christ said (v. 3). *Fourth,* He would enter the encounter with a power that is expressed by vulnerability, by the cross. Our Lord conquered the cosmic powers on the cross (Col. 2:15), and we can expect to be "partakers of Christ's sufferings" (1 Pet. 4:13). This year in a South Asian country, a Muslim leader became a follower of Christ. A mob gathered to kill him. He prayed and someone shouted that someone else had been critically injured. The mob disbanded and ran to the other man's house.

Christ's instructions included, "Carry no purse" (Luke 10:4). Yet, elsewhere the disciples are told to take one and even to get a sword (Luke 22:35, 36). This suggests, *fifth,* that He would alter his approach according to the timing and the context. We note historical cycles in the more extraordinary signs and wonders, with the greatest concentrations being when there are major expansions of the Church.

Jesus goes on to tell the disciples, "Whenever you

enter a town and they receive you, . . . heal . . . and say
. . . 'The kingdom of God has come near you.'" Conversely, they are told to leave any place that does not
receive them while they announce that "the kingdom of
God has come near" (Luke 10:8-10). *Sixth,* He would
focus on the receptive but still leave a witness with those
who are not. Currently, folk Muslims are more receptive
than the orthodox, suggesting that we should focus on the
former while we still give a witness to others.

The disciples' instructions were to "heal the sick" and
proclaim the nearness of the kingdom (v.9), and they
reported that the demons were subject to them (v.17).
Seventh, He would engage in a holistic ministry of healing
and announcing God's rule, of demonstration and proclamation in which healing is a sign of the Kingdom. In South
Asia, country doctors declared a three-year old girl to be
within hours of death. A Christian couple prayed for her
and she was healed. Four followed Jesus. The villagers
were given instruction during the next few months and
nine more believed. With the subsequent combination of
demonstration and proclamation in the area, the numbers
have mushroomed into the thousands.

The unresponsive are told, "Woe to you . . . for if the
mighty works done in you had been done in Tyre and
Sidon, they would have repented" (v.13). *Eighth,* He
would note that power ministries lead to opposition as well
as faith. As in our Lord's day, both responses are found.
Where hundreds became Christians in a South Asian local-
ity a mob estimated at 10,000 came with petrol to kill a
convert. They got sidetracked on learning of an *imam* in
the area who had also become a follower of Jesus. The latter was able to calm all but two who then began rolling on
the ground in pain and had to be hospitalized. The news
led about 200 more to follow Christ.

The disciples returned and reported that "even the demons are subject to us in your name." Jesus responded, "I saw Satan fall like lightening from heaven" (v.17, 18). *Ninth,* He would show that world views need .to be expanded to include the spirit world and the cosmic battle there. This lack in most Western world views is what Paul Hiebert has called "the flaw of the excluded middle."[9]

Jesus gave the disciples authority over "serpents and scorpions, and over all the power of the enemy" (v.19). *Tenth,* He has given and continues to give authority in both the physical and the spiritual realms. The story above, of Christians praying for the flooding and erosion to stop, illustrated how God responded to prayer concerning the physical elements. One of the lessons that Christians who are oppressed by spirits need to learn is that they have authority to command them to leave.

The disciples are warned, "Do not rejoice in this, that the spirits are subject to you; but rejoice that your names are written in heaven" (v.20). *Eleventh,* He would prioritize evangelism over exorcism. Some involved in a ministry of exorcism have found it monopolizing so much of their time that other areas of ministry like evangelism have suffered.

Then Jesus addressed God as "Father, Lord of heaven and earth" (v.21). *Twelfth,* He would demonstrate that instead of being a place of fear of potentially harmful beings and forces, the universe is under the control of a personal, loving Father. The previous analysis of folk Islam has demonstrated that the folk Muslim lives in fear.

Christ's prayer then recognizes that God has "hidden these things from the wise and understanding and revealed them to babes" (v.21). *Finally,* He would observe that, for understanding such spiritual realities, simple faith and teachableness are more important than erudition. Most of us in academia or in foreign missionary service have had to learn about the spirit world and spiritual warfare from the common people we serve. Richard De Ridder observed how unprepared his formal training in traditional Reformed Theology left him for dealing with the spirit world in which his people lived. He concluded, "This is a chapter of Reformed Theology that has still not been written, and perhaps which cannot be written by the West."[10]

How Paul Would Encounter Power in Folk Islam

Ephesus in Paul's day, as described in Acts 19 (*RSV*), contained the major elements found in folk Islam. It had *spirit* powers (v. 11-20) and power *objects* in the silver shrines of Artemis (v. 24) and the sacred stone that fell from heaven (v. 35)—a meteorite like the Black Stone in the Ka'ba in Mecca. It had a power *place*, the temple of Artemis (v. 27), and power times when there were celebrations in honor of the goddess. There were power *rituals*, the Jewish exorcists who tried to use the name of Jesus as a power word (v. 13). Other rituals would have been used by those who practiced the magic arts (v. 18, 19). We can infer from what Paul said and did in this context what he would say and do among folk Muslims.

In Ephesus "he entered the synagogue and for three months spoke . . . about the kingdom of God." Then he "argued daily in the hall of Tyrannus. This continued for two years, so that all . . . heard the word of the Lord" (v. 8-10). The *first* principle is that he would engage in power ministries in the context of teaching. The spiritual effectiveness of Inayat's power ministry in Pakistan, to which we have referred, is that it is always carried on in the context of teaching. Healings and exorcisms that are not in the context of extended teaching seldom make much permanent impact on the Church. Such teaching was necessary in an African country when a folk Muslim sorcerer followed Christ. Deception had become such a way of life for him that it was a difficult habit to break, a task needing all the spiritual reinforcement possible.

We read that "when some were stubborn and disbelieved, speaking evil of the Way before the congregation [of the synagogue], he withdrew" (v.9). The *second* principle has already been seen in Luke 10: he would focus on the receptive.

The account continues, "God did extraordinary (lit., not the ordinary) miracles (lit., powerful deeds) by the hands of Paul" (v.11). *Third,* God would use him in the miracles but God would be the one accomplishing the task. Conversely, folk Muslims tend to focus on the human instrument as the power person. *Fourth,* the word "extraordinary" reminds us that there is also an ordinary way that God works; so we may note: God would also use him in ordinary ways. We need to remember that the God who does extraordinary things is also the one who established the works through the laws of nature such as healing through medicine. Even the gift of grace to endure unchanged suffering is a work of God.

The extraordinary works are described, "handkerchiefs or aprons were carried away from his body to the sick, and diseases left them and the evil spirits came out of them" (v.12). *Fifth,* He might let objects convey the power, but the power would be God's, not the objects'. As Jesus used saliva in enabling eyes to see, a Coptic Orthodox priest in Egypt used to send some of his saliva in a bottle to the sick who could not come to him, and God would sometimes heal them.

"Itinerant Jewish exorcists," we read, "undertook to pronounce the name of the Lord Jesus over those who had evil spirits" (v.13). Here, and elsewhere where the activities of those other than Paul are described, the principles are stated without reference to Paul. *Sixth*, real evidence of the power of God is often accompanied by counterfeits. Folk Muslims have fabrications of the works of the Spirit. Some exorcise spirits in the *Zar* cult, speak in tongues, prophesy concerning the future or collapse in unconsciousness in a state like being "slain in the Spirit." Thus, discernment is needed to decide between: what is real and what is an illusion; what is of God and what is of the devil; and, what has a physical or psychological or a spiritual cause, or any combination of these.

The evil spirit answered the exorcists, "Jesus I know, and Paul I know; but who are you?" (v.15). *Seventh*, spirits recognize the authority of Jesus and those in whom He resides. Folk Muslims try to appease or threaten spirits, but the Christian can speak with authority because Christ is over all such powers (Eph. 1:20, 21). God's superior power was evident in an African country where a Muslim tried to put a curse on a Christian convert. It backfired, and he got deathly sick. No medicine man could help him; so he had to contact the Christians who prayed for him. He was healed and became a Christian.

The passage continues "the man in whom the evil spirit was leaped on them, mastered all of them, and overpowered them" (v.16). *Eighth*, spirits have real power, using the bodies they inhabit. In the same African country just described, a sorcerer put a curse on three people who became insane though they were later restored to mental health through Christian prayer.

The result in Ephesus was that "fear fell upon them all" (v.17). *Ninth*, evidence of power elicits fear which can only be balanced when God is seen as a loving Father. As has been demonstrated previously, the mood of folk Muslims is that of fear.

The verse continues, "and the name of the Lord Jesus was extolled" (v.17). *Tenth,* signs of the power of the kingdom should lead to the exalting of the King. This is often not the case since folk Muslims just want healing and usually do not care from where it comes. In Mindanao the sick may go to the Muslim Shaman, the Catholic priest, the government hospital and the Protestant missionary.

In Ephesus, many new believers confessed their practices of magic and burned their books on magic (v.18, 19). *Eleventh,* Christian converts often continue magical practices. In Faisalabad (formerly Lyalpur) Pakistan people cast off their Muslim amulets at an evangelistic meeting and then outside bought St. Christopher's medals for stronger Christian amulets. A Christian holy woman in the capital city of Islamabad wrote Bible verses, rather than quranic verses, for amulets.

Twelfth, magic seeks mechanically to manipulate rather than submit to the will of God. This is a temptation to Christians as well as Muslims. *Thirteenth,* materials associated with magic need to be destroyed. If a former Muslim sorcerer in an African country had not burned his paraphernalia, he said, he probably would have used it to discover and curse those who stole his boat and fishing net, his only means of support for himself and other converts who had lost their jobs and homes.

The result in Ephesus was that "the word of the Lord grew and prevailed mightily" (v.20). *Fourteenth,* the demonstration of God's power should lead to the increase of the message rather than be an end in itself. This is why significant church growth has only resulted when power ministries have been combined with teaching.

330 Wrestling with Dark Angels

Finally, the story concludes with the silversmiths, because of their economic interests, stirring up the populace by appealing to their religious concerns and civic pride. Then the legal and governmental institutions are identified as means of expressing complaints or redressing wrongs (v.24-39). *Last*, the "powers" with which the Christian must contend are not only spirits but human institutions, be they commercial, religious, legal or governmental. These are included in the biblical definition of the "powers."[11]

Current converts in the countries described have lost their jobs, their families, and in some cases their lives. They have been called disbelievers and faced court cases to deprive them of their property. In such situations those Christians with a means of livelihood have provided for others. In another case they have tried to form a cooperative. Though the New Testament leads Christians to expect suffering with no guarantee of escape in this life, God did avenge such treatment in one African town where Muslims have been persecuting Christians. A friend, whose judgment I trust, personally saw and reported that, for five months this year in daylight, balls of fire struck the fences and later the homes of Muslims who persecuted the Christians. God's power comes in judgment as well as mercy.

Last year my wife, youngest son and I visited Ephesus. The Temple of Artemis, one of the seven wonders of the ancient world, had all sunk into the marsh except one pillar which bore witness to the glory that had been. Nearby stands the Isa (Jesus) Mosque, representing the orthodox faith that has replaced the old paganism. Yet the mosque is surrounded by homes in which are hung glass replicas of blue eyes (nazars) to ward off the evil eye—reminders of the folk beliefs and practices that are mixed with the orthodox. Yet, like the temple before, these too will pass away. All that will be left is the name on the mosque—Jesus—since, as the previous residents were told, he sits "far above all . . . power" (Eph. 1:21).

Notes

1. Shems Friedlander, *Ninety-Nine Names of Allah* (Lagos: Islamic Publications Bureau, Karachi: London Book House, n.d.).
2. Nagasura T. Madale, "Kashawing: Rice Ritual of the Maranaos," *Mindanao Journal*, I: pp. 74-80.
3. *Mishkat al-Masabih*, translated by James Robson. 4 vols. (Lahore: Sh. Muhammad Ashraf.), Book 22, chap. 3, Para. 1.
4. Ibid.
5. Many categories have been adapted from Paul Hiebert, "Power Encounter and Folk Islam, *Muslims and Christians on the Emmaus Road*, ed. J. Dudley Woodberry (Monrovia, CA: MARC, 1988), pp. 52-54, and Bill Musk, *Popular Islam: An Investigation into the Phenomenology and Ethnotheological Bases of Popular Islamic Belief and Practice* (Pretoria: University of South Africa, 1984, unpublished Doctoral dissertation), p. 164.
6. Ibn Hisham and Abd al-Malik, *The Life of Muhammad: Ibn Ishaq's Sirat Rasue Allah*. Translated by A. Guillaume. (London: Oxford University Press, 1955), pp. 14-16.
7. Vivienne Stacey, "The Practice of Exorcism and Healing," *Muslims and Christians on the Emmaus Road*, ed. J. Dudley Woodberry, (Monrovia: MARC, 1988), pp. 317-331.
8. Ibid., p. 322.
9. Paul Hiebert, "The Flaw of the Excluded Middle," *Missiology*, January 1982, 10: pp. 35-47.
10. Richard R. DeRidder, *Disciplining the Nations* (Grand Rapids, Baker Book House, 1975), p. 222.
11. Walter Wink, *Naming the Powers: The Language of Power in the New Testament* (Philadelphia: Fortress Press, 1984).

RESPONSE
BY
DEAN S.
GILLILAND

The Relevance of Power Ministries for Folk Muslims

The context of my response to Mr. Woodberry's paper is West Africa, especially Nigeria. This is a special place to study folk Islam in light of evangelism. This is because of the nearly equal distribution between Muslims and Christians and, because there are several notable evangelism projects now underway to convert Muslims. Political and ethnic tension is critical. It all boils down to, "Power, power, who's got the power?" The paper is in three parts, and I want to respond briefly to each.

Formal and Folk Islam

The distinctions Mr. Woodberry made between formal and folk Islam hold true, in general, for West Africa. A further note must be made that West African manifestations of folk Islam are of two varieties. There are the highly institution-alized types (for example, Hamaliyya, Wahabiyya) with stylistic rituals and sectarian beliefs, and there is a loose, practically illiterate expression of Islam which, though dominated by ancestral religion, is still Islam.

I want to emphasize that in this context, the term *power encounter* is a legitimate, positive concept for evangelization among Muslims. This is true in the generic Muslim context, not just in folk Islam. There is considerable ambivalence in the ranks of formal Islam about folk practices. It has always been this way. What Islam strictly forbids is tolerated unofficially at least, and often practiced openly. Ideally, the power shifts more to God, as Woodberry has pointed out, in orthodox Islam. But in a place like Nigeria, and West Africa in general, this would be true for only a small minority of Muslims.

I got the impression Woodberry feels that orthodox Muslims now keep quite a clean space between themselves and folk Muslims, even though it was not so in the beginning. In Nigeria this is only theoretically true. Who can best meet the manifest need will have status as these two illustrations demonstrate.

First, on Muhammed's birthday (1965) the *ulama* marched round and round in Bauchi town center, beating drums and singing ancestral songs and spitting on the ground. This was a cry for Allah to send rain. What a sight they were in their white gowns! The king of Bauchi, an *alhaji* (one who made the pilgrimage), watched. Such utilization of folk practice even by Arabic-speaking Muslims is common.

Second, an Apostolic Church in Ilorin (looked down on by evangelicals) sang, prayed and danced around a Muslim woman who had been thrown out by her husband because she was barren. Being evicted in this manner is more symbolic than actual. And within a month she became pregnant. The high ranking Muslim husband took her back and allowed her to become a Christian.

My point is to push the viability of a power methodology even further to include all Muslims. What verbal encounter has rarely accomplished at any level of Islam, wise Spirit-guided power encounter can. Why are there

African independent churches more successful in convert-
ing Muslims than historical churches? Since we are not
prepared to approach Muslims with power, why should we
complain about the questionable Christianity of the independent churches? They have the converts from Islam.
We have the right doctrine.

Taxonomy of Power

The second section of Woodberry's paper was fascinating.
So much is there for the missiologist. I refer to the taxonomy of power confrontation in world view. He does mention that the categories of *helpful* and *harmful* tend to slide
across lines. I want to compare this with the folk Islam we
find among Islamized traditional people in northern Nigeria. The important point of difference with the Middle East
context is that in Africa there is a quite well defined *neu-
tral* category of powers. What lies behind this phenomenon is the encounter that Muslim power structures had
with traditional structures when Islam first arrived. This
resulted in a synthesis which changed both Islam and the
ancestral system. From the illustration, note that the *neu-
tral* features can recombine on either the helpful or the
harmful side. But it is important that folk Islam sees
baraka (blessing) in terms of both the *helpful* and the *neu-
tral* categories. Only the harmful forces/beings are associated with *la'ana* (curse). See fig. 2.

It is helpful to note that traditional practitioners imitate
Muslim paraphernalia and vice versa. Clients utilize either
Muslim or traditional clerics; "belief" is not required.

There is a similarity here with certain of the designa-
tions of the *powers* used by Paul. Not all of the powers
were evil or intrinsically bad. While, difficult for us to con-
ceptualize, the *stocheia,* for example (Gal. 4:9; Col. 2:20)

Figure 2

Helpful	*Neutral*	*Harmful*
(angels) malaiku	iskoki (winds)	sihiri (divination)
(gods) alloli	aljanu (jinn)	shaitani iblishi
(ancestors) kaka	ruhoh (spirits)	maita (witchcraft)

BARAKA	LA'ANA
(blessing)	(curse)

were those *elemental spirits,* all of which had some kind of semi-benevolent function before Christ. This kind of reality calls for patience and care on our part in West Africa. It is also a lead to a contextualized power theology. There is more in the African power world that is disposed toward the good than to the bad. The ambiguous categories could be claimed for the gospel. Paul's argument in Colossians shows quickly the new faith can slip into a syncretism with these outmoded, passé powers. The preeminent Christ must now reign! (Col. 2:15)

A pastor-in-training (1962) had an intestinal disorder, from which he got no help at the mission hospital. He went to a Muslim doctor. I tried to stop him. The *malam* read verses from the Quran to him periodically for ten days. His diagnosis: a *ruhu* (spirit) had to be blown from the pastor by an *iska* (wind) from the west. The patient came back and went on with his training. He is an ordained pastor today. Note the formula: Christian + Muslim + traditional = healing. The church and the hospital had done nothing.

Common Teachers

Woodberry's paper turns to a thoughtful application taken from Jesus' commissioning of the 70 and Paul's ministry in Ephesus. This was done with special exegetical eyes. No one could have seen what is in these passages for power ministry among folk Muslims without having lived in the real world of Islam. We thank Woodberry for this.

I want to emphasize the observation on Luke 10:21, that God uses the common people to teach us. In the high tradition of Islam, as in any religion, the intellectuals (theologians) must defend the dogma and perpetuate the tradition. The babes transparently tell the story, call for help and usually accept when it is offered. I confess that in my evangelical way I was closed off from Islam even though Nigeria was predominantly Muslim. This was because I had a doctrine that Muslims had to accept or reject. All of my interaction was with the thinkers. Then I met an untrained Muslim man who said he had had a vision and heard a voice. He saw Jesus and the voice said that he should pray to Allah in the name of Jesus. I was embarrassed that God would be so anti-intellectual, but it was a start on a new paradigm for me.

A final observation on Paul's ministry at Ephesus. Acts 19:11,12 reads, "And God did extraordinary miracles by the hands of Paul, so that handkerchiefs or aprons were carried away from his body to the sick, and diseases left them and the evil spirits came out of them" (*RSV*). This is a unique narrative as to the means Paul used. Nowhere was magic more pervasive than in Ephesus. We are here in the center of a charged field of power. The magicians practiced contagious magic. The open, innovative, Spirit-led Paul contextualized his methods. The methodology had to be a familiar one. These magic sweat clothes from his body communicated instantly with power. What a risk he took! The orthodox would have accused him of syncretism. Much could be said about the means of power encounter. Paul's method was that of contagious magic alright, but the consequence was healing, demonic confrontation and, "the name of the Lord was extolled." Dynamic contextualization of this kind requires intimate, intense direction from the Holy Spirit. And it probably will draw criticism from the home church.

chapter 13

Trends and Topics in Teaching Power Evangelism

F. Douglas Pennoyer

F. Douglas Pennoyer, coeditor of these lectures, is director of the Intercultural Institute of Missions at Seattle Pacific University. He is an anthropologist, church planter, two-time Fulbright scholar and former corporate executive. Dr. Pennoyer teaches courses in anthropology and missiology, and conducts seminars on spiritual warfare.

EIGHT years ago Fuller Theological Seminary took a bold step and offered an experimental course on signs, wonders and church growth. The course found its way into the School of World Missions curriculum because students from all over the world were coming to Fuller, excited about the quantam leaps of church growth in their countries. They reported demonstrations of spiritual power that doubled, tripled or exponentially multiplied congregations. "Why aren't missiologists studying this pattern of church growth?" they asked. "This is what we do and it works."

Fuller's experiment, with a course taught by John Wimber and Peter Wagner on evangelism and the miraculous, has also helped to spawn growth of another kind. Institutions all over the country are beginning to offer courses on power evangelism topics, and it is occurring at a time when publishers report that these are hot topics for the 1990s. Frank Peretti's novels on human, divine and demonic battles are some of the most read books by Christian readers today. Suddenly the subject has come off the streets and into classroom discussions.

Turn on the television set almost any day, anytime, and you will discover talk show hosts interviewing New Agers who channel communications from spirit guides, or Satanists who sacrifice animals and even babies. In the 1990s the world is obsessed with power: supernatural power. How do we find it, harness it and use it to reduce the stressful uncertainties of life?

The Church is called by God to provide the answers to the world's call for power. Christians have the right power source and there is a needy world trying to find it. Christians must learn the best biblical ways to unleash the power. It is critical that institutions of higher learning teach their students to search the Scriptures on these issues and discover appropriate methods of impacting the world with God's power.

Power evangelism classes belong in missions training centers, Bible schools, Christian colleges and seminaries. Wherever the Word of God is taught, we cannot separate the proclamation from the power, and we dare not teach a gospel message or methodology that presents a caricature of God's power. It is all-powerful for He is omnipotent. It is relevant for everyone today for He is omnipresent now and in every age, everywhere. It transcends human knowledge and experience for He is omniscient.

Several trends in providing such courses emerged during the presentation of the preceding papers at the Academic Symposium on Power Evangelism at Fuller Seminary in December 1988. In this section we list eight of these trends, then present ten specific courses as examples of the variety currently offered at Christian institutions.

Trends

1. *Mission training schools, Bible schools, colleges and seminaries are starting to teach power evangelism topics.* In previous decades power evangelism was ignored or given cursory treatment by mission training centers. Most missionaries arrived on the field ill-prepared to meet situations involving demonic interference. Training curricula focused on basic biblical principles and concentrated on enhancing the candidate's knowledge of the Scriptures. Cross-cultural methods of communication were taught and, while candidates went to language school to study local languages, they did not go to spiritual warfare classes to learn how to handle demons. And only Pentecostals were emphasizing healing as a method of evangelism.

Now increasing numbers of mission agencies are

including seminars on spiritual warfare as part of their basic training or in-service workshops. For example, Youth With a Mission includes a module on the devil and demons in their Discipleship Training Seminars. Overseas Crusades has a vice-president (Dr. Ed Murphy) who travels the globe lecturing on spiritual warfare, and The Evangelical Alliance Mission has a veteran missionary in South America whose growing ministry is to help local pastors understand and practice deliverance. Arab World Ministries and the Evangelical Free Church have sponsored workshops on power encounter, by Dr. Timothy Warner, for their missionaries.

The gathering at the 1988 symposium at Fuller Seminary alone is evidence that different aspects of power evangelism are receiving notice at schools other than seminaries. Fuller's Signs and Wonders course, taught by Wimber, can be credited with some of the expansion into Bible schools and colleges. As graduates have assumed teaching positions around the nation, they have instituted new courses on the topic, or revised existing ones to include it. Other seminaries, recognizing the validity of the subject as an academic course, have followed Fuller's example. Therefore, this topic is beginning to be taught at missionary training centers, Bible schools, Christian colleges and seminaries. It is possible that within the decade of the '90s power evangelism in its various forms will become a required part of missions courses at many of these schools.

2. *These schools represent a broad spectrum of denominational and nondenominational schools, and come from both Pentecostal and non-Pentecostal traditions.* The power evangelism scene with its focus on the Holy Spirit's power would appear to be a natural fit with the Pentecostal or charismatic traditions. Certainly some institutions that

have taken narrow stands on theological issues concerning the work of the Holy Spirit have resisted attempts to include power evangelism topics in their curricula. Individual faculty members who have suggested courses on the topic have either been discouraged or actively prohibited from teaching the subject.

But power evangelism as a subject, and in particular the power encounters and spiritual warfare issues, seem to be bridging a gap between theological traditions. Besides, more than one Pentecostal academician at the symposium remarked that we cannot assume power evangelism is a best fit with Pentecostals because even Pentecostals need to put the Spirit back in the curriculum today. And, non-Pentecostals are becoming more aware of the Holy Spirit's power, even leading to revival movements characterized by renewal trends within mainline denominations. These factors have shortened the gap, and power encounter and spiritual warfare seem to be the bridge or common meeting ground.

3. *An increasing number of academicians are moving into researching and teaching power evangelism topics.* Signs and Wonders as an academic subject at Fuller was birthed in the dynamic, multi-disciplinary, global-experienced School of World Mission. Several professors sat in on that class, including Chuck Kraft. Kraft's personal journey from curious onlooker to avid practitioner is recounted in his book *Christianity with Power.* We can expect that as the number of classes on power evangelism increases at a wide range of institutions around the nation, they will act as a net pulling in professors from a variety of disciplines. This will be a strengthening infusion of energy because the field needs a broad base of theologians, social scientists, psychologists and others who will continue to research and teach on the subject.

4. *Most courses on the subject concentrate on power encounters between the divine and the demonic.* Fuller's pioneer course on power evangelism originally contained an emphasis on healing and in-class demonstrations of healing power. However, a review of course syllabi provided by symposium participants reveals that the major emphasis in power evangelism courses today is not healing but power encounters. It is not the restoration of sick people to good health, neither is it the supernatural healing of individuals with congenital problems. Most instructors have focused their classes on the battle between the Kingdom of Light and the Kingdom of darkness. Building from Old and New Testament scenarios of this clash, the courses move from a theological understanding of the principles involved to modern-day case studies of personal encounters, and the methodology employed. Deliverance from demons is observed by students in the classroom through audiovisual materials, or outside of school session. Power encounter is mainly studied as an academic research subject with little participant observation. However, at the seminary level some instructors and students, especially career missionaries, have had experience with demonic battles and their stories help to personalize the subject.

5. *Various methodological approaches to deliverance are being taught, including a "truth encounter" model.* Deliverance from demons is usually portrayed as a power encounter in which an exorcist drives out the resident demons with God's power. Dr. Neil Anderson of Biola University is developing a model that emphasizes the catalytic role of the counselor-facilitator working with the individual—who then applies God's truth—leading to a kind of self-directed liberation. He teaches a Pastoral Care elective class at Talbot School of Theology at the M.Div. and Th.M. level. It has become the largest elective class, growing over a

four-year period from 15 students to 120. He also conducts conferences on "Spiritual Conflicts and Counseling."

Anderson's approach is for Christians; non-Christians
must first be led into the Kingdom of Light. Then Satan
and his demons are prayed into silence and bound from
interfering in the process. Anderson uses a confidential
inventory to discover background facts used in diagnosing
spiritual problems, and a steps-to-freedom format leading
the counselee through seven areas of demonic attack: cult
and occultic involvement, deception, unforgiveness, rebellion, pride, sin and the sins of ancestors, including curses.
Along the way the counselee renounces sins, affirms biblical truths and communicates with the counselor if he is
hearing thoughts in the mind (demonic interference).
These lies are refuted by God's Word. Gathering sufficient
strength as the process proceeds, eventually the counselee, not the counselor, commands the demons to leave.

Anderson's model is explained in this book in his paper,
"Finding Freedom in Christ" and a response by John Ellenberger follows.

6. *Teaching on power evangelism topics has produced a
whole range of on-campus reactions, from revival to resistance.* One Bible school campus reports that their denomination suggested the introduction of a course, Signs and
Wonders, with one-half of the course a practicum, hands-
on experience. The course was designed and offered following chapel. It has caused a mini-revival on campus,
leading to early morning prayer meetings and an extra
chapel session per week. Chapel attendance is no longer
required because students want to come to chapel. From
chapel they go into the Signs and Wonders class in an attitude of praise and worship.

A seminary professor surveyed his campus informally
about the introduction of a course on power evangelism

covering the Old and New Testament foundation, church history and current applications. He encountered three reactions from his colleagues. Some were concerned that he may be going off the "deep end" and relying on experience, rather than the Word. Another group was sympathetic and open. Although they claimed no personal experience with the subject, they would not oppose the introduction of the course. A third group stood in silent opposition to the idea but undoubtedly would become vocal if the course were actually considered. These individuals had some experiences that led them to comment that the subject was full of "fraud and fakery." The president of the seminary supported the idea in principle because he came from an Assembly of God background and understood the reality of spiritual power. His closing remark was, "You can teach it and do it, if the faculty are behind you."

At another seminary, a course on evangelism and the church contains a single lecture on power evangelism. A professor reports that he was invited in by his colleagues to lecture on the topic. When students complained during the lecture of feeling pressure on their arms, he conducted spiritual warfare praying and the pressure stopped. The students were very attentive during the second half of the lecture. At this seminary power evangelism topics are mainly addressed in summer or extension courses. John White, for example, came in and taught a course entitled, "Whitfield, Wesley, and Wimber." However, when Wimber came to the city to do a power evangelism workshop sponsored by local churches, professors at the seminary were buzzing with negative comments. One professor is reportedly considering introducing a course on power evangelism, but may face an uphill struggle in a school with a strong pedantic tradition, and little praxis orientation.

7. *Institutions have a tendency to place restrictions on in-class or in-office "hands-on" healing or deliverance practices.* Here the teacher is presented with a real classroom problem. Signs and wonders cannot effectively be taught without confirmation, for the student who investigates the biblical record will yearn for personal validation of biblical truths. People don't want to just read about the miraculous; if it truly works, they want to experience it. If it is an evangelistic method that students will use as a ministry tool, they will want to try it out now in classroom settings to solve real, personal problems. Case study research or lectures cannot answer the ultimate questions, "Does this really work?" and, "How do I use it?"

Detroit car workers are trained to assemble car parts so that a complete vehicle rolls off the line. In the assembly process they know that when finished, a turn of the key will unleash the power to run the car out of the shop. Factory testing laboratories validate this, and after work each day workers get in their own automobile and turn the key and unleash the power that takes them home.

Professors teaching power evangelism without classroom practicum experiences are like Detroit assembly line trainers without factory testing laboratories, who simply tell the workers, "If you assemble this car and turn on the key, it will work, believe me. We have a company policy against testing power in the factory, so the vehicles are rolled outside the gate to test them out." While this may sound unusual to the worker, he, unlike the inexperienced student, experiments with his own vehicle every day because out of necessity he must use the power to get home.

There are, of course, some serious issues weighed by administrators when placing restrictions on healing or deliverance practices on campus or in the classroom.

Administrators at Fuller, Biola (since amended), Moody
Bible Institute and other schools have considered legal
implications and academic strength issues. Restrictive
rulings limiting praxis, hands-on experiences to out-of-
class or off-campus settings are sometimes formally
argued as a question of maintaining the academic formal
content of the course, the adequate cognitive knowledge
required by students to gain a full understanding of the
topic. It is also argued that the student can pursue his own
experimentation outside the classroom or campus, thus
preserving the classroom as a place where knowledge is
transmitted, but not subject to experiment. Fuller's
revised Signs and Wonders course, for example, requires
that students visit local church healing services.

There is no doubt that some schools' restrictive reactions have been motivated by internal opposition to the
whole subject of power evangelism, or, in a sense, fear of
the unfamiliar. But whatever the motive, more than one
institution has placed restrictions on on-campus or in-class
healing or deliverance practices, making it a trend to watch.

8. *The terminology of power evangelism is the topic of
considerable discussion, with several underlying theological
suppositions about believers and demons in debate.* "Power
encounter," Alan Tippett's phrase, and "power evangelism," John Wimber's term, have become standard terms.
While there may be differences in broad or narrow applications of these terms, they are standard, easily understood
cover words used by all. There is a growing trend, however, to dispose of the term "possession" in favor of
"demonization." This then allows for degrees of demonization, such as Kraft's scale of 1-10, indicating the observ-
able degree of resistant power or supernatural strength of
the demon or demons. This avoids what many consider to
be a terminology problem since the terms "possessed" or

"inhabited" do not actually occur in Scripture. Rather, the Greek term *daimonidzomai* is used.

This shift from the use of "possessed" to "demonized" may not have attracted much attention except that it is naturally linked to a larger, older issue, "Can Christians be demon possessed?" or in current terminology, "Can Christians be demonized?"

It is on this issue that we have some polarization into two camps. The Assemblies of God have taken an official position, decreeing that believers cannot be possessed. A detailed discussion of this position is given in Opal L. Reddin's *Power Encounter: A Pentecostal Perspective.* This volume was written partly as a response to the issue of demonization of believers which surfaced at the 1988 Fuller symposium. In the introduction Reddin says, " . . . some are saying that believers themselves can be inhabited by demons . . . " and she calls this position "unscriptural and therefore dangerous" (p. 3). Elsewhere she remarks that, "Those who are saying that Christians can be demonized have taken the term, *daimonidzomai*, transliterated it (given it an anglicized pronunciation), and then given it a definition that has no scriptural basis" (p. 12).

In the same volume, Douglas Oss coins the term "DC-theologians" to refer to individuals who believe that Christians can be demonized. Oss emphasizes, as do others in the book, that this view is not "based on careful interpretation of the Scriptures, but rather on experience and human reason" (p. 24). Harold Carpenter, in this same book, echoes this point: "Previously theological positions were determined on the basis of scriptural statements. Currently they are being determined on clinical observations as well as scriptural declarations" (p. 91).

On the other hand, as Wagner points out in *How to Have a Healing Ministry*, almost everyone involved in deliverance ministries believes that Christians can be demonized, and several Christian leaders have recently changed from denial to affirmation that believers can be demonized (p. 190). Among those are Fred Dickason and Merril Unger. Chuck Kraft, Ed Murphy, Tom White, Neil Anderson and others conduct seminars using a variety of emphases and approaches which are designed to free demonized Christians.

This, then, is not just a terminology discussion; it is an arena of both theological and experiential difference. However, it's a friendly debate. Wagner, described by Oss as a "DC-theologian," wrote an endorsement for the back cover of Reddin's book, stating that she and her colleagues "have done the Christian world a singular favor," and it "opens new vistas of understanding." There are enough common issues, jointly held beliefs and mutual respect in both camps to ensure continued, substantive discussions.

Topics

1. *Power Encounter in Missionary Ministry, a Trinity Evangelical Divinity Seminary course by Dr. Timothy Warner.* Warner's course is the most popular elective course at Trinity. He has described the course in an article published in *Evangelical Missions Quarterly* (Vol. 22, No. 3, pp. 66-70) entitled, "Teaching Power Encounter." He begins the course with a discussion of the philosophy of balance in this subject. Warner emphasizes that there are two extremes to avoid—seeing demons in everything and seeing demons in nothing. He also makes it clear that power encounter is "not a panacea for missionary ills nor a strategy or methodology which can or should dominate missionary ministry. It is simply one approach which is essential."

Other topics covered include the concept of world view, the contrast between the animist, Western and biblical views. Since angels and demons are part of the biblical world view, this takes the course into the biblical teaching on Satan and demons, and the conflict Christians are involved in today. Here Warner discusses the position of the believer "in Christ" resulting in positional authority and victory. Christ's absolute victory over Satan and his demons, a victory in which Christians participate, is a key concept he teaches to counter the fear of the demonic. Resources available for the Christian's use in confrontation are also studied, as well as schemes Satan employs to attack people.

With this biblical foundation laid, Timothy Warner then begins a section on applications for the missionary. He addresses possible areas of Satanic attack, and ways in which missionaries can go on the offensive through prayer, evangelism, the destruction of demonic related objects, healing, confrontation with demonic backed practitioners and the casting out of demons. The course ends with a discussion of the practical methodology employed in confronting demons. Warner uses audiovisual materials to illustrate this process, and tapes are available from Faith and Life Publications, 632 N. Prosperity Lane, Andover, KS 67002.

While Warner has an active off-campus ministry in dealing with demonized people, he does not bring a practicum experience into the classroom; rather he uses some of his personal experiences as case studies or illustrations.

2. *Signs and Wonders, a Western Evangelical Seminary course by Dr. Donald Hohensee.* Hohensee's two credit course takes the student through an understanding of the biblical doctrine of signs and wonders, and the historical uses by the Church. The course also examines

Wesleyan teaching on the subject, and seeks to distinguish between the Wesleyan and the Pentecostal or charismatic positions. Hohensee hopes that each student will determine areas where they feel comfortable using signs and wonders in their ministry.

Lecture and discussion topics include: Signs and Wonders in the Bible; The Holy Spirit and Power; John Wesley on Signs and Wonders; Spiritual Gifts; Enabling Gifts and Serving Gifts; Divine Healing; Miracles; Tongues/ Languages; Demon Possession and Exorcism; and Power Encounter.

The course requires readings from an article by Hohensee, "Signs, Wonders and Power: A Wesleyan Perspective"; three books by Wagner, *The Third Wave of the Holy Spirit, How to Have a Healing Ministry Without Making Your Church Sick* and *Signs and Wonders Today;* Lewis Smedes' *Ministry and the Miraculous;* Chuck Kraft's *Christianity with Power;* John Wimber's *Power Evangelism,* and *Power Healing;* John White's *When the Spirit Comes with Power;* Wesley Duewel's *Touch the World Through Prayer;* and, Wayne Caldwell's article on Contemporary Wesleyan Theology (Vol. II, p. 1043-1097) entitled, "Angelology and Demonology."

3. *Power Encounter: Theology and Practice, Assemblies of God Theological Seminary course by Dr. Opal Reddin.* This course explores the conflict between two kingdoms from the biblical, historical and contemporary perspectives. Special attention is given to Christ's total triumph and the believer's authority over Satan and demons.

Reddin's lectures include Scriptural Usage of *daimonidzomai;* Power Encounters in the Old Testament; The Kingdom of God as Related to Power Encounter; The Hermeneutics of Power Encounter; Power Encounter in the Gospels, Acts, Epistles, Revelation, and Church History; Gods of the New Age; Discussions of Peretti, Wimber and Springer; Humanistic Influences in American Culture, and the Occult; Evangelism and Church Planting; Spiritual Warfare; Missiology and Territorial Spirits; Counseling; Healing and Casting out Demons; and Ministerial Training. Reddin has edited a book, *Power Encounter: A Pentecostal Perspective,* and readings from it are required in addition to Kevin Springer's *Power Encounters Among Christians in the Western World,* Wimber's *Power Evangelism,* and other books and articles.

4. *Power Encounter Evangelism, Central Bible College course by Dr. Jesse K. Moon.* Moon's course is a study of the relationship of the supernatural to the ministry of evangelism through the examination of the Old Testament background, the New Testament mandate, Church history, Pentecostal/Charismatic/Third Wave movements, and contemporary applications.

He divides the course into four main sections: The Biblical Precedent; In the Pristine Church; An Historical Sketch; and, Contemporary Applications. His lecture topics include the Old Testament background, the New Testament mandate, and New Testament Power Encounters by Jesus, Paul, and other Apostles and Disciples; The Principles and Methods; The Post-New Testament Era (Middle Ages, Reformation, and Modern); the Pentecostal Movements; Contemporary Methods (Prayer, Fasting, Exorcism, Witnessing and Counseling, Preaching and Teaching, Worship and the Gifts); Demonic Influences in Culture (Territorial Demons, Political and Social Injustice, Paganism and Idolatry, Immigrant Enclaves, and Other People Groups, Cults and Occult and the New Age Movement, Secularism/Humanism/Materialism); Demonic Manifestations (Spiritual and Moral Depravity, Demonic Activities, Illness, Sexual Immorality, Drug Addiction and Alcoholism); Guidelines for Evangelism; and, Spiritual and Practical Preparation. Required textbooks for this course are Reddin's *Power Encounter: A Pentecostal Perspective;* Wimber's *Power Evangelism;* and Wayne Warner's *Touched by the Fire: Patriarchs of Pentecost.*

5. *Theology of Power Encounter, an Alliance Theological Seminary course by Dr. Gerald McGraw.* McGraw's course centers on biblical and theological data, while examining ethnographic, historical and contemporary approaches to spiritual warfare. It explores different approaches on principles and methodologies for ministry to people involved with forces of evil. Theology of Power Encounter notes the relationship of power encounter to world evangelism, healing occultism, human behavior and pastoral activity.

Students hear lectures on topics like Encounter Principles, Selected Biblical Power Encounters; The Demonic Realm: Existence and Activities; Deliverance Methodologies; Controversial Issues; Healing; Evangelism; Revival; Deliverance; Occultism; False Strategies Creating Bondage (Cultism, Satanism, Animism, and World Religions). Required and recommended books are Kurt Koch's *Occult Bondage and Deliverance;* John W. Montgomery's *Demon Possession: A Medical Historical, Anthropological and Theological Symposium;* Conrad Murrell's *Practical Demonology: Tactics for Demon Warfare;* Ernest Rockstad's *Enlightening Studies in Spiritual Warfare;* John White's *When the Spirit Comes with Power: Signs and Wonders Among God's People'* and Walter Wink's *Naming the Powers: The Language of Power in the New Testament.*

6. *Special Studies—Spiritual Warfare, a San Jose Bible College course by Dr. Ed Murphy.* Murphy's course, taught once a year, is an outgrowth of his personal experience with demons who affected his family, and a series of

encounters with demonized students while he was teaching at Biola University. He has also taught power evangelism topics within some theology courses at San Jose Bible College, such as the Book of Acts. The course is also given in a shorter seminar version, or on tape (32 tape studies and a 112-page training manual).

For textbooks, he uses Mark I. Bubeck's *The Adversary,* and *Overcoming the Adversary,* and his own Spiritual Warfare syllabus.

Murphy's course explains evil supernaturalism, the activity of Satan and demons and emphasizes spiritual warfare with the flesh, the world and the demonic. He teaches that Christians are involved with warfare on at least three levels: the *objective,* reaching unbelievers with the gospel; the *subjective,* protecting ourselves and our families; and the *Christian,* helping to free demonized Christians. Other topics in his course include: The Believer's Warfare with the Flesh, and Victory over Evil Supernaturalism. Students learn some of the practical principles of warfare praying, aggressive resistance of the enemy and delivering oneself and fellow Christians from demonization.

7. *The Devil, Demons, and World Missions, a Five-Hour Lecture Series at Seattle Pacific University by Dr. F. Douglas Pennoyer.* Pennoyer has designed a five-lecture module that fits into a number of missions and anthropology courses he has taught at Seattle Pacific University, including Culture and Religion, and Principals and Strategy of the Christian Mission. It begins with the biblical background of spiritual warfare and the four scenes of confrontation between Satan and God, man, Christ and the believer. The duties and tactics of demons are investigated in light of Scripture and experience.

The first commission and Jesus' modeling of compassion and authority is studied in Matthew 7-10, as He commissions the disciples to drive out demons, heal and preach.

Using case studies from his research among the Tawbuid of Mindoro, Philippines, Pennoyer illustrates how individuals, and an entire society, can become dominated by demons. Parallels are drawn between spiritism in this isolated tribe and the channeling techniques of the New Age Movement. The class analyzes a video performance by a channeler, and a slide scenario of a Philippine psychic healer operating on a woman's stomach with only his bare hands.

The series closes with a strong emphasis on the characteristics of all-powerful, victorious God; the position of the believer in Christ; and ways in which the believer can win spiritual warfare battles.

8. *The Ministry of Healing in World Evangelization, a Fuller Theological Seminary course by C. Peter Wagner.* This course is a successor to the well-published MC510 Signs, Wonders and Church Growth taught for four years (1982-1985) primarily by John Wimber with Wagner as professor of record. Due to negative reactions, particularly among faculty of the School of Theology, the course was suspended for one year, then reorganized, renamed and begun again in 1987. The course meets during the winter quarter for ten evenings, one session of which is taught by John Wimber. Wagner does most of the lecturing, but also invites Chuck Kraft of the School of World Mission and Ray Anderson of the School of Theology to participate. On one evening Cathy Schaller and David Rumph, two members of Wagner's healing team at Lake Avenue Congregational Church share a lay perspective of healing.

While there is no laboratory or clinic for the class as a whole to experiment with and witness divine healing, the members of the class break up into small groups at the final part of each class session for sharing and prayer, frequently with laying on of hands, for one another.

The required textbook is *A Force in the Earth* by David Shibley (Creation House), with five additional books selected from a list of works by Ken Blue, Colin Brown, Rex Gardner, Morton Kelsey, Francis MacNutt, Peter Wagner, Lewis Smedes and John Wimber.

9. *Pentecostal Strategies of Missions, a Church of God (Cleveland, TN) School of Theology course by L. Grant McClung, Jr.* While this is primarily a course on strategy, lectures are included on the role of the Holy Spirit, spiritual gifts, signs and wonders, power encounter and spiritual warfare. Michael Harper's *Spiritual Warfare* (Bridge) is required. Among optional books are titles by Mark Bubeck, Michael Green, Vinson Synan, Peter Wagner and John Wimber.

10. *Power Evangelism, a LIFE Bible College course by John Louwerse.* The stated purpose of this course is to "investigate the relationship between miraculous signs and wonders and the growth of the church." Louwerse examines the issues involved from the Scriptures, from church history, from theology and from contemporary missions around the world. As texts he uses John Wimber's *Power Evangelism* (Harper & Row) and Kevin Springer's *Power Encounters Among Christians in the Western World* (Harper & Row). Supplementary reading includes works by Jim Montgomery, Carl Lawrence and Peter Wagner.

This course does include a weekly practicum in which different models of healing are demonstrated in the class. Each student is required to submit an eight-page paper summarizing and synthesizing the varied experiences in the practicum, with a personal application.

Index

Abd Al-Malik, 331
Academic Symposium on
  Power Encounter, 6-12
Acts, sign phenomena, 24-26
Africa, 102, 303-312
African Revival, 305-312
Ajah, Friday Thomas, 76, 90
Alliance Theological
  Seminary, 8, 354
Amstutz, John L., 7
Amundsen, D.W., 235
Anaheim Vineyard
  (see Vineyard, Anaheim)
Ananias and Sapphira, 219
Anderson, Neil T., 7,125-168,
  344-345, 350
Anderson, Ray, 356
animism, 315
Apostle Paul, 225-227
Arab World Ministries, 342
Argentina, 81
Asbury College, 8
Ashcraft, Nancy, 177,183
Assemblies of God, 15,
  76,186,190, 213, 346, 349
Assemblies of God
  Theological Seminary,
  352-353
astrology, 320
Awasu, Wilson, 87
Azusa Street and Beyond, 203

Bangladesh, 321

Bangs, Nathan, 181
Barrett, Charles K., 236
Bartlemann, Frank, 95
Benedict, Ruth, 270
Bermuda Triangle, 83
Biola University, 7, 344,
  348, 355
Black Stone, 317, 326
Blue, Ken, 216, 235, 357
Bodine, Walter R., 8, 238-247
Bosworth brothers, 15
Branham, William, 15
Brazil, 81
Brengle, Samuel Logan,
  175,182,183
Bresson, Bernard, 189,193
Brewster, Betty Sue, 8
Bridge, Donald, 48
Brown, Colin, 48, 357
Brownlee, William H., 69, 72
Bruce, F. F., 79, 90, 236
Brumback, Carl, 247
Bubeck, Mark I., 159, 202,
  206, 213, 355, 357
Buckingham, Jamie, 80
Buhid people, 251-270
Burgon, J. W., 20
Burkina, Faso, 321

Cabezas, Rita, 81, 84-85, 94
Cabrera, Omar, 6, 84
Caldwell, Wayne, 352
Calvinism, 282-283

Canty, George, 201, 204, 212, 213
Carpenter, Harold, 349
Carter, Charles, 182
Cartwright, Peter, 180,183
CBN University, 8
Central Bible College, 8, 353-354
cessationist teaching, 246
charismatic movement, 5-7,10,11, 239, 240, 305
Charles E. Fuller Institute of Evangelism and Church Growth, 15
Cho, Paul Yonggi 6, 81
Christenson, Larry, 99
Christianity with Power, 343
Church Growth Movement, 77, 203, 211, 340
Church of England, 200
Church of God (Cleveland, TN), 15
Church of God School of Theology, 8, 357
Cirner, Randall J., 198, 200, 207 212, 213
Clinton, J. Robert, 45
cognitive captivity, 262-263, 272-273
contextualization, 336-337
cosmic-level spiritual warfare, 11
cosmic-level spiritual warfare, dangers of, 86-88
Costa Rica, 81
Council of Carthage, 200
Cruz, Nicky, 190,193
Cunningham, Loren, 82

Dale, Stan, 286
Dallas Theological Seminary, 8
Davids, Peter H., 8, 215-247
Dayton, Donald, 187
Dayton, Wilber T., 175,177,182,183
deception, 101-123
Deere, Jack, 8
deliverance, 49-72, 125-168, 195-214
demon possession, 56-57
demonic activity, levels of, 276-278
demonization, 56-58, 249-279
demonization of Christians, 61-71,121-123,130,190-193, 206-207, 277, 349-350
demons, 76-77,195-214, 221, 228-229, 249-279
DeRidder, Richard R., 326, 331
DeWet, Christiaan, 212, 214
Dickason, C. Fred, 64, 65, 71, 350
Dieter, Melvin E., 187,193
dispensationalism, 15, 246
divine healing, 189, 223-225
Dobson, E. G., 235
Donald, Bob, 288, 293-295
Douglas, J.D., 212
Dowey, Alexander, 15
Duewel, Wesley, 352
Duffield, Guy P., 196,198, 202, 209, 212, 213, 214

East African Revival, 305-312

Eastern Church, 200
Eastman, Dick, 6
Ebel, G., 236
Edward VI, 200
Ellenberger, John, 8,161-168, 345
Ellens, J.H., 235
Elliston, Edgar J., 8, 297-301
Elwell Walter, 48
Elymas, 219
Engelbrecht, Johan, 8
Ethiopia, 298
Evangelical Free Church, 342
evangelism, 303-312
evil eye, 318, 330
exorcism, 200, 328
exorcism see also deliverance

Fee, Gordon, 47, 236
First Prayer Book, 200
flesh, 105-106
Friedlander, Shems, 331
Fuller Seminary School of World Mission, 6-7, 8,15-16, 26, 74, 93, 340-343
Furnish, Victor P., 236

Gardner, Rex, 357
Garrison, Mary, 213
Gartner, B., 236
Germany, 81
Gibb, Sir Hamilton, 314
Gibbs, Eddie, 8
Gilliland, Dean S., 8, 332-337
Glasser, Arthur F., 8,167,168, 203, 213

Gordon-Conwell Theological Seminary, 8
Gorman, Jack, 47
Great Commission, 9-12,19-23, 44, 75,118-119
Greece, 82
Green, Michael 24, 42,197, 200, 202, 205, 207, 208, 209, 211, 212, 213, 214, 357
Groothius, Douglas, 99
Grudem, Wayne, 8

Hancox, Phil, 21-22, 41
Harper, Michael, 200, 202, 209, 210, 211, 212, 214, 357
Hayford, Jack, 6
healing, 204-205
Henry, Rodney, 114
Herod Agrippa, 219
Hiebert, Paul G., 8,16, 331
Hills, A.M., 179,183
Hills, E.F., 20
historical-critical interpretation, 36-37
Hoekema, Anthony A., 193
Hohensee, Donald, 8,169-193, 351-352
Holland, 282-284
Holy Spirit, 200
Horton, Stanley M., 193
How to Have a Healing Ministry Without Making Your Church Sick, 74, 80, 349
Hughes, Phillip E., 236
Hunter, James Davison, 39, 42

Ibn Hisham, 331
Ibn Ishaq, 321
Illich, Ivan, 45
Inayat, 322
Indonesia, 321
inner healing, 246
Irian Jaya, 284-296
Islam (see Muslims)

Jacobs, Donald R., 8, 303-312
Japan, 89-90
Jessop, Henry E., 182
Jesus' ministry, 16-23,170-
    174,196-197, 322-326
Jones, E. Stanley, 173,182
Jorgensen, Knud, 8

Karen people, 177-178
Kelsey, Morton, 357
Kingdom of God, 17-48, 78-
    80,191
Klaus, Byron, 8, 92-98
Koch, Kurt, 354
Korea, 81
Kraft, Charles H., 8,16,
    42,118,164,165,166,168,
    271-279, 343, 348, 350,
    352, 356
Kumuyi, William, 6
Kwast, Lloyd E., 7

Ladd, George Eldon, 16
Lake, John G., 15
LaSor, William S., 48
Lausanne II Congress on
    World Evangelization, 6

Lawrence, Carl, 357
Lee College, 8
Lenski, R.C.H., 20
Leslie, John, 176,182
Lewis, C.S., 36,106
LIFE Bible College, 7, 357
Lindors, Barbnabos, 48
Lindsay, Gordon, 199, 206,
    208, 212, 213
Lindsay, Hal, 59
Loewen, Jacob, 85, 91
Longley, Arthur, 204, 213
Louwerse, John, 7, 281-
    301, 357
Lowery, Thomas Lanier, 213
Lurker, Manfred, 91
Luther, Martin, 12, 97,190

McAll, Kenneth, 83, 90
McClung Jr., L. Grant, 8,195-
    214, 357
McGavran, Donald A., 16, 90,
    211, 213, 214
McGraw, Gerald, 354
McKendree, William, 181
McQuilkin, J. Robertson, 193
MacNutt, Francis, 48, 357
Madale, Nagasura T., 331
Maggay, Melba, 114
Mallone, George, 8, 238
Masters, Phil, 286, 287
Masters, Phyllis, 286
Mecca, 317
mental illness, 128-129
Menzies, William, 99
Messer, Dollas, 213
Michaelis, W. 236
Middle Ages, 200

Mission Aviation Fellowship, 288
Mitton, C. Leslie, 48
Moberly, Elizabeth R., 8
Montgomery, J. Warwick, 72, 354
Montgomery, Jim, 357
Moody Bible Institute, 348
Moon, Jesse K., 353-354
Muhammed Ibn Hisham, 321
Murphy, Edward, 8, 49-72, 342, 350, 354-355
Murray, John, 192,193
Murrell, Conrad, 354
Musk, Bill, 331
Muslims, 212, 309-310, 313-337

Navajos, 81
New Age Movement, 85, 96,126, 311-312, 356
Nicholson, Steve, 82
Niehaus, Jeffrey J., 8
Nigeria, 332-337
Non-Christian Spiritual Experience Inventory, 148
Numbers, R.L., 235
Nysewander, Mark, 8

Olofson, Harold, 270
Opler, Morris, E., 270
Oral Roberts University School of Theology and Mission, 8
Oss, Douglas, 349, 350
Overseas Crusades, 342

Pakistan, 314, 329
paradigm shift, 36

Paul, Apostle, 225-227
Paul's ministry, 326-331
Payne, Gunner, 14
Penn-Lewis, Jessie, 113
Pennoyer, F. Douglas, 8, 9, 249-279, 339-357
Pennoyer, Virginia, 270
Pentecostal Holiness Church, 15
Pentecostal Movement, 5-7,10,11,15,184-193, 239, 305, 341
people movement, 296
Peretti, Frank, 340
Philippines, 81, 249-270
Phypers, David, 48
Pierson, Paul E., 8
Plumtre, E. J., 69, 72
Pommerville, Paul, 45, 211, 214
power, 108-113, 170-193
power encounter, 31-32, 36, 74,129-130, 321, 332-333, 343, 348
power evangelism, 7,11,13-48, 281-301, 340-357
Power Evangelism, 16,18, 27, 29
Power Healing, 27
power, satanic, 108-113
praise, 11
prayer, 11,180, 323
Prosser, Peter E., 8

Reddin, Opal L., 8,184-193, 349, 352-353, 354
Reed, Barbara Flory, 254, 270
Reed, Russ, 254

Rees, Paul, 176
Rees, Seth C., 181,183
Reformed Theology, 326
Regent College, 8
Regions Beyond Missionary Union, 288
resistance-receptivity theory, 77
Revival, East African, 305-312
Richardson, Carl, 209, 212, 214
Richardson, Don, 286
Robinson, Bud, 181,183
Robson, James, 331
Rockstad, Ernest, 354
Roman Catholic Church, 200
Rumph, David, 356
Russell, J.B., 99

Salvation Army, 175
San Jose Bible College, 8, 354-355
Satan, 55-58, 75-76
Scanlan, Michael, 198, 200, 207, 212, 213
Schaller, Cathy, 356
Schatzmann, Siegfried, 47
Schippers, R., 236
Schlier, H., 236
scientific method, 36-39
Seattle Pacific University, 8, 355-356
Sharp, O.J., 190,193
Shaw, R. Daniel, 8
Shibley, David, 357
sickness, 215-247
Sierra Leone, 77
Silvoso, Edgardo, 81

Simpson, James D., 8,115-123
sin, 51-54, 218
Smedes, Lewis, 352, 357
Smith, Amanda, 180
Smith, Timothy L., 182
Southern California College, 8
spiritual gifts, 264
spiritual warfare, 10-12, 29-30, 49-72, 303-312, 342, 343
Spittler, Russell, 16, 36
Springer, Kevin, 41, 42, 353, 357
Stacey, Vivienne, 331
Stedman, Ray, 61
Steele, Daniel, 176,181,182,183
suffering, 215-247
Sumrall, Lester, 81,193
Synan, Vinson, 193

Talbot School of Theology, 7,134, 344
Tawbuid people, 249-270, 271, 278, 279
Taylor, Richard S., 177,183
temptation, 105
territorial spirits, 73-99, 259, 279
territorial spirits, names of, 84-85
Tertullian, 202
Thailand, 80-81, 177-178
The Evangelical Alliance Mission, 342
Third Wave, 5, 98, 240, 305
Third Wave of the Holy Spirit, The 80

Third World, 16
thorn in the flesh, 226-227
Thornton, Philip, 8
Tippett, Alan, 348
tongues, 241-242
Toon, Peter, 200, 212
Torrey, R.A., 179
Trinity Evangelical Divinity
    School, 8, 74, 350
truth, 106-108
truth encounter, 129,133,
    165-167
Two-Thirds World, 201, 272

Una people, 289-296
unclean spirit, 200
Unger, Merrill F., 72,198,
    202, 212, 350
Uruguay, 81

Van Cleave, Nathaniel M.,
    196,198, 209, 212, 213, 214
Van Engen, Charles, 8
Vest, Lasmar, 118
Villanueva, Clarita, 190
Vine, William, 53, 71
Vineyard, Anaheim, 27, 31
Vineyard movement, 7,
    27, 82

Wagner, C. Peter, 8,16, 40,
    42, 73-98,189,193, 213, 214,
    240, 247, 259, 340, 349-350,
    352, 356-357
Wallace, Anthony F.C., 270
Walvoord, John F., 193
Warfield, B.B., 246
Warner, Timothy M., 8, 74,
77, 87, 90,101-123,167,168,
    342, 350-351
Warner, Wayne, 354
Watney, Paul B., 8, 43-48
Watt, James, 80
Wesley, John, 186-187,188
Wesleyans, 169-193
Westermann, Claus, 48
Western Evangelical
    Seminary, 8, 351
White, John, 346, 352, 354
White, Tom, 350
Whyte, H. A. Maxwell, 213
Wilkerson, David, 190
Williams, Don, 41
Williams, Herman, 81
Wimber, Carol, 14
Wimber, John, 7, 8,13-48, 82,
    99, 205, 207, 212, 213, 276,
    340, 342, 346, 348, 352, 353,
    354, 356, 357
Wink, Walter, 98, 99, 331, 354
Wolter, Albert, 46, 48
Woodberry, J Dudley, 8,
    313-337
word of knowledge, 32-33
worldview, 29-31, 310-312
worship, 11

Yali people, 286-289
Yorba Linda Friends
    Church, 14
Youngblood, Ronald, 48
Youth With a Mission,
    82, 342

Zam Zam water, 317